Language Teaching and Skill Learning

Applied Language Studies
Edited by David Crystal and Keith Johnson

This new series aims to deal with key topics within the main branches of applied language studies – initially in the fields of foreign language teaching and learning, child language acquisition and clinical or remedial language studies. The series will provide students with a research perspective in a particular topic, at the same time containing an original slant which will make each volume a genuine contribution to the development of ideas in the subject.

Series List

LANGUAGE TEACHING
AND
SKILL LEARNING

Keith Johnson

BLACKWELL
Oxford UK & Cambridge USA

First published 1996

Blackwell Publishers Ltd.
108 Cowley Road
Oxford OX4 1JF
UK

Blackwell Publishers Inc.
238 Main Street
Cambridge, Massachusetts 02142
USA

British Library Cataloguing in Publication Data

A CIP catalogue record for this book is available from the British Library.

Library of Congress Cataloging-in-Publication Data
Johnson, Keith.
  Language teaching and skill learning / Keith Johnson.
    p. cm. — (Applied language studies)
  Includes bibliographical references and index.
  ISBN 0–631–16876–1 (alk. paper). — ISBN 0–631–16877–X (pbk. :
alk. paper)
    1. Language and languages—Study and teaching—Great Britain.
2. Languages, Modern—Study and teaching—Great Britain. I. Title.
II. Series.
LB1578.J63 1995
418'.007—dc20   95–11582
                                                                        CIP

Typeset in 10½ on 12½ pt Ehrhardt
by Graphicraft Typesetters Ltd., Hong Kong
Printed in Great Britain by Hartnolls Ltd., Bodmin, Cornwall

This book is printed on acid-free paper

Contents

Figures

Acknowledgements

The author and publishers wish to thank the following for permission to use copyright material:

The Guardian for figures from articles by Roger A. Redfern, 'Shades of sunsets past', *The Guardian*, 24 August 1990 and 'Photocopier', *The Guardian*, 23 October 1990 (both adapted);

Longman Group Ltd for figure 5.2, from W. E. Rutherford, *Second Language Grammar: Learning and Teaching*, 1987, p. 163;

Thomas Nelson & Sons Ltd for illustrations from Keith Johnson, *Now for English, Activity Book I*, illustrated by Margaret Chamberlain, 1982, p. 11.

Every effort has been made to trace all the copyright holders but if any have been inadvertently overlooked the publishers will be pleased to make the necessary arrangement at the first opportunity.

Introduction

This book's ultimate concern is the relationship between language teaching and the teaching of skills other than language. We hope to show that there is much to be learned about the business of language teaching by considering what teachers in other subject areas have to say, and what practices they have followed. Our ultimate concern is indeed language teaching, but it is not our starting point, and a considerable part of our study will deal with language learning and with the nature of language itself. Indeed, an accurate title for the book would be: 'Language and Skills, Language Learning and Skill Learning, Language Teaching and Skill Teaching'. But this does not have much of a ring to it!

Language teachers and applied linguists have regularly used similes with other skills to talk about language teaching. 'Learning a language is like learning how to ride a bicycle . . .' is one such observation, and it generally elicits a wise nod from any listening audience. Since it *is* nods all round, the question immediately arises why it is necessary to devote an entire book to the language/skills comparison. Is any convincing necessary?

Throughout the history of language teaching there is another sort of comparison that language teachers and applied linguists have found highly fruitful. It is that 'learning a second language is like learning a first language'. Examples are manifold; one of the most famous is of the French scholar Gouin who, having failed to learn German as a second language (L2) through diligent study, was fascinated to watch his nephew, a three-year-old, and no scholar at all, learning French as a first language (L1) without apparent intellectual effort. The nephew appeared to do it by the direct linking in his mind between experiences and the words used to describe them. This led Gouin, along with others, to develop a version of the Direct Method, in which that same direct linking of experience and words was captured. Many other examples could be cited; for obvious and perfectly sensible reasons it is a quite acceptable justification of any L2 teaching method to say that it is based on insights about how L1s are learned.

The L1/L2 parallel is then a common one throughout applied linguistic history, and it has been applied as much to learning as to teaching studies. Hence – again for quite acceptable reasons – the study of second language acquisition has always displayed the influence of L1 acquisition studies. But in recent years the influence has been particularly dominant. This dominance reveals itself in many ways. In research methodology, for example, techniques originally used for the study of L1 development have found their way into L2 studies. Views on language teaching are similarly affected by the parallel. Ever since Newmark and Reibel, in their seminal 1968 paper, pursued the L1/L2 parallel and reached a conclusion concerning language teaching, there has been a plethora of naturalistic, 'acquisition-based' approaches to language teaching. So much so that Krashen (1983) is moved to comment that 'acquisition [not learning] is where the action is'. We find in his work, as well as in the work of others such as Prabhu, the desire to approximate as far as is feasible in the classroom the conditions which hold in L1 acquisition. So the teacher does what a parent does (tuning input in the same rough, not fine, way; avoiding much overt error correction), and the student does what a child does (incubates, for example). To borrow a phrase from Hymes (1970, who himself borrowed it from elsewhere) the 'representative anecdote' of the day is along the following lines: The language learner has a language acquisition device (an LAD). Though this may have its 'critical period', it can – if certain conditions are met – be put to use for L2 acquisition. The L2 class cannot of course totally replicate the environmental, cognitive and affective conditions of L1 acquisition, but the anecdote suggests an instructional strategy which does this as far as possible – through motherese-like input, attempts to clear the 'affective filter', and in other ways. 'Rusty' LAD is, in short, 'oiled' back into service; it is the representative anecdote of the 'student as child, teacher as parent'.

Where does this view come from? Why has it such predominance today? The reason relates clearly to Chomskyan views about L1 acquisition. As is well known, Chomsky's view is that we are all possessed of an LAD which equips us for L1 acquisition. The aspect of this LAD which is important here is that it is language-specific; that is, it works for the acquisition of language, but not other skills. In this way, language is viewed as unique, not just to humans (as opposed to other creatures), but also in humans, for language (as opposed to other skills). Language is 'unique and uniquely acquired'. This view of language strongly suggests two things relevant to us here. The first is that if applied linguistics is to seek any parallel at all to L2 learning, it should be with L1 acquisition. The second is that any comparison between language learning and the learning of other behaviours is inappropriate, because language is unique. To parody Pope: 'the proper study of language acquisition is indeed language acquisition'. The doors allowing us to link language teaching and riding bicycles are thus firmly slammed. Any hidden treasures (in the form of insights) lurking behind those doors remain well and truly forbidden.

It is not our intention in any part of this book to deny the value of this representative anecdote. Viewing the process of L2 mastery as acquisition has brought important and fresh insights to the field. But what about learning as opposed to acquisition? What about those closed doors?

The view of language as 'unique and uniquely acquired' can be, and has been, challenged. It remains an issue of contention today, such that Anderson (1980) can claim: 'little direct evidence exists to support the view that language is a unique system . . . in my opinion the status of language is shaping up to be a major issue for cognitive psychology'. If language shares important characteristics with other forms of behaviour (and is hence not unique), then it is unlikely to be 'uniquely acquired'. And once language is deprived of its unique status, then the acquisition of non-linguistic behaviours becomes an area of study likely to provide information relevant to L2 learning. A second type of parallel, in other words, presents itself: between L2 acquisition and the acquisition of non-linguistic behaviours.

The starting point for this book is, therefore, a second representative anecdote – of learners who approach a second language in much the same way as they might learn to play tennis, pilot an aircraft, play a musical instrument. The aim is to ask what it would mean for language teaching to regard itself as skill training. What, in the most rough outline, would language teaching as skill training look like? Would such a view offer a coherent theoretical alternative to approaches based on an L1/L2 acquisition parallel? It is the aim of this book to consider issues like these.

The reader will soon observe that during the course of this book we develop not one but three different positions, which differ in terms of specificity. On the most general level is the view that language can fruitfully be viewed as a skill, with language learning seen as skill learning, and language teaching as skill teaching. But we shall also be looking at specific types of learning models – those associated with information processing, and utilizing such concepts as automization. Thirdly, we shall pay particular attention to one model, that associated with the cognitive psychologist John Anderson. It is important to say at the outset that the first of these positions is by far the most important. It may be that a reader wishes to discount the Anderson model, and may even find information-processing models in general unacceptable (a possible complaint being that the concept of automization is essentially a behaviourist one). But if through this book the reader is led to accept the view that language learning is comparable to other kinds of learning, then we shall feel we have been successful.

Some while ago, a book appeared called *The Inner Game of Tennis* (Gallwey 1974). The 'Inner Game' takes place in the mind, where the opponents are such things as nervousness and self-doubt, and the book develops techniques for the teaching of tennis which enjoyed an amount of success (culminating perhaps in the Wimbledon title for one of its adherents, Asher). The techniques have been applied elsewhere, and other *Inner Game* volumes have also appeared, including *The Inner Game of Music* (Green and Gallwey 1986). Perhaps a further one might very fruitfully be written, *The Inner Game of Second Language Learning*. If so, the approach to language teaching it would imply might have very little to do with the Anderson model, and ideas like automization might not even get a mention. But such a book should still be welcomed; Anderson and automization are secondary to a preparedness to talk about language learning, tennis, and music in the same breath. This present book is not 'selling' any specific model; but it is 'selling' something – a way of looking at language learning and teaching.

The book is organized in the following way. In Chapter 1 we consider the relationship between language and cognition, outlining the conflict between the Piagetian view that they have similar bases and Chomsky's position that they develop distinctly. Chapter 2 widens the debate to consider parallels between language and skills in general, showing what characteristics language shares with other skilled behaviour. Chapters 3 and 4 focus on L2 acquisition. Chapter 3 looks at the proposition that L2 acquisition develops following the mechanisms of a Universal Grammar - mechanisms that are quite distinct from those which control other aspects of cognition. In chapter 4 we review L2 acquisition theories which do utilize the mechanisms of general cognition. We outline one theory in particular (Anderson's) and the concepts it is based on – particularly those of declarative and procedural knowledge. Chapter 5 switches the focus onto language teaching, and we consider ways of developing declarative knowledge (knowledge about) in learners. In chapter 6 we turn to procedural knowledge (knowledge how to) and show how an emphasis on information processing would have implications for one particular area, that of error correction. Chapter 7 stays with the notion of procedural knowledge and considers ways in which language teaching might facilitate the proceduralization, or automization, of knowledge in learners. Chapter 8 looks at other outstanding issues, particularly to do with syllabus design. It considers other ways in which a skill-based view of language will have implications for language teaching. In our final chapter we relate the conceptualization of language teaching we have been developing to other language-teaching approaches. In particular we claim associations between our conceptualization and communicative methodology.

Sooner or later the reader will realize that many of the pedagogic examples given in these pages relate to the teaching of grammatical items, and this raises the question of whether what is being put forward is relevant to the teaching of all language areas. The bland answer would be yes; but this would be to conceal particular problems relating to the teaching of specific skills – the problems involved in teaching language use (pragmatic, functional areas) being perhaps the most acute. But most pronouncements on language teaching face the same problems of generalizability.

Among those to whom thanks are due are David Wilkins, for his encouragement (rather a long time ago!) to put pen to paper in the first place, and Philip Carpenter, not only for being such a patient and encouraging publisher, but also for useful feedback, particularly on Chapter 1. I am indebted to Martin Bygate, Vivian Cook and David Crystal for extremely useful and detailed comments on a draft of this book. Vivian has also been very generous both with his time and in making available a good deal of relevant reading material. Needless to say, none of these individuals bears any guilt.

Thank you, Helen, not just for your support, but also for the (as ever) perceptive feedback you provided on some portions of this book. It is dedicated to you, and to Hugh Charles who came into the world in the middle of draft 3 of chapter 5. Welcome to him.

1 Language and Cognition

If there is any skill in the human repertoire of a sufficiently high level to be compared with the skill of language, one might suppose that it is likely to be the skill of being able to 'think'. Since we are interested in the relationship between language and other skills, we might therefore fruitfully pursue the issue in relation to language and cognition. Are language and thinking quite different, incomparable, phenomena? Or are they, conversely, similar skills – perhaps even manifestations of the same thing?

The nature of the relationship between language and thought is an age-old problem, at least as old as Aristotle. We shall begin our consideration of it earlier in this century by briefly looking at the two most common positions which, for reasons that will become clear, we call the Shelley and Johnson views. We then turn to more recent discussion and focus on the debate between Chomsky and Piaget which took place in the mid-1970s. We shall identify three central issues in their debate, and our discussion of them will take us beyond Chomsky and Piaget to more general considerations of the positions that have been taken regarding each.

The language–cognition debate is both a highly complex and an unfinished one. Conclusions are difficult to reach, but the result of our survey will be to side with a position we outline at the end of the chapter – that of Karmiloff-Smith (1992). She argues that the balance of evidence is for early language growth separate from cognition; but with time the structures of language become generalized for the child and available for general processing. Language may start off as separate from cognition, but does not end up so.

We need a term to refer to the view that language and cognition are closely related. Cromer (1991 and in earlier publications) uses the phrase 'cognition hypothesis', and we shall follow this usage.

The Shelley and Johnson Views

Much of the huge amount of discussion on this issue in the literature is concerned with establishing dominance: which came first, language or thought – which is the 'senior partner'? The two main positions in this debate may be easily summarized: some see thought as dominant, language is merely a 'vocalized' version of it. Others have language dominant, with thought characterised as silent language.

The Shelley view

Crystal (1987) associates the view that thought depends on language with the poet Shelley, following a quotation from *Prometheus Unbound*: 'He gave men speech, and speech created thought'. Early arguments along these lines in this century were developed by the father of behaviourism, Watson (1930), who argued that thought was subvocalized speech. This view fits in well with behaviourism, with its desire to avoid recourse to any concept of unobservable brain activity, and to a concept of mind. In this tradition there were various studies seeking evidence for subvocalized speech activity when people were thinking. The idea received something of a death blow from Smith et al. (1947). Smith allowed himself to be given a curare which paralysed him; he was kept alive on a respirator. No body movements, including subvocalized speech, were possible. Yet he reports being able to 'think' under these conditions. The clear suggestion is that thought is something different from subvocalized speech.

Working in a rather different tradition (that of Humboldt and the emphasis on the value of the diversity of languages) were the American linguist and anthropologist Sapir and his pupil Whorf. The Sapir–Whorf hypothesis has it that the native language affects the way the world is seen; in Whorf's (1956) words: 'we dissect nature along lines laid down by our native languages'. One of Whorf's often quoted examples concerns the English sentence 'the light flashed'. We have to have a subject, something to do the flashing; it is impossible to report the occurrence of flashing without any statement of what caused it. The Hopi Indian language does not have this. Whorf speculates that this is perhaps why 'we frequently read into nature ghostly entities which flash and perform other miracles. Do we supply them because some of our verbs require substantives in front of them?'

A number of experiments test the validity of this hypothesis. One, by Carroll and Casagrande (1958) notes that in the Navaho language, verbs of handling (e.g. 'pick up', 'drop') require a form of the verb to be selected according to the shape of the object of the verb. The verb form will be different if the object being picked up is long and flexible as opposed to long and rigid. Carroll and Casagrande hypothesized therefore that Navaho speakers should learn to discriminate shape attributes earlier than those whose dominant language was not Navaho. At first this hypothesis seemed to be true. Navaho bilingual children dominant in Navaho did better on a shape discrimination task than Navaho children dominant in English. But when the task was given to native English speakers, they did as well as the first group. Thus doubt was cast on the validity of the hypothesis.

Other research, particularly on codability and colour recognition (but also on taste – see O'Mahoney and Muhiudeen (1977) for English and Malay differences in the expression of saltiness), also raises problems by suggesting that there are in fact 'perceptual universals' – universal ways of seeing the world irrespective of one's native language.

The strong version of the Sapir–Whorf hypothesis thus gave way to a weaker one – that language does no more than exert an influence on the way we perceive and remember. This hypothesis is indeed a weaker one, and experiments do show that people recall things more easily if the things correspond to readily available words or phrases.[1]

The Johnson view

In the Preface to his 1775 *Dictionary of the English Language*, Samuel Johnson says that 'language is only the instrument of science, and words are but the signs of ideas' (cited in Crystal 1987). 'Johnson's view', then, is that language depends on thought. In this century, this old view has been concerned with attempts to identify cognitive and perceptual universals which can account for the linguistic universals which linguists have identified.

In Chapter 3 we shall explore the issue of universals, including implicational ones, in detail. We here offer one brief example. Greenberg (1963) observes that languages may be coded according to whether they order verbs before objects (VO) or vice versa (OV). He then notes a remarkable number of other similarities amongst VO languages on the one hand, and OV languages on the other. For example, VO languages tend to have the order noun + relative while OV languages have relative + noun. Bartsch and Vennemann (1972) attempt to account for these clusters of similarities in terms of cognitive processing variables. They distinguish between the operator, which specifies and determines the operand, and the operand which is specified, determined by the operator. Clark and Clark (1977) exemplify this by means of the (VO) phrase 'eat apples'. Here 'apples' is the operator, specifying or determining what is eaten; 'eat' is the operand. In VO languages one consistently finds operand followed by operator (as in 'eat apples'). In OV languages the order is consistently operator followed by operand. Bartsch and Vennemann account for this consistency in terms of a 'principle of natural serialization', according to which 'constituents in surface structure all tend to have the same order, either Operand + Operator, or Operator + Operand'. In this way, language differences are seen to reflect different processing principles, or 'ways of thought'.

For a detailed and accessible description of this and other work concerned with the language–thought relationship, see Chapter 14 of Clark and Clark (1977); also Cromer (1991).

The Shelley–Johnson debate and language–cognition similarities

We need to be clear about what information this debate does, and does not, provide us with *vis-à-vis* the issue that interests us here: establishing a relationship between language and cognition. What does not concern us is which of the two 'wins' the debate. Whether it is language or thought that is shown to be more primary or dominant is irrelevant to our concern. But this work clearly has relevance. For if any sort of true dependency relationship is shown to hold (that is, something more than statements that language 'has an influence on' thought, or vice versa), then this would appear to be evidence for similarities between the two behaviours. Hence there is a sense in which either view – that language is vocalized thought, or that thought is silent language – is positive evidence helping to establish a relationship between thought and language.

We turn now to the views of two protagonists much more sharply delineated in terms of the issue that centrally concerns this chapter. One relates language and thought, the other has them as separate, quite different phenomena.

The Chomsky–Piaget Debate

In the middle of this century the most dominant figure in the field of the development of thought in the young child was arguably the Swiss psychologist, Jean Piaget. A similarly dominant figure in another relevant field – the development of language in the child – is the American linguist Noam Chomsky. It is therefore to be expected that when these two scholars met together, as they did at a 1975 conference at Royaumont in France, the result would be highly relevant to our discussion – especially since their views on the language–thought relationship are diametrically opposed. The debate between them, their supporters and other interested parties, is recorded in Piatelli-Palmarini (1980), which is a report of the Royaumont conference.

It is useful to focus on Royaumont because the issues that interest us are so well covered there. We shall begin with a short general statement of the two opposing views, and will then identify three central 'arenas of debate' treated at the conference. But there is a clear danger in concentrating on Piaget and Chomsky: that relevant work of others is ignored. Following consideration of Royaumont we shall indeed widen the discussion to encompass the views of others, but there remain individuals (Bruner and Vygotsky in particular) whose work would need to be represented in a comprehensive consideration of these matters.

Chomsky

Chomsky's attempt is to find a solution to what he calls 'Plato's problem'. The problem in its most general form is: how comes it that human beings, whose contacts with the world are brief and personal and limited, are able to know as much as they do know (the formulation is from Chomsky 1988). The association of this issue with Plato comes about because in *The Meno* Socrates is able to demonstrate that an ignorant slave boy knows the principles of geometry – Socrates leads him through a series of questions to discovery of geometric theorems. Chomsky discusses Plato's problem in relation to language in various sources; we here mainly use Chomsky (1980). The problem is: how does the child learn such a complex system of language in such a short space of time? The acquisition is quick, and the constructs that are acquired are complex; the achievement needs explanation.

Two sorts of explanation are possible. One is that the child receives excellent teaching, from the 'environment' in general and caretaker (mother) in particular. Chomsky has always denied the feasibility of this explanation. In Chomsky (1965) he speaks of the degenerate nature of motherese, and the lack of linguistic exemplars that the child receives. Although more recent studies of motherese (e.g. Snow and Ferguson 1977) have suggested that it is not nearly so 'degenerate' as Chomsky once assumed, the point stands. It is part of Plato's problem that the child acquires language without much help; there is, in the phrase much used to evoke this argument in the recent Universal Grammar literature (which we cover in chapter 3), a 'poverty of stimulus' for the child in the task of first language acquisition. This 'poverty of stimulus' is not just restricted to the correct forms of language; it is also the case that the child does not receive examples of ungrammaticality, crucial to enable it to discount otherwise logically possible hypotheses which we might expect to occur if language were being acquired through a normal process of hypothesis formation. In White's (1982) words: 'the input data are deficient in that they lack direct evidence of ungrammaticality'. Cook (1985) also argues in this way.

The inadequacy of this first possible explanation leads Chomsky to the second. This is that the child is born with a powerful piece of machinery – the language acquisition device (LAD) – which enables it to do the complex task. Chomsky (1987) notes that his answer to the problem is not dissimilar to Plato's. For Plato also the learner brings a complex machine to the task, but for him this was explained through reincarnation – we bring the machine with us from a previous existence. Today (in the tradition of Western thought, at least) reincarnation is no longer acceptable as an explanation, though the effect of an innately endowed LAD is comparable.

For Chomsky, the LAD is specific both to the species (man being characterized as *Homo loquens*), and to language. There is for the species no general-purpose learning strategy which will apply to all skill domains; that there should be is (for Chomsky) as theoretically unlikely as that there exists some general mechanism to account for the growth of different physical organs, such as heart and lungs. For language, as for other cognitive areas, humans have 'highly specific capacities' (Chomsky 1980). To describe growth he adopts a revealing phrase from Cellerier (1980): it is a process of 'successive maturation of specialized hardware'.

Piaget

Piaget's position is in opposition to Chomsky's in important respects. He identifies a number of discrete stages in the child's cognitive development; these are shown in table 1.1, with rough ages at which they occur given in years.

Piaget dubs his theory 'interactionist', because the process by which the child proceeds from one stage to the next involves interaction with the

Table 1.1 Piaget's main developmental stages

Developmental stage	Age (years)
Sensori-motor	0–2
Pre-operational	2–7
Concrete	7–12
Formal operations	12 onwards

environment. 'Autoregulation', the mechanism involved in this interaction, has two components: assimilation and adaptation. The child assimilates new forms and experiences into his rapidly growing picture of the world; but he also adapts to these forms and experiences. His world picture is modified by interaction, enabling him to pass from one developmental stage to the next.

Piaget (1962) describes the change from sensorimotor to pre-operational at around the age of two as a 'Copernican revolution' in cognitive development. It is characterised by the onset of representations, and heralds the beginning of symbolic behaviour. As Inhelder (1980) has it, 'representation beyond the here and now [is] the culmination of sensorimotor intelligence'. This representational ability manifests itself in various ways. One is deferred imitation, where the child imitates a person or object when it is not present; another is symbolic play, as when the child pretends that a pebble is a car and plays with it (Sinclair 1971). A third is language, and in this way language is seen to develop within a general cognitive framework, alongside other cognitive activities. Hence Piaget's system (unlike Chomsky's) postulates a unitary and general learning theory.

Three 'Arenas of Debate'

The Chomsky–Piaget debate is a highly complex one, and our discussion of it is complicated by the fact that very often the central issue for them will be a question such as innateness, which though relevant to us is not our main focus of attention. From the web of concerns covered in Piatelli-Palmarini (1980), we have here identified three questions of central relevance to the language/cognition relationship issue – three main 'arenas of debate'. These may be stated in the form of questions.

1   How plausible is it that the same mechanisms are involved in both language and cognition? If language is seen to involve processes not found in any other form of behaviour, this argues strongly for the uniqueness of language.

2   How comparable are the developmental patterns of language and cognition? If the two develop side by side and in a comparable way, then this suggests a relationship between the two.

3   Is one ever found without the other? This involves the issue of whether animals have language – since they have intelligence, one would also expect to find evidence of communication, if language and cognition are related. But animals are not the only possible test case areas. Humans who for one reason or another have either linguistic or cognitive deficits will be of interest too. Is it possible, for example, for someone to have a cognitive deficit which leaves language unaffected?

Focusing on these three questions provides a useful path through the complexities of the debate. But it also oversimplifies the issue; these relatively simply stated questions do indeed hide complications and many difficulties. Quite where the answers to these questions will take us is not always clear (what exactly, for example, would the answer 'very comparable' to question 2 lead us to conclude?). Also, there is a degree of overlap in the questions. We shall find, for example, that the issue of whether or not animals have language (question 3) depends on how one defines language, which in turn depends on what mechanisms are associated with language (part of question 1). Bearing these caveats in mind, we shall now consider each of these questions.

How Plausible is it that the Same Mechanisms are Involved in Both Language and Cognition?

Structure-dependent rules: Chomsky's claim

Chomsky claims that language involves constructs that are not found in skills other than language. His answer to question 1 above is therefore 'not plausible at all'.

In various sources, Chomsky's example of a language-specific construct (and it is just one of a number of possible examples) is the 'structure-dependent' rule. His discussion of structure dependency is usually in the context of the L1 acquisition of syntax, and the basis of his argument is that since language acquisition involves mastery of such specialized (structure-dependent) rules, it cannot be achieved by general learning mechanisms. The following example is taken from Chomsky (1980; see Cook and Newson 1995 for a fuller discussion with further examples). As well as exemplifying the structure-dependency question, it also well illustrates Plato's problem and the 'poverty of stimulus' type of argument referred to earlier.

The example concerns English interrogative formation, as in pairs like these:

(1.1)   (a)   The man is here – Is the man here?
       (b)   The man will leave – Will the man leave?

The following two hypotheses are, Chomsky argues, ones which might be developed by a learning organism to account for example 1.1.

H1:   Process the declarative from beginning to end (left to right), word by word, until reaching the first occurrence of the words 'is', 'will' etc.; transpose this occurrence to the beginning (left), forming the associated interrogative.

H2:   Same as H1, but select the first occurrence of 'is', 'will' etc., following the first noun phrase of the declarative. (p. 39)

H1 is a structure-independent rule, because it does not involve any concept of hierarchical structure within the sentence (you do not have to know what a noun phrase is to operate the rule). H2, on the other hand, is structure-dependent, and involves the ability to recognise that there exists a hierarchical structure: noun phrase. H1 is 'simpler' than H2; therefore we might expect a child (like a linguist attempting to be 'scientific' by opting always – in the absence of contrary evidence – for the simplest solution) to prefer it over any more complex hypothesis.

But H1 is of course incorrect, and does not work for data like example 1.2.

(1.2)   (a)   The man who is here is tall – Is the man who is here tall?
       (b)   The man who is tall will leave – Will the man who is tall leave?

H1 incorrectly derives the following:

(1.3)   (a)   *Is the man who here is tall?
       (b)   *Is the man who tall will leave?

Because H2 is sensitive to the notion of noun phrase, it recognizes 'the man who is here' in 1.2(a) and 'the man who is tall' in 1.2(b) as single entities. It is hence able to recognize that the first instance of 'is' in 1.2(a) and the 'is' in 1.2(b) are not verbs of the main clause in each example. It can therefore move the right verbs to the beginnings of the sentences.

'How', Chomsky asks (1980), 'does a child know that H2 is correct (nearly), while H1 is false?' (p. 40). The idea that the child would proceed by the use of general learning mechanisms (as Piaget would have it) is for him unlikely, partly because of the sheer complexity of the structure-dependency concept. The notion of 'noun phrase', essential to H2, is an abstract one (not physically marked in any way). Furthermore, if the child were to operate like a scientific linguist, adopting H1 then modifying it on the basis of incoming data, one would expect evidence of mistakes of the sort found in example 1.3, made before H1 was discounted as a valid hypothesis. But sentences of the example 1.3 type never occur. In addition (and this is the 'evidence of ungrammaticality' argument mentioned earlier), the environment provides the child with no negative instances like the example 1.3 sentences; and (the argument goes) it is very difficult indeed to indulge in a process of logical hypothesis modification without negative instances.

Structure-dependent rules: the counterarguments

A number of papers in Piatelli-Palmarini (1980) take exception to his characterization of the structurally dependent rule. Because the nature of linguistic rules (whether they are 'unique' or otherwise) is such an important issue for us, we shall consider the counterarguments in some detail.

In discussion of the Chomsky (1980) paper, Premack (1980, p. 127) cites a case of chimpanzee learning which for him is 'logically parallel' to Chomsky's 'the man who is here is tall' example. The chimpanzee Sarah was taught a language using pieces of plastic, and one piece of plastic was associated with the noun plural morpheme 's' (henceforth referred to as 'pl'). Sarah was trained to pluralize by putting 'pl' after the verb 'is' – so 'is + pl' = 'are'. Sentences like 'apple banana is + pl red' were produced, but the experimenters began to have doubts as to the exact nature of the rule Sarah had internalized. It may have been of a mechanical nature, simply placing 'pl' after 'is' when two elements preceded 'is' (as in the 'apple banana' example above). To test this the experimenters gave Sarah sentences with blanks, of the kind:

(1.4)   (a)   'red apple _____fruit'.
       (b)   'orange grape _____fruit'.

Sarah correctly filled the blank in (a) with 'is', and in (b) with 'is + p1', indicating that it was indeed a 'grammatical feature' rather than a 'physical feature' (in Premack's words) at work here. The suggestion is that Sarah's rule exemplifies something more akin to Chomsky's H2 than his H1; so apes (whose possession of language is, as we shall see in a later section, highly questionable) seem able to manipulate these so-called 'structural-dependent' rules.

Putnam (1980) provides a more complex example. He claims that Chomsky is 'pulling a fast one' with the 'the man who is here is tall' example. Putnam also draws on chimpanzee language, this time involving Gardner and Gardner's (1969) attempt to teach the chimpanzee Washoe to use deaf-mute sign language. Putnam notes that among Washoe's achievements are the following:

1   the realization that a certain class of words correspond to what we call nouns – words such as 'grape', 'banana' etc.;
2   a sentence frame of the type 'X gives Y to Z', where the Y is often a noun of the 'grape', 'banana' sort. Washoe can use this sentence frame in novel ways, creating 'original' sentences as and when new lexical items are learned. Hence when she learns a new word for the Y category, she can use it in the sentence frame forthwith;
3   the ability to use 'and' to combine sentences. If she knows what Sentence A means and Sentence B means, she can figure out what 'Sentence A and Sentence B' means.

Putnam's claim is that the 'X gives Y to Z' frame and the sentence combining ability entail structure-dependent rules, involving grasping a syntax which operates on units. Washoe has acquired these rules, thereby apparently demonstrating that apes can handle structure dependency. But the essential point for Putnam is that Washoe is learning not structural but semantic rules. That is, when Washoe (and the child learning English also – this extrapolation is crucial) manipulates language, she is not dealing with syntactic building blocks (nouns, noun phrases, verbs), but semantic ones – things, actions etc. Now semantic rules are, according to Putnam, of their very nature structure dependent: they 'cannot be stated without the use of structure-dependent notions. There aren't even plausible candidates for structure-independent semantic rules' (p. 294). Chomsky, Putnam continues, 'presents us with a picture of the child as being like an insanely scientific linguist . . . both are interested in an occult property of "grammaticality"'. But in fact the child is trying to understand English, and this involves it, like Washoe, in structure-dependent notions. For this reason, it is not at all the case that H2 seems more complex to the child than H1; on the contrary, attempting to process sentences like 1.3 above will be as (semantically) difficult to the child as to the reader here, while the results of H2 will be consistently interpretable.

What precisely does Putnam's interpretation of the Washoe data tell us? If we wished to claim that the same mechanisms were involved in both language and cognition, we would really need to show two things: firstly that structure dependency can be learned through general learning mechanisms, and secondly that it occurs in other, non-linguistic behaviours (which the child masters). Putnam's argument strongly suggests the first of these, because he shows how structurally dependent rules are acquired by an ape 'without the benefit of an innate template for language' (Putnam 1980:293). It might be possible to argue logically that since apes are able to acquire these sorts of rules (viewed by Chomsky as unique to language), that they too must have an LAD. But this is implausible, and if apes are able to handle structure dependency, then this does indeed suggest that such rules are available to general cognition; they are not unique to language.

Regarding the second point: Putnam's argument concerns language behaviour in Washoe, as opposed to some other form of behaviour, so strictly speaking it does not provide evidence of structure dependency in the general cognitive sphere. But one of Putnam's main points is that what appears to be structural is in effect semantic. 'Semantic as opposed to syntactic' appears to connote two things in this debate. Firstly, it means 'less complex': if you regard language acquisition as the acquisition of mathematically complex structures (by that 'insanely scientific linguist' Putnam refers to), then you do indeed have to postulate a powerful mechanism for acquisition. Viewed in terms of semantics, the task becomes less complex (just 'trying to understand English' in Putnam's phrase again), and the mechanism to account for it needs to be less powerful. Secondly, semantic means 'non-unique'. Just 'trying to understand English' seems to suggest a task related to learning to come to terms with the world outside in general. This in turn implies that the child learning language as a semantic system would not perceive language learning as that different from other tasks it is undertaking. To utilise a phrase often found in this context, language would not be viewed as a unique 'problem space'. Anderson (1983), a psychologist whose work we shall consider in some detail in chapter 4, illustrates the kinds of production rules that will account for structural dependency, in general cognitive areas (i.e. not just in language).

'Semantic versus syntactic'

It will be clear from the above that the issue of 'semantic versus syntactic' is a central one in the language–cognition debate. The positions we have so far considered approach this issue from a theoretical point of view, the question being whether structure dependency can be accounted for in semantic terms. An alternative approach to the same issue would be to ask whether the young child does in fact process in a semantic or a syntactic way. Karmiloff-Smith (1992) has things to say on this question. She does concede that where semantic development is concerned, there is a relationship between language and cognition. Citing Mandler (1988), she argues that semantic development is controlled by schemas which begin life as modes of perceptual analysis in which the child analyses perceptual primitives such as SELF-MOTION/CAUSED MOTION/PATH/SUPPORT/AGENT. These perceptual primitives guide the child's semantic development.

But Karmiloff-Smith goes on to point out that there is evidence that from an early age the child develops syntactically in a way which appears not to relate to development in other spheres. She cites Katz et al. (1974), who show that 17-month-olds can use syntactic information to distinguish between a noun referring to a class of objects and one functioning as a proper noun. Their experiment uses the invented word 'dax'. They found that when the infant hears 'a dax' it chooses a doll similar to one which the experimenter has already called 'a dax'; but when they hear 'Dax', they choose the individual doll which the experimenter has named 'Dax'. This suggests to Karmiloff-Smith (1992) that 'language is a problem space per se for infants'; they are thinking linguistically from an early age, perceiving language as an entity which needs special attention. Moreover, infants perceive language in this way 'well before they are producing much language themselves' (p. 44).

Karmiloff-Smith provides a good deal of (post Royaumont) evidence in general support of the Chomsky position and the notion of language having its own problem space, not related to cognition. Petitto (1987) exemplifies. This study concerns the child's acquisition of the personal pronouns 'I' and 'you' in American Sign Language (ASL). Most signs in ASL do not resemble natural gestures, but these two pronouns are exceptions – 'I' is encoded by pointing at oneself, and 'you' by pointing at the addressee. Because these are such natural gestures one would expect these pronouns to occur early in ASL, if sensorimotor intelligence is the basis of language acquisition. One would also expect ASL learners to avoid the temporary error that children learning other languages go through, of mistaking 'you' to refer to one's self. Neither of these expectations is in fact met – ASL learners learn the pronouns at the same time that learners acquire them in other languages, not before; and the temporary error is found in ASL as elsewhere. The child seems to be regarding language as a formal system with its own rules, not necessarily related to other aspects of the outside world. In Karmiloff-Smith's words: 'the deaf child ignores the indexical aspects of the signs (the pointing gestures that correspond to semantic information) and focuses on the formal aspect of the signs (personal pronouns as a formal linguistic system)' (p. 39).

Our conclusion regarding this particular issue must be that however much force an argument linking cognition and language has, it cannot be the whole story. Ample evidence exists, and continues to accrue, that language is to some extent a unique problem space for children, involving mechanisms that are not found in general cognitive growth.

How Comparable are the Developmental Patterns of Language and Cognition?

If the cognition hypothesis is correct, then we would expect the general patterns of cognitive and linguistic development to be comparable. We would further expect to find evidence of similar levels of capacity in both areas at any given point in time. We shall consider these issues in turn.

General developmental patterns

Those concerned with the biology of language, particularly Lenneberg (1966), argue that language development follows the pattern of other biologically controlled onsets of behaviour in occurring through 'leaps and bounds'. It is, according to Lenneberg, a trait of 'maturationally controlled' behaviours to develop through significant 'milestones', the baby's transition from crawling to walking being an oft-quoted example. Development does, of course, occur between milestones, and gradual transition is hence present, but nevertheless milestones are distinguishable. When attempting to compare the development of language and thought, we therefore need to ask whether cognition follows the same general milestone pattern, and whether any specific milestones in both areas coincide.

It is possible to find evidence of both cognitive and linguistic milestones in the child's development and, with a certain amount of imagination, to find some degree of coincidence between them. In the cognitive sphere, we have already noted the Piagetian stages; the transitions between these are clear candidates for milestones. Piaget also identifies substages: pre-operational thought, for example, being divided into the preconceptual (aged two to four and a half) and intuitive (four and a half to seven) substages. The first and most salient of the linguistic milestones occurs at around the age of 24 months, coinciding with the onset of pre-operational thought, and Lenneberg (1966), among others, notes the rapid growth of two-word phrases at this age. A consideration of the literature makes it possible to discern a further series of linguistic milestones between two years, when the first milestone takes place, and the age of nine, by which time most acquisition of syntax has occurred. An enthusiastic Piagetian would be able to link these with the cognitive milestones; a case might be made.

But there is plenty of counter evidence to this position. Citing Mandler (1983, 1988), Karmiloff-Smith (1992) provides cogent evidence to suggest that symbolic representation exists in early childhood, long before Piaget has it occurring. In her own words (1992): 'the data which have accumulated since the early 1980s call into question the very notion of a purely sensorimotor stage of human development prior to language' (p. 33). This introduces the question of why language acquisition, if related to cognition, occurs so late; the convenient developmental parallel between the end of the sensorimotor and the onset of language disappears with this view.

Levels of capacity

In the early days of transformational grammar, some of Chomsky's supporters used the apparent mismatch between what the child can do linguistically and what it can do cognitively at a given age as argument for the uniqueness of language. McNeill (1966), for example, studies the use of the two Japanese postpositions (a word class roughly comparable to the English preposition) 'wa' and 'ga' in two-year-old children. He concludes that their usage is apparently at odds with cognitive development: children are not claimed to be able to perform mental gymnastics of this order until they reach the age of seven or eight. This suggests different developmental patterns for language and cognition.

There are two main avenues of attack for those who attempt to reconcile this apparent gap between the child's linguistic and cognitive behaviour. One is to argue that the child's *linguistic* achievement is exaggerated in Chomskyan accounts, and is not in fact nearly so impressive. The other is to claim that the child's *cognitive* growth is in fact more impressive than appears at first sight. By these two means – de-emphasizing linguistic ability and emphasizing cognitive ability – the attempt is made to bridge the apparent gap between the two.

We have already exemplified one major instance of the first sort of argument – that what Chomsky analyses as structurally dependent syntactic rules are in fact semantic ones which of their very nature must be structurally dependent. Sinclair (1969) further propounds this same type of argument. She utilizes the distinction of Piaget (1954) and others in the semiotic literature between symbols and signs, and claims that: 'language, though it is a system of signs . . . that can be used for rationale discourse and communication . . . need not be used as such. In fact linguistic forms can be used as signals "to be reacted to" rather than "to be understood" (p. 364).' She, along with others, further notes how easy it is to overemphasize the child's linguistic ability on the basis of behaviour taken at face value. Her 1969 example is often used as illustration, where the child produces passives like 'John is washed by Mary' to indicate not passivity at all, but reciprocal action (John and Mary wash each other).

The second line of argument, that the child's cognitive growth level is underestimated, is commonly argued by those of the Genevan school who seek to show that cognition contains the roots of language acquisition. At the early stage, the belief is that the cognitive systems the child has developed in the sensorimotor stage are enough to lead it to develop symbolic thought, one version of which is language. Inhelder (1980), for example, looks at the bases for sensorimotor thought and attempts to show how they are reflected in early linguistic performance. She quotes Sinclair (1971):

> at the sensori-motor level, the child can establish connections of order, time, and space; he can classify objects – in other words he can use a class of objects for the same actions or apply sets of programmed actions to a single object. He is able to connect objects with actions, as well as to interconnect actions among themselves. The linguistic equivalent of such structures would be concatenation and categorisation, especially the essential categories of P, SN, and SV as well as functional grammatical relationships: subject of, object of, etc. (Inhelder 1980, p. 134)

Inhelder adds: 'Sensori motor schematizations would thus provide the child with heuristic procedures allowing him to approach the syntactic and dialogical structures of his language' (p. 134). More recently, Smolak and Levine (1984) study the development of object permanence – the concept that allows children to retain a representation of an object when it is not present. One might imagine object permanence to be a cognitive prerequisite for the growth of what they call representational language – referring to past events and absent objects. They do indeed reach the conclusion that a particular stage of object – concept development is reached before representational language can occur.

Looking beyond the sensorimotor to other levels, Inhelder (1980) is generally concerned to indicate parallels in cognitive and linguistic development. She considers, for example, the passive and the onset of concrete operations, and also notes work by Bovet on the acquisition of length, indicating similarities there with the processes involved in the acquisition of gender. Karmiloff-Smith (1992) and Cromer (1991) contain useful references to the extensive research in this area, and Sinclair (1971, 1987) is also worth consulting as a principal proponent of the language–cognition relationship.

But detailed parallels like this are disputed. Karmiloff-Smith (1992) comes out clearly against the notion that sensorimotor mechanisms control language development, and part of her argument concerns such details: 'syntax', she claims, 'does not simply derive from exploratory problem solving with toys, as some Piagetians claim. Lining up objects does not form the basis for word order. Trying to fit one toy inside another has nothing to do with embedded clauses. General sensorimotor activity alone cannot account for specifically linguistic constraints' (p. 11).

Debate on these issues at Royaumont goes beyond consideration of detailed parallels, and includes the epistemological. Behind the claim that sensorimotor structures contain the basis of symbolic thought is Piaget's (1980) general belief that 'the previous structure already contained something of the subsequent one, containing it not as structure, but as a possibility' (p. 150). But for Fodor (1980), 'it is never possible to learn a richer logic on the basis of a weaker logic, if what you mean by learning is hypothesis formation and confirmation' (p. 148).

Our brief consideration of the literature might lead to the conclusion that some parallels between the development of language and thought could indeed be established. But even if these parallels are accepted without dispute, it is important to note that they may provide no more than corroborative evidence for the cognition hypothesis. This is because so many types of relationship other than a straight causal one would involve parallels. It is in fact accepted even by the Chomsky camp that the innate structures of language will not come to light until cognitive prerequisites are met. But this is a far cry from saying that cognitive structures account for language development. A degree of cognition is unarguably a necessary condition for language acquisition; but this is not to say that it is a sufficient prerequisite.

Is One Ever Found without the Other?

Animal communication

Animals display various degrees of intelligent behaviour. If they are shown not to have any means of communication through something like language, then we have a clear case of 'thought' without language, potentially an argument for the two being different.

The conclusion one reaches regarding this question much depends on how one defines language. Taken in the clearly over-narrow sense only to include means of communication using the auditory–vocal channel, then many systems of animal communication (such as bee dances) would be precluded. The broader one is prepared to be in one's definition, the more able one is to include behaviours like bee dancing as a form of 'language'. Hockett (1960) represents one systematic attempt to characterize language, by means of thirteen design features. We shall not enumerate these design features here, but note that Hockett has a table that considers a number of animal 'languages' in terms of these features. Along with bee dancing, the list includes stickleback courtship, western meadowlark songs, and gibbon calls. The table reveals that most of these forms of communication share some, but not all, of the characteristics of language, and it must be concluded that most of the animal communication systems are not readily comparable with language in any meaningful sense.

The chimpanzee experiments

More hopeful are the attempts to teach chimpanzees (as a highly intelligent animal species) some form of language. The most famous are the Gardners' work with Washoe in the 1960s (Gardner and Gardner 1969); and the

Premacks' experiments with Sarah which began in 1954 (Premack and Premack 1972).

There is much disagreement regarding the outcome of these experiments, largely concerning whether what was learned was really language or just an ability to imitate in a rather sophisticated way. It is relatively uncontentious to claim that apes' cognitive level is sufficient to permit the appearance of language. Premack's (1980) position is suitably modest. He avoids any 'strong' claim that human syntax arises from 'general cognitive factors'; but he does conclude that there are 'factors that both participate in human intelligence and play a role in language' (p. 208), and that apes have these. He discusses some of these factors. 'Representational capacity' is one, and he notes that apes have 'impressive representational competence' (p. 213). Mere possession of representations is not, however, enough. The species must also have accessibility to the representations, and be able to do manipulations with them. Many species, from insects to apes, possess 'cognitive maps', for example; yet the way in which insects utilize these may be highly restricted. The ape is able to make the map available for all sorts of tasks.

A third factor is 'causal inference', the capacity to perceive and represent cause–effect relationships, as exemplified in language by 'if–then' clauses, for example. Premack reports a series of impressive experiments that demonstrate that apes have understanding of cause–effect relationships. In one, apes are given pictures of an intact object and a changed one – for example, a whole and a cut apple, a dry and a wet sponge. They are also given pictures of objects that have 'caused' the change – a knife and a bowl of water, in the example above. Three of the four apes that Premack reports being tested were able to link the cause (e.g. knife) with the effect (e.g. cut apple) by matching the pictures. Other experiments reveal that the ape has similar capacities even when pictures are not used, and – to conclude as Premack does – 'chimpanzees not only have a schema for cause–effect relations, but they have one that can be activated by noniconic representations' (p. 219).

One may therefore conclude that apes do indeed exhibit a kind of sensorimotor intelligence, not unlike that which Piagetians would see as the basis for language in humans. If the cognition hypothesis is correct, one would therefore expect to see the development of language in apes. Is this in fact found? As we have just exemplified, apes are able to handle symbols in language-like way. But, as Karmiloff-Smith (1992) puts it: 'despite rich representational capacities, the most intelligent of chimpanzees can at best be taught – through incredibly extensive training – strings of manually encoded lexical items (Gardner and Gardner 1969) or a simple form of language-like logic (Premack 1986). . . . But this is not language (Premack 1986; Seidenberg 1985)' (p. 62).

In this debate the 'semantic versus syntactic' issue comes to the fore again. In an earlier section we noted Putnam's claim that Washoe's linguistic capacity may be accounted for in semantic terms. We also noted that early in his development the human child begins to display something different: mastery of syntax as formal system. As Brown (1970) notes: 'grammatical relations are defined in purely formal terms, and while they may, in early child speech, be more or less perfectly co-ordinated with the semantic rules, the two are not the same' (p. 222). It is this coming to grips with syntax as formal system that ape language lacks. Cromer (1991) cites an example from Brown (1970) of this crucial difference between human children and apes. Washoe was able to produce quite complex strings of 'words', but there was no evidence that word order (for example) played any role in meaning. This is in sharp contrast to the children Brown was studying, where word order, as a syntactic measure, came to carry meaning relatively early. In a later section, we shall see how Karmiloff-Smith also places great importance on this difference between children and apes.

It seems that we are left with a situation where apes have the sensorimotor intelligence for language, but do not produce it. This is something of a severe blow for the cognition hypothesis, which is left to explain why language has not apparently appeared spontaneously in apes. Chomsky (1987) illustrates just how severe a blow it is when he draws attention to the 'enormous selectional advantages' (in evolutionary terms) of language, and observes that it is almost inconceivable for apes to be potentially able to produce it yet not to do so; this would be like humans having the ability to fly but never doing so because 'no one ever told them the right way to move their arms around'.

Linguistic savants

Chimpanzees provide just one of a number of possible 'test-case' areas of whether 'one (language or cognition) is found without the other'. Among the other test case areas are humans whose strokes or other pathologies cause linguistic deficits, but apparently no others.[2]

Particularly interesting cases are the so-called linguistic savants. Savants (sometimes referred to as idiot-savants) are individuals who in most areas have gross deficits yet who shine in one area. A linguistic savant called

So I'm gonna have to, at some point, settle down, somewhere, [Uh-huh] somehow. Mum didn't mind me moving about, but Dad objected to it because he knew it was bothering me and it was bothering my schoolwork. [Um-hmm]. And now I'm [getting on] like a house on fire and he doesn't want to destroy it. He said I'm not going to destroy this for her, she can just keep going. [Uh-huh]. I love to move around with my Dad because of his work. (Um-hmm]. But he feels if he keeps on doing that to me, I'm never gonna get anywhere. [Um-hmm]. Which is fair enough. I've got friends here.

Figure 1.1   Sample from a transcript of D. H. in conversation with Richard Cromer (Cromer's contributions are given in brackets; from Cromer 1991).

Christopher is studied by Smith and Tsimpli (1991, 1995). Christopher has a low IQ and is institutionalized as being incapable of looking after himself. Yet he has learned around 16 foreign languages. Smith and Tsimpli admit that their study is in its early stages and that as yet no conclusions can be reached. But they acknowledge that Christopher 'provides a test case for the role of cognition in adult language learning'. Admittedly his case concerns not a first language-learning child but a foreign language-learning adult; yet his very existence is something of an embarrassment to the cognition hypothesis.

Cromer (1991) discusses another such case. Cromer was long an advocate of the cognition hypothesis. His book reviews the current research situation regarding the cognition hypothesis, and one of his findings is that there remains a good deal of evidence in favour of it, which he discusses at length. This evidence does not, however, prevent him from reaching a contrary conclusion, that 'language acquisition proceeds on a different course, basically independent of general cognitive development' (p. 135). A main piece of evidence that leads this lifelong advocate of the cognitive hypothesis to such a conclusion is related to the case of D. H., a child who has spina bifida with arrested hydrocephalus. A large number of cognitive ability tests have been run on the child, and she consistently appears as severely retarded, not just in intellect but also in the functions of everyday life (she cannot, for example, cope with money). But her language is both fluent and appropriate. Figure 1.1 is reproduced (slightly abridged) from Cromer (1991) and well illustrates the linguistic ability she possesses.

Cromer's 'conversion' from the cognitive hypothesis (as set out in chapter 2 – written just before his death – of his 1991 book) illustrates that linguistic savants, like apes, provide difficult evidence for the hypothesis to handle.

'Specialized Hardware' in the Young Child

Where does this brief consideration of the literature take us? In the Foreword to his discussion of the Royaumont conference, Piatelli-Palmarini (1980) asks the question regarding the Chomsky–Piaget debate: 'who won?' The answer is not a straightforward one. Many participants came to the conference with entrenched positions they were unlikely to change. Piatelli-Palmarini does, however, recognize a degree of impartiality among the biologists, who have no particular affiliation with either school. And they, it is remarked, 'seemed closer to Chomsky than to Piaget' (p. xxxi). Chomsky the winner by a head?

If one goes beyond the Royaumont confrontation to the debate at large, one must conclude similarly – that there is some weight of evidence in the direction of the 'specialized hardware' camp (to utilize the phrase from Cellerier we quoted earlier). Such evidence places clear limits to the efficacy of the cognition hypothesis as a means of explaining language acquisition.

But there is more to say. Returning to the issue of ape language for a moment, Karmiloff-Smith (1992) makes the point that even if there are some similarities between a child's early language output and that of a chimpanzee (to do with semantic processing), what the child very soon does with that language goes far beyond what any animal would be capable of. This leads her to ague that however language-specific the capacity underlying the early use of language, this is far from the final product – the language that is developed by the time the child reaches adolescence. We shall now consider how, in Karmiloff-Smith's model, language is seen as developing.

The 'Representational Redescription' (RR) Model

Karmiloff-Smith's 1992 book is entitled *Beyond Modularity*, and it is concerned with the child's entire development, not just in language. The mention of modularity is taken from the title of Fodor (1983) – *The Modularity of Mind* – a book that argues through the case for the 'specialized hardware' view of human development. Although, as her title states, Karmiloff-Smith goes beyond (and has the child going beyond) this modularity, her position is that the force of evidence weighs in favour of modularity in early growth.

Her position is thus not that of Piaget, even though she once worked as a researcher within the Piagetian Genevan school. She now feels that 'Piaget's strong anti-nativism and his arguments for across-the-board stages no longer constitute a viable developmental framework' (p. 11). In her discussion of the Chomsky–Piaget debate, she argues that supporters of the Chomsky position would look for, and would find, plenty of linguistic precursors to language. 'Attention biases', she says, 'and some innate predispositions could lead the child to focus on linguistically relevant input and, with time, to build up linguistic representations that are domain-specific. Since we process language very rapidly, the system might with time close itself off from other influences – i.e. become relatively modularised' (p. 36).

Karmiloff-Smith hence accepts a degree of domain-specific growth of language at the early stages. But the crux of her model is that eventually the child is able to generalize this specialized knowledge so that it becomes available for general cognition. This generalizing comes about through a process of what she calls 'representational redescription' (RR). She approaches this concept by means of an example related to the skill of piano playing. In the early stages of playing, one practises a piece until it can be played more or less automatically. But the automaticity is constrained by the fact that the learner can neither start in the middle of the piece nor play variations on a theme. There is no flexibility; the piece has been learned as a routine. But at a later stage, this flexibility develops so that the pianist may start at different points, change the sequential order of the notes, add improvisations and so on. This change is the result of a restructuring of the representation of the piece that the learner has – what Karmiloff-Smith calls a representational redescription. Using a word that we shall be discussing at length in chapter 4, she describes the early representations as 'procedural'; with time they change to become 'available as manipulable data'. Although she concedes that some pianists never go beyond the stage of procedural representation (just playing the piece automatically), it is characteristic of human learning that it goes beyond mere behavioural mastery of the skill, to an ability to understand it, to manipulate its component parts, and to make them available for other activities and tasks.

Karmiloff-Smith's model postulates various levels of representation which become progressively more generalized. The first level she calls Implicit (I), in which the child has knowledge, but in the form the novice piano player above has it. Gradually, this knowledge becomes more 'explicit' at levels E1, E2 and E3 (where E = explicit). Her model holds for all areas of learning, including language. One of the language learning examples she uses to illustrate this process concerns the child's ability to segment the continuous speech stream into appropriate word boundaries. It relates specifically to the definite article form 'the'. Speech stream segmentation is, of course, no easy task; it uses reasoning processes and general learning mechanisms, yet by an early age children are able to do it, and their usage clearly indicates that for them 'the' is a word – it operates like one in their speech; they have an I-representation of it. There is plenty of evidence, however, that it is not until about age six that the child recognizes 'the' (and other closed-class 'grammatical' words) as true words. Ask the child under six if 'table' is a word and the reply will be 'yes'; but ask the same child if 'the' is a word and the answer will be 'no' – young children asked to count words will omit all closed-class items in their total. After the age of six, both are recognized as words, and the older child may therefore be said to have an E2–3 level representation. A Karmiloff-Smith, J. Grant, M.-C. Jones and P. Cuckle (unpublished observations) set out to show that there is an intermediary stage, E1. They designed tasks that required some level of 'grammatical understanding' to accomplish, but fell short of an expression of metalinguistic knowledge of the sort 'Is X a word?' One of the tasks they devised involved the children listening to a story which was frequently stopped, with the children being asked to repeat 'the last word'. The RR theory predicts that the young child with I-representation would not identify closed-class items like 'the'. The six-year-old with E2–3 would, of course; but between the two, they predicted, there would be an E1 level, where five-year-olds would recognize 'the' as a word in the story-telling task, but not if asked the direct question: 'Is "the" a word?'

Although at the I level of representation, human and ape language may have things in common, the essential difference lies in the animals' inability to go beyond behavioural mastery and develop E representations. She cites an interesting example from Premack (1988) of the plover, who practises a kind of 'deception' by leading potential intruders away from its fledglings. This behaviour is apparently innate. It can be modified by learning (the plover can eventually discern the degree of risk a given intruder poses, and takes appropriate action), but it is not generalized into behaviours other than those of protecting fledglings; it cannot 'deceive' in a general sense. In Premack's words: 'the bird is analogous to a human who could tell lies about pilfering fudge; he could not tell lies about dirtying the carpet, breaking the lamp, talking money from his mother's purse . . .'. (p. 161). There is, one might say, an I but no real E.

Similar points may be made about the chimpanzee's behaviour in general, and its use of 'language' in particular. The chimp does not go beyond successful mastery as the child does. Karmiloff-Smith notes that in her communications with Premack, the latter was unable to recall any 'case of a chimpanzee's spontaneously analysing the components of successful behaviour in a way the child does' (Premack 1988, p. 191). This leads Karmiloff-Smith to conclude, in relation to language, that 'even if the chimpanzee were to have an innately specified linguistic base, . . . it would still not go as far as the normal human child' (p. 63). We shall return to Karmiloff-Smith's view of this child/animal difference in chapter 5.

Conclusion

Karmiloff-Smith's RR theory manages a kind of reconciliation between Piaget and Chomsky. The concluding section of her chapter dealing with language is headed 'From the nativist infant to the constructivist linguist'. We have suggested in this chapter that there is indeed a strong argument for nativism in the early stages of L1 acquisition. But there is equally strong evidence for an eventual constructivist linguist. However domain-specific early language growth is, the eventual result of L1 acquisition is a system where language becomes available to domain-general processes and knowledge. In the terms of this book, we end up with a product that is like a general skill, even if it does not begin life as such.

Notes

1   See, for example, Carmichael et al. (1932).
2   See Cromer (1991) for discussion on what research into aphasia and other conditions might imply for the language–cognition relationship.

2 Language as Skill

We concluded the last chapter with the argument that whatever language starts life as, it ends up being something that contributes to general cognition. This conclusion does not in itself mean that language is a skill comparable with others. But it does leave open to us the possibility of exploring ways in which language shares characteristics with other skilled behaviour. We shall undertake this exploration in the present chapter.

We shall argue here that language may indeed be convincingly characterized in skill terms. One reason why this need cause no surprise is that the predominant models of skills psychology have been applied to language in an explicit way. Similarities are evident because the same descriptive models are being used. But this is in itself significant. Psychologists and linguists have chosen to utilize such models for language, and their choice clearly involves the implication that language may be regarded as a skill; the same models are used because the behaviours are felt to be comparable.

Motor and Cognitive Skills: Are They Comparable?

A good proportion of the skills literature deals with skills that have a large perceptual motor component, like playing tennis, driving a car, operating a lathe. This immediately raises the general issue of the extent to which discussion of skills like these is relevant to higher level skills in general, of which language may be one. Is anything about operating a lathe relevant to playing chess, conducting an orchestra, writing poetry? There are certainly those who stress the need to be cautious in comparing; Holding (1989) warns that 'extending the idea of skill to include cognitive skills introduces quite different research issues, explanatory concepts, and kinds of methodology' (p. 1). But it is a generally accepted view that all perceptual motor skills, however 'low level' they may seem, do have a cognitive element to them; Colley and Beech (1989) refer to this element as 'substantial', and Welford (1968) claims that 'all skilled performance is mental in the sense that perception, decision, knowledge and judgement are required . . . There are thus many features common to both sensorimotor and mental skills . . .' (p. 21). Similarly, many skills which we may think of as predominantly cognitive also have a perceptual motor component. Language is a case in point because all the four skills of listening, speaking, reading and writing entail motor actions (involving ears, lips, tongues, glottises, eyes, hands, and various other parts of the body). Factors like these lead many to focus on similarities rather than differences between the perceptual–motor and the cognitive. Hence Fitts and Posner (1967) speak of the 'close relationship of perceptual–motor and symbolic processes', while more recently Bechtel and Abrahamsen's (1991) (connectionist) model recognizes the centrality of pattern recognition to all levels of processing, from basic perception to complex cognition. It was the feasibility of similarities and common elements that led Fitts and Posner in the 1960s to attempt to develop a 'Human Performance Theory' that would account for all human skills, including language. One finds similar attempts at work today, and Langacker's (1987) 'cognitive linguistics' is one of a number of models that utilize general cognitive processing mechanisms to describe language behaviour.

One major apparent difference between motor skills and language (together with other cognitive skills) causes concern to those not convinced that useful comparison can be made. It is that language production does not seem so related to stimuli as in other skills. As Herriot (1970) puts it: 'in a skilled task like tracking, the performance is judged by its success or failure in responding to the stimulus situation. In language behaviour, language output need not be correlated with stimulus conditions to the same degree' (p. 21). The point is important because so much of the skills literature deals with models developed to 'handle interaction with the environment' – to respond, that is, to incoming stimuli. But two further points need making. One is that not all non-linguistic skills are closely related to stimuli. Indeed, Poulton (1957) finds it possible to make a distinction between 'closed' and 'open' skills. In closed skills, reaction to restricted external stimuli is required; playing a stroke in tennis would be an example. In open skills, there is more unpredictability, less direct reaction to environmental stimuli, and the skill of diving might be an example. Language would clearly fall into this open category. The second point would be to argue that language use clearly involves some relationship to stimuli; after all, the phrase 'interaction with environment' that we use above contains the word 'interaction', which is commonly applied in the description of language use. One is not being Skinnerian and adopting a stimulus–response model of language use in recognizing that responses in conversational interaction (for example) must take account of, and be relevant to, environmental stimuli. Note the wording of the above sentence: it is not 'be derived from' (which would be the behaviourist's words), but 'take account of' and 'be relevant to'.[1]

Characteristics of Skills

What is a skill? We shall now consider the characteristics of skilled performance, particularly within an information-processing model. We shall then turn to language, to ascertain whether it shares these characteristics, and hence may be regarded as a skill.

The cybernetic base

In 1948 the American psychologist Norbert Wiener suggested the name cybernetics for the scientific study of communication systems, and the advent of cybernetics had a great influence on skill theory. The cybernetic model was prominent from the end of the 1940s until into the 1960s, but its influence extends far beyond this, and it is recognized that in the cybernetic approach lie the foundations of present-day cognitive psychology and learning theory. Cybernetics is to do with information processing, and the concepts which we are about to discuss in relation to it are as important and useful today as they were in the 1960s. Anderson (1980) – whose work is discussed in chapter 4 – recognizes this influence when he notes that 'while other types of analysis in cognitive psychology exist, information-processing is the dominant viewpoint' (p. 9). While it is true that cognitive learning theory goes well beyond cybernetics, its basis lies there, which is why we need to spend time on it here.

A central metaphor for the cybernetic approach is that of the servo-mechanism. This is a mechanism constructed to reach and maintain certain desired states. If the mechanism receives feedback from the environment that the desired state is not being maintained, corrective action takes place. A central heating system offers a clear example. The system might be set to maintain a 'desired state' of 20° centigrade. A thermometer receives feedback from the 'environment' (using this word in its general sense to refer to some aspect of the 'outside world'), and keeps the system informed about the actual temperature. If this falls below the required figure, the boiler raises the temperature until the discrepancy between actual and desired is eliminated. We therefore have the following ingredients: a mechanism with a desired state (the system); input received from the environment (about temperature, from the thermometer); output geared to eliminate discrepancy (the boiler switching on and off).

It was in the spirit of the age to attempt to apply mechanical concepts to areas of human behaviour (Wiener's wartime work was on guided missile systems, and his study of electronic devices encouraged comparison between them and human processes). Hence it was regarded as insightful to view the skilled performer as a kind of servo-mechanism. The three important ingredients referred to above are present in the skilled performer. A desired state exists, information is received from the 'environment' concerning the present state of affairs, and the performer takes whatever action is necessary to achieve his aim, bearing in mind the information he receives from the environment. We shall now put flesh onto this skeletal description by considering six important concepts involved in this basic model, illustrating these concepts with reference to non-linguistic skills.

1   **Skills are hierarchically organized**. Miller et al. (1960) show how the notion that skills are hierarchically organized goes at least as far back as the turn of the century. The example they take from Book (1925) well illustrates the role that hierarchical structuring plays in the learning process. Book describes how novices learn typing skills. Learners first develop 'letter habits', identifying each letter one at a time and finding it on the keyboard. Then 'word habits' are formed, with some words being learned as special routines. Finally, the learner works at the level of the phrase (with 'phrase habits'), processing text a phrase at a time. As we shall see in chapter 4, the notion of 'automizing' lower hierarchical levels ('letters' in relation to 'phrases') in order to concentrate on the next higher level plays an important role in skill learning. Later writers, such as Shaffer (1975), similarly recognize a hierarchical structure to typing skills, and Miller et al. add to the typing example their own detailed description of the skill of hammering, divided into hierarchies. Holding

(1989) notes that various skill models recognize and give importance such hierarchical characteristics.

2   Skills are goal-directed behaviour. The notion of *directed action* is a central one. Servo-mechanisms contain within them an 'intention' – what MacKay (1972) calls the 'internal "target" criterion' (we have referred to this above as 'desired state') – and this guides their behaviour. To illustrate from the skill of playing tennis, the player will have a hierarchy of aims. In the longish term, one may be to win a particular tournament; this will involve a shorter term aim of winning a particular game against a particular opponent, and an even shorter one, at a specific moment, to play a fast low stroke into the back right-hand corner of the court. Note that once again one is dealing with a hierarchy, this time of 'desired states'. Models of skilled performance and learning must take the directed nature of skilled actions into account; and in Miller et al. (1960) this is reflected by their notion of 'Plans'. One might further argue that goals should clearly stand in adequate skill models as the starting point of any description of performance. In the Anderson model which we shall outline in chapter 4, the computer-like rules for skilled production begin with a statement of intention, and have the form: 'IF the aim is to achieve X, THEN do Y'.

3   Skills involve evaluation of data. It is the existence of goal-directedness that invests with importance the concept of *evaluation* in the cybernetic model: an aim provides something against which to evaluate the current state of affairs, the input the mechanism receives. Here is the quotation from MacKay which includes the phrase noted in the paragraph above: 'directed action by an organism is distinguished from mere undirected activity by an element of evaluation: a proccess whereby some indication of the current or predicted outcome is compared against some internal "target criterion" so that certain kinds of discrepancy or "mismatch" (those "negatively valued") would evoke activity calculated to reduce that discrepancy' (p. 11). Reed (1968) puts it like this: 'skill depends upon an active temporal/spatial organisation which is responsive to, and continually regulated by, discrepancies between activity and intention' (p. 110). In human skills, the relationship between action and intention is rarely so simple as it is in basic servo-mechanisms, but it is nevertheless there. To elaborate the tennis example: players are constantly evaluating the speed the ball approaches them, its angle, its likely position of contact with the court were it not to be hit, and so on. If the player does hit the ball, the stroke is the result of an evaluation all these pieces of information mediated by the intention of playing the winning stroke (delivering it in a certain part of the court, at a certain speed, etc.).

4 Skills involve selection. When we come to consider the 'output' that the mechanism produces in response to the input it receives mediated by an aim, the concept of *selection* becomes important. Skilled performers are seen as choosing what action to perform from a choice available to them; in the case of skilled tennis players, they have a considerable repertoire of strokes available for them to choose from in any given situation. There are some important points to be made about the nature of the choices made in skilled performance. One is that the number of choices available at any one time may be very large. There are exceptions, of course, and in operating a lathe the courses of action available at any given time might be highly restricted. But for more complex skills like playing tennis, there may be a large selection. The player may respond to a particular input' received (an opponent's stroke) in a large variety of ways; for a skilled player the repertoire of types of stroke to play will be huge. A second point is that in many skills the choices must be made quickly, in 'real time'; the tennis ball crosses the net at speed, and the player must respond in a split second. Selection from the vast repertoire of options must be made with speed.

5 Skills involve 'combinatorial skill'. An important point that emerges from characterizations of skill is that good performance involves a lot of what may be called 'combinatorial skill' – doing more than one thing at the same time. The tennis example above illustrates well. The stroke that the player eventually makes is the response to many inputs combined together. Some of the controlling input factors are: the speed the ball approaches, its angle, an evaluation of where it will go if it is not played at all (in or out of the court), where the opponent is placed, what the opponent is expecting. We might say that the player must 'get it right' in relation to all these parameters at the same time, and when in later chapters we come to consider language learning and teaching, we shall argue that training the novice performer to 'get it right' on various levels at once is vitally important. A metaphor from Craik (1943) makes this point well. The skilled performer is compared to 'a kind of calculating machine capable of receiving different inputs and producing an output which is derived from the various input parameters acting in concert' (Welford 1970, p. 31). The important words in this context are 'in concert'.

6 Skilled behaviour is non-stereotyped. Another important aspect of the selections the skilled performer makes is that they are non-stereotyped, and it is this aspect of skill that enabled the cyberneticists of the 1950s to do something historically very important for them to do: to distinguish skills from habits. This was important because the latter were the basis of behaviourist theory; in behaviourism, skills were habits. Oldfield (1959) uses notions of choice and versatility to make the distinction: 'habit demands conformity to a prescribed, standard sequence of motor acts, while in skilled behaviour the same act is, strictly speaking *never* repeated . . . in a skill the effectiveness of the behaviour is *dependent* upon the absence of stereotyping' (p. 34). The unique nature of a skilled action ('never repeated', in Oldfield's words) is indeed an essential part of what distinguishes it from a stereotyped habit. Craik (1943) makes a similar point when he speaks of skilled performance resulting 'in a response which is unique on each occasion, although it is determinate and based on constants which are, at least in principle, discoverable'; and more recently we have Summers's (1989) statement that 'human skills are seldom performed in exactly the same way twice' (p. 58).

Legge and Barber (1976) retell a story, taken from Johnson (1961), where the moral is that versatility is indeed a hallmark of skilled behaviour. It is the story of the 'Wood Chopper's Ball'. This is about a contest between two woodsmen, both highly skilled with the axe. On a large number of tests they come out as equal, and the judge has the problem of distinguishing them. Eventually it is decreed that they should swap axes, and chop with each other's axes, rather than the ones they are used to. The champion emerges as the one who can adapt to the situation better. Skill demands flexible responses, not just a fixed set of actions.

There are other concepts related to the cybernetic view of skills which we might note in passing. As is clear from what has so far been said, servo-mechanisms involve a feeding back of information about perfomance, a 'matching or comparison of "output" with "input"', to use yet another formulation from Reed (1968, p. 113), and this involves *information processing*. For this reason it is natural for skill psychologists to utilize the concepts of communication or information theory. One such is the notion of *doubt* or uncertainty. A concern of information theory was to establish the means for measuring information, and this was done in terms of the amount of doubt it eliminates. Reed's (1968) example is linguistic. The word 'yes' in reply to the question 'Is it a boy, doctor?' is exceedingly informative because it eliminates all possible alternatives, and hence all doubt. A further key concept from information theory is that of *channel capacity*. Signals are conveyed along channels, whose capacity can measured in terms of the number of pieces of information they can carry. Reed (1968) notes that is has long been known that when two stimuli (e.g. lights) are presented in rapid succession, the time taken to respond to the second stimulus is delayed. Welford (1952) argued that this is because the human nervous system cannot handle two stimuli presented in rapid succession. The system can, in other words, be regarded as a single communication channel of limited capacity.

To conclude this section, below is an attempt to summarize the view of skilled behaviour set out in the paragraphs above.

> Skills are goal-directed, hierarchically organized, non-stereotyped behaviours. From the environment, the performer receives information along various parameters. The performer's response is selected from a large repertoire of possible responses. It must be appropriate along all the relevant parameters (hence exhibiting considerable 'combinatorial skill'), and in many cases must be executed speedily.

Language as Information-processing Skill

How well does the above characterization of skill fit language? Cybernetics and information-processing concepts have certainly had influence on language studies, and even on language teaching. A linguist whose view of language relates closely to the cyberneticist's view of skill is Halliday, and one also finds in influential texts such as Lyons (1968) considerable recourse to cybernetic, information-processing principles. We shall consider these influences by looking at each of the above six characteristics of skilled behaviour, and showing how they may be said to apply to language. Although we are thus engaging in a point-by-point comparison, our aim is in fact far more general – to produce convincing argument that a view of language as skill is persuasive, insightful, and useful for language teachers.

1   **Language is hierarchically organized.** A glance at the index of almost any introductory textbook to the study of language is likely to find an entry under 'hierarchy', with the associated discussion revealing some way that language is indeed a hierarchically organized system. Herriot's (1970) entry (for example) refers to discussion of the basic language hierarchy of phonology, grammar and semantics, with sub-hierarchies like

First-order goal: to express particular intention
Second-order goal: to decide on topic
Third-order goal: to formulate a series of phrases
Lower-order goals: to retrieve lexicon needed
to activate articulatory patterns
to utilise appropriate syntactic rules
to meet pragmatic conventions

Figure 2.1 The hierarchical task structure of speaking (from McLaughlin 1987, based on Levelt 1978)

the morpheme level also being identified. Transformational psycholinguists were fond of pointing out that language processing does not work on a purely linear level, but takes account of hierarchical structure. Hence the verb following the phrase 'the friends of his brother' will be plural, not singular, even though linearly the last word ('brother') is a singular one; the user knows that the verb must agree with an entity higher on the hierarchical structure than that of the immediately preceding word. The generative grammarians' tree diagrams are instruments for indicating hierarchies in syntax, and all linguistic theories are obliged to adopt some means or other of indicating the hierarchies that exist in all languages' syntax – look up 'hierarchy' in the index of Bolinger (1968), for example, and you will be led to the tagmemic version of the tree diagram, while linguistic models like Halliday's (1961) 'scale and category' grammar clearly place hierarchical levels at their very basis.[2] On another level, an example of the way the complex task of speaking is divided into sub-tasks is found in Levelt (1978). Figure 2.1 is McLaughlin's (1987, p. 135) table based on Levelt's description.

2 **Language is goal-directed behaviour.** In the quotation about 'directed action' given earlier, MacKay (1972) is in fact talking about communication systems in general. His concern is to differentiate true communication from what he calls communication-like activity – activity which informs, but where the intention to communicate is lacking. His example of the latter is a spotty face, which may inform of the presence of measles, but is not an act of communication. Hence 'directed action' is seen virtually as a defining characteristic of communication systems, including language. The starting point of linguistic analysis for linguists like Halliday is the user's 'desire to mean' – a concept of goal-directedness. Linguistics should therefore (it may be claimed) study language in

relation to its uses. 'The more', Halliday says (1973), 'we are able to relate the options in grammatical systems to meaning potential . . . the more insight we shall gain into the nature of the language system' (p. 85). Note that McLaughlin's hierarchical task structure of speaking, shown above, specifies its hierarchy in terms of 'goals' at the different levels.

3   **Language involves evaluation of data.** Psycholinguists have long realized that the processes of listening and reading, once referred to as 'passive' skills, are very far from being so. The language receiver (listener/reader) is involved in active processing of input, one important part of which is evaluative. In some models of listening, the evaluative element relates to the listener's attempts to discern the speaker's intentions, one example being Demyankov's (1983) so-called 'new model of understanding'. Rost (1990) criticizes such models not only because they are not 'new' at all, but more importantly because they fail to recognize the goal-directed starting point for understanding: 'what such a . . . model essentially overlooks is that people listen for a purpose and it is this purpose that drives the understanding process' (p. 7). In models where listener/reader purpose is central, part of the evaluative element will involve searching for what Cherry (1957) calls 'pragmatic information'. This is not equivalent to semantic information; it is that part of the total information conveyed which contributes to the information 'required' by the speaker. It is, in short, information which the listener/reader wants to receive. In listening and reading with some clearly identifiable purpose – reading a text for some specific piece of information, for example – this process and the evaluation it implies is most obvious. Of course, in most listening and reading such readily identifiable and discrete purposes are not always so obvious, and are likely to be more complex. In some cases they may add up to no more than sifting 'new' from 'known' information content. A further part of the evaluation process involved in listening and reading involves evaluating input in the light of knowledge of the world and knowledge about the speaker/writer.

The above observations relate to language reception (listening/reading), but language production (speaking/writing) also involves evaluation, as the producer evaluates feedback to his own output in order to gauge its effectiveness and appropriateness. Levelt (1989) makes the point that 'a speaker is his own listener' (p. 13), and ennumerates the questions a speaker asks in self-monitoring. They are: 'is this the message/concept I want to express now?; is this the way I want to say it?; is what I am saying up to social standards?; am I making a lexical error?; are my syntax and my morphology all right?; am I making a sound-form error?; has my articulation the right speed, loudness, precision, fluency?' (p. 460).

4 Language involves selection. For MacKay (1972) it is the concept of 'selection from a repertoire' that provides the central link between communication engineering and the study of biological communication. 'By viewing', he says, 'an organism as a system with a repertoire, and its environment as imposing a running pattern of demand for actions selected from this repertoire, we find ourselves talking essentially the same language as the communication engineer' (p. 11). The concepts of doubt and choice (implying selection) have found a place in the work of communication-minded linguists. Here is Lyons's (1968) expression of notions discussed earlier concerning doubt and information content: 'if the hearer knows in advance that the speaker will inevitably produce a particular utterance in a particular context, then it is obvious that the utterance will give him no information when it occurs; no "communication" will take place' (p. 413). Cherry (1957) indicates how the notions of doubt and selection are linked: 'Information', he says, 'can be received only when there is doubt, and doubt implies the existence of alternatives – where choice, selection or discrimination is called for' (p. 168).

Selection is also a key concept in Halliday's view of language. This is well exemplified (Halliday 1973) where he imagines a situation in which a child comes home with an object picked up on a building site. Mother disapproves, and has various ways of expressing disapproval. Halliday characterizes these in terms of available selections. Some are non-linguistic (a smack, for example). If the mother selects a linguistic course of action, then various choices of what to 'mean' are open to her (at another point in the paper, he says, 'we shall define language as meaning potential' (p. 72)). the mother might for example, decide on a threat, or an appeal, or reference to some rule ('that's not allowed'). Having decided on one type of meaning, various structural ways of expressing that meaning will be open to her. Hence instead of 'that's not allowed', we might find 'you're not allowed to do that', and so on. Halliday views these systems of choices as networks, and they are, of course, substantial in any given situation. Language use involves (in Halliday's (1970) words again) 'a simultaneous selection from among a large number of interrelated options' (p. 142).

5 Language behaviour involves 'combinatorial skill'. The term 'doing more than one thing at the same time' was used earlier in relation to this aspect of skilled activity, and language performance is a clear

example of this. Among the linguists, it is again Halliday who most
overtly recognizes this aspect of language skill; in the quotation given in
full in the preceding paragraph, he speaks of 'simultaneous selection',
while in the same paper he says that 'speech acts involve planning that is
continuous and simultaneous in respect to all the functions of language'
(p. 145).

If one asks the question: 'what are the things one does more than one
of at the same time?', then the most obvious answer is in terms of the
core linguistic areas. Hence when one responds to a question, one's reply
must conform to the syntax of the language, to its phonology and its semantics. The response must be 'well formed' in all these respects. But it
must conform in many other respects also, and Levelt's self-monitoring
questions cited earlier imply some of these. It must, for example, be
appropriate to speaker intention – saying what the speaker wants it to
say. It must also be appropriate to what has been asked, conforming to
rules and conventions of cohesion and coherence. It must also not con-
travene socially expected norms concerning role relationships (by, for
example, being too formal or informal). Since the beginning of the 1970s
and the emphasis on appropriateness in the work of sociolinguists like
Hymes, we have more awareness of what these parameters are, and in the
syllabus design work of the Council of Europe (e.g. Trim et al. 1980) we
find attempts to list parameters of appropriateness for the purposes of
syllabus construction. One way of viewing such attempts is that they list
some of the ways in which speakers must 'get things right' when they
plan utterances.

One further formulation of the same point might be useful. Grierson
(1945) characterizes the Aristotelian view of rhetoric as 'the study of how
to express oneself correctly and effectively, bearing in mind the nature
of the language we use, the subject we are speaking or writing about,
the kind of audience we have in view . . . and the purpose, which last is
the main determinant'. Johnson (1983a) links this statement with the
communicative teaching of writing, and uses it as the basis for a consideration of the levels on which appropriateness must be achieved.
Using the Hymesian categories of the 'appropriate', the 'possible', the
'feasible' and the 'performed', he produced figure 2.2 to indicate the
ways in which an utterance must conform. The number of boxes in
the diagram is insignificant, and could be considerably increased in number; one of the context ones would be 'role relationships', another would
be 'setting', and so on. The speaker 'gets it right' on all these levels when
he produces a successful utterance (output):

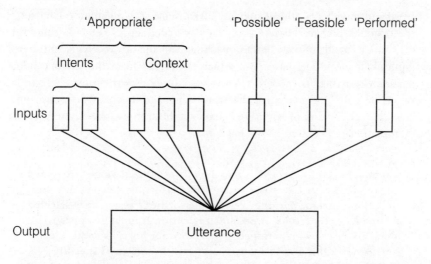

Figure 2.2 Input and output parameters in language use (from Johnson 1983a)

It is worth noting how easily a similar diagram could be used in relation to the tennis stroke discussed earlier. In that situation, the input parameters leading to the final stroke (output) would then be things like speed and direction of the ball, position of the opponent, and so on. The diagram well suggests the similarity in this respect between non-linguistic skills and language use.

6 Language behaviour is non-stereotyped. As we have already seen, there is, in Oldfield's terms, an 'absence of stereotyping' in the choices which are made in skilled performance. The Oldfield quotation was cited earlier in the context of discriminating skills from habits, and that discussion is reminiscent of one which occurred in the linguistics literature, where Chomsky argues against Skinner's view of language exhibiting SR bonds. In Oldfield's characterization of skilled behaviour, an action is 'strictly speaking never repeated' – there is a sense in which a tennis stroke is a unique event. In Chomsky (1964) the formulation is that 'except for a ridiculously small number (e.g., conventionalised greetings, etc., . . .), all actual sentences are of a probability so low as to be effectively zero' (p. 37). Though of course in both the skill and the linguistic case there are (Craik's formulation this time) 'determinate' underlying principles, what we are speaking about here is rule-governed creativity.

If we add together all the elements so far discussed in relation to language, the result is a characterization of language production very close indeed to Craik's 'kind of calculating machine capable of receiving different inputs and producing an output which is derived from the various input parameters acting in concert'. Below we take our own earlier characterization of skills and exchange the word 'language' for 'skills' throughout. The characterization of language behaviour that results can certainly stand examination:

Language is goal-directed, hierarchically organized, non-stereotyped behaviour. From the environment, the performer receives information along various parameters. The performer's response is selected from a large repertoire of possible responses. It must be appropriate along all the relevant parameters (hence exhibiting considerable 'combinatorial skill'), and in many cases must be executed speedily.

Language Teaching and Cybernetic Principles

This chapter is not about language teaching, but in a later one which is (chapter 9), an attempt is made to create links between an information processing-based learning theory and communicative language-teaching methodology. To provide background for this discussion we shall here make brief mention of ways in which some of the principles we have been discussing have already made their way into language teaching – particularly communicative language teaching. This is doubtless partly through the influence of Halliday, whose effect on communicative language teaching has been considerable, and certainly greater than generally thought. One of the notions we discuss above at length is that of 'doing more than one thing at the same time'. The term 'fluency' is associated with this notion, and the development of fluency may be seen as one of the prime concerns of communicative language teaching. Indeed, Brumfit's influential (1984a) book on communicative methodology is subtitled *The Roles of Fluency and Accuracy*, reflecting communicative language teaching's recognition of the need to provide students with practice at 'doing more than one thing at the same time'.

Johnson (1979) makes heavy use of some of the principles discussed above to argue in support of information-gap and information-transfer exercises in communicative methodology. These latter exercises reflect the central role of purpose in listening and reading. They lead away from listening and reading activities where there is no purpose other than 'understanding' (as would occur in practice based on models like Demyankov's mentioned earlier), and they move towards exercises where a purpose is stated, which to be met characteristically involves extracting information to be used in some other activity. Providing such purpose (Johnson argues) requires the important process of evaluation to take place. For production exercises, particularly in speaking, Johnson claims that it is important for the process of getting many things right at the same time, and for selections to be made quickly, that real time conditions should be simulated. This can only occur where there is an information gap, and interactants do not know in advance what is going to be said to them. With this condition met, processing and formulation of utterance must be done in real time. Johnson links these ideas with the concept of doubt mentioned earlier, quoting Cherry and Lyons, and claiming that in language teaching terms 'doubt' implies 'information gap'. Johnson also utilizes these concepts to account for communicative approaches to the teaching of writing. For him (1983a), the Aristotelian view of rhetoric as represented in figure 2.2 is the basis of communicative writing practice. Figure 2.2's boxes represent the parameters which control written language. They are many and complex, so much so that great combinatorial skill is involved in producing written text. This leads him to argue that the only sensible approach to communicative writing is one which begins with written exemplars (*not* models), and explores how their form and content relate to the 'boxes' – exploring the relationship between written word and intent and context.

Recent Concepts from Cognitive Psychology

Our view of skill in this chapter has focused on cybernetics and information processing, the justification for this being the central role such a view continues to play in cognitive psychology. But concepts developed more recently in that field have also been related to language. We shall not here attempt a comprehensive survey of these concepts, and will exemplify by means of just one illustration. It is related to discourse analysis (an area in which the importation of concepts from cognitive psychology has been particularly common).

Schemas

Anderson's (1980) definition of schemas is that they 'are large, complex units of knowledge that organise much of what we know about general categories of objects, classes of events, and types of people' (p. 128). As this definition suggests, one of the areas in which schemas have been studied in psychology relates to how we categorize. Anderson reports studies (e.g. by Rosch 1977) on the configurations of features which make up a familiar concept such as that of 'bird'. A number of studies reveal that in some Western societies, the robin is a more characteristic 'bird' than the chicken or the eagle – robin fits the bird schema more centrally than the other two. Anderson (1983) discusses how schemas may be incorporated into plans for actions in relation to skilled performance in general. Schemas for sequences of actions are known as scripts, and studies show how our pre-existing scripts colour the way we interpret stories we read or hear for the first time; we bring our scripts with us to the business of reading and listening comprehension. A common, oft-quoted example of this is Bartlett's (1932) *The War of the Ghosts* story. This is a story originating from the oral literary tradition of West Coast Canadian Indians. It contains many features alien to a society such as that of pre-World War I England, where Bartlett's subjects come from. He notes how in recall tasks his subjects tended to change the story to fit in with what they would expect to happen in such a situation. The changes involved not just omitting strange details, but also actually adding non-existent information which might be expected in the context. One extreme example is the subject who changes the original story, about two young men going down a river to hunt seals into 'two brothers going on a pilgrimage' (Bartlett 1932, p. 77). The relevance of this to language is clear from this example – what is heard or read depends greatly on the schemas we bring with us to the hearing or reading. For this reason it is not surprising that although the schema concept has relevance for all areas of language use, its influence on reading and listening studies has been particularly profound, and theories of both the processing and acquisition of reading skills have been based on this concept (for example, Anderson and Pearson 1988, and Carrell and Eisterhold 1988, respectively).

Characteristics of a Skilled Performer

So far we have largely been concerned with the issue of what characteristics a skill possesses. A further question, and one which Reed (1968) considers perhaps more fruitful to ask, is: what characteristics do skilled performers possess? – what distinguishes the skilled from the novice performer? Reed has the following list.

1 **Skilled performers work speedily.** This statement needs, according to Reed, to be interpreted with caution because of the widespread belief that improvement in a skill can be assessed wholly in terms of speed. He points out that this is not always the case, and indeed there are times when speed may decrease with proficiency, though in such cases as likely as not there will be a redistribution of speed allocated to the different components of the task. Where performance does get faster it will be because of restructuring of the task, plus automization of the subcomponents, issues we shall discuss later in this book.

2 **Skilled performers 'suppress flourishes'.** The term is Bartlett's (1947) and is used to describe the economy of action which distinguishes the expert from the novice. In mental tasks this is due, Reed suggests, to ignoring inessentials and maximizing information from information available. In Reed's (1968) words: 'in fact, one aspect of most skill development is that the subject becomes able to carry out the task with less information' (p. 108).

3 **Skilled performers quickly detect and throw out errors.** According to Bartlett, this is 'the best single measure of mental skill'. This may be viewed as a speeding up of the checking (feedback) process, and it is the case that the expert performers needs to run fewer checks on their action than novices.

4 **Skilled performers anticipate.** They can 'think ahead' and prepare what to do next. Part of the reason for this is that the size of units being processed increases with skill (a further case of restructuring).

5 **Skilled performers automize responses.** This is particularly true of the more 'low level', mechanical aspects of the task, which require less conscious attention to perform, freeing the conscious attention for higher level activities. One result of this is that skilled performers will be less consciously aware of performing the activities they have automized.

6 **Skilled performers are reliable.** Their performance will be less resistant to unfavourable conditions, as we saw in the case of the woodcutters mentioned earlier. As Reed (1968) notes: 'the top rank golfer or chess player is not necessarily *always* better than the competent club player; the point is that his performance is more *consistent*. His level is less likely to disintegrate in distracting or disturbing situations'.[3]

We shall not attempt to spell out links between these performer characteristics and language use. Many of them will strike resonances with the
reader. Some are already discussed in relation to language teaching and
testing – it may (for example) be said that cloze tests assess not only the
ability to anticipate, but also the ability to operate with less information, not
utilizing all the cues. If resonances are indeed struck, perhaps applied linguists should seek more applications and implications in the skill psychologist's view of the skilled performer.

Since Reed's account, a good deal of attention has been given to the
analysis of expertise, and the methods of doing this have been recently
tabulated in Ericsson and Smith (1991). One common method involves
expert–novice comparisons, and an example of this is found in Dreyfus and
Dreyfus (1986, cited in Bechtel and Abrahamsen 1991). They place great
importance on *holistic recognition of similarity* between situations the performer meets. They discuss this in the following terms:

> with enough experience in a variety of situations, all seen from the same
> perspective or with the same goal in mind but requiring different tactical
> decisions, the mind of the proficient performer seems to group together
> situations sharing not only the same goal or perspective but also the same
> decision, action, or tactic. At this point not only is a situation, when seen as
> similar to a prior one, understood, but the associated decision, action or tactic
> simultaneously comes to mind.
>
> An immense library of distinguishable situations is built up on the basis of
> experience. A chess master, it has been estimated, can recognise roughly
> 50,000 types of positions, and the same can probably be said of automobile
> driving. We doubtless store many more typical situations in our memories
> than words in our vocabularies. (p. 32)

This concept helps them towards a characterization of skill development
which has five stages. The *novice* employs precise rules, which apply to
objectively specifiable circumstances that can be recognized independently
of other aspects of the situation encountered. Their example of such a
principle is: shift to second gear when you obtain a speed of 10–15 m.p.h.
Since these rules are applicable independently of what else happens in the
context, they are *context-free*. Next, the *advanced beginner* begins to recognize the role of context, and to realize that in some situations the rules are
to be modified. These exceptions typically are not specified in terms of
additional context-free rules, but in terms of previously encountered situations. The *competent performer* is distinguished by developing a set of goals
that facilitate coordination of rules and known facts. Rules are no longer

applied simply because they will enable the performer to reach a goal. Since the competent performer sets the goals for particular situations, he or she no longer simply responds to events, but directs activity. The competent performer has become an agent responsible for his or her actions.

Dreyfus and Dreyfus' next stage is that of the *proficient performer*, who is able to rely extensively on recalling previous events similar to the current one. This recollection is not based on specific features, but on *holistic similarity*. With the *expert*, the whole process of responding becomes smooth and fluid (in contrast to the unevenness of the proficient performer), and the expert no longer exhibits any of the deliberativeness of competent performance. The expert sees the situation, and sees what to do. The expert also responds *intuitively*.

In this chapter we have attempted to persuade that what is said about skills and those who perform them may be equally applied to language and those who use it. We shall now turn our attention to language learning, to explore whether models of skill learning may be used to explain and describe L2 acquisition.

Notes

1 Gilhooly and Green (1989) make use of a distinction between 'adversarial' and 'non-adversarial' skills which has some relevance here. In 'adversarial' skills (e.g. chess, tennis), the presence of an adversary considerably increases the degree of unpredictability of input. Although a conversational interactant is not usually an 'adversary', the effect on input is the same.

2 See also Sinclair and Coulthard's (1975) model for analysing classroom discourse, which similarly uses hierarchical categories.

3 Vivian Cook (personal communication) has various points to make about some of Reed's characteristics of skilled behaviour: Regarding speed, he notes that books on calligraphy often explicitly warn against speed, and that fast speakers are not 'better' than slow speakers in any sensible use of the term. He further asks what a 'flourish' is in language use terms, noting that 'over-elaboration' is a valued skill in relation to some genres. Regarding reliability, he observes that he cannot imagine an unskilled player disintegrating in the way Ivanisevic did against Sampras in the 1994 Wimbledon tennis finals. 'Consistency', he claims, 'is only a virtue on rote tasks.'

3 Second-language Learning and Universal Grammar

Learning, Acquisition and General Cognitive Processes

Where we have so far in this book been concerned with language learning it has been first language (L1) learning. The issue of whether or not second language (L2) acquisition is comparable to L1 acquisition has a long and respectable history, with both sides of the argument having been developed fully in the literature. We shall not review that literature here, but note that in recent times various commentators have come to accept that there is more than one pathway to mastery of a second language, and that one of these may follow the L1 pattern, while others may not. The best known expression of this view is found in the work of Krashen (1982 and elsewhere). He has two pathways, which he calls 'learning' and 'acquisition'. For Krashen, learning is marked by the presence of feedback and rule isolation, and it is what happens in classrooms. Acquisition is the pathway which follows the L1 pattern in that it is what Dulay and Burt (1973, 1974 and elsewhere) call a 'creative construction process'. It is achieved 'without conscious focusing on linguistic forms' (Krashen 1977).

Many have been highly critical of the way Krashen sets up his distinction (see particularly McLaughlin 1987 and Gregg 1984). One major criticism concerns Krashen's insistence that the two systems (learning and acquisition) are, in Tarone's (1983) words, 'independent' and 'apparently homogeneous'. For this reason, Tarone refers to Krashen's model as the 'Dual Knowledge Paradigm'. She calls her own model the 'Capability Continuum Paradigm' because it allows for the gradual appearance of (a continuum of) forms being internalized over time. But it is important to note that even Tarone recognizes the existence of two different processes at work (her difference with Krashen lying in how these two processes are felt to relate to each other). Hence she notes (1983) that the Capability Continuum 'allows for two means of internalization of IL [Interlanguage]. In one means, the learner spontaneously produces simple structures in the vernacular style' (p. 155). In the other means, rules appear first in formal contexts, and spread to other styles over time. These two processes might sensibly be called 'acquisition' and 'learning'. Others (like Ellis 1985b) similarly accept the existence of two processes while operating within frameworks quite distinct from Krashen's, and it is hence quite acceptable to talk about learning and acquisition without any implication that this involves adherence to Krashen's Monitor Model. This is what we shall do here.

The issue we shall be considering in this chapter is whether or not mastery of a second language involves general cognitive mechanisms, or whether it can follow its own, separate pathway. Since (as we have just argued) there may be two possible processes by which 'mastery' may be reached – learning and acquisition – we need to consider the potential role of general cognitive mechanisms in both these processes. The questions, in other words, which we are asking are, 'is there evidence for a cognitive hypothesis for second language learning?' and 'is there evidence for a cognitive hypothesis for second language acquisition?' In this introductory section we shall consider some of the positions which may be taken regarding both these questions.

It is not a logical necessity that the 'learning pathway' should involve general cognitive mechanisms. But common sense suggests that it does, and although we may take this to be a relatively uncontentious claim, we shall approach the literature seeking for confirmation. If we find it, we shall be able to say that a second language *may* be mastered following a strategy utilizing general cognition. The 'acquisition pathway' is more problematic. One possibility is that general cognitive mechanisms are involved in L2 *acquisition*, but that the mechanisms are somehow different from those in L2 *learning*. Krashen himself (e.g. 1977) suggests as much when he relates his learning – acquisition distinction to what Lawler and Selinker (1971) call two types of 'general cognitive structure'. One is 'automatic language performance' (associated with acquisition, presumably), and the other is 'problem solving performance' (associated with learning?). Other similar distinctions are also found in the general cognitive skills literature, the best known being Schneider and Shiffrin's between 'controlled' and 'automatic' (Shiffrin and Schneider 1977; Schneider and Shiffrin 1977). One difference between these two which will be important to us in later chapters is that controlled processing consumes cognitive capacity, while automatic processing consumes little or no such capacity.

So it may be that both pathways involve general cognition, but with different sorts of processing. On the other hand, Krashen clearly associates L2 acquisition with L1 acquisition which, as we saw in chapter 1, in the early stages at least follows a pathway different from that of other cognitive structures. Thus, in regarding the acquisition pathway we have contrary views to decide between: one which applies a cognition hypothesis to L2 acquisition, and one which does not.

In this chapter we shall seek in the literature for arbitration concerning this issue. Before we do so, mention should be made of one model of L2 acquisition which recognizes two pathways and is clearly committed regarding how they relate to general cognition – Felix's 'Competition Model'. Felix (1986) begins by accepting the Chomskyan view that the young L1 child is unable to do cognitively what she or he can do linguistically; it is only with the onset of formal operations around the age of twelve in the Piagetian scheme that the child can manipulate formal structures in the cognitive domain (though, as we saw in chapter 1, the child seems able to manipulate complex formal structures in the linguistic domain at a much earlier age). Felix also agrees with Chomsky that the application of general learning procedures will not allow the young L1 child to arrive at the structures of natural language. He therefore accepts the notion of a language-specific learning strategy for L1 acquisition. This he calls the 'LS-system' (LS = language specific). But he also admits a role for general cognitive learning in L2 acquisition, particularly in the classroom, and this he refers to as the 'PS-system' (PS = problem solving). Since the PS-system is not available to the learner before Piaget's formal operations stage, L2 learning before the age of twelve is controlled by the LS-system only. But thereafter one sees both systems at work: 'there is some evidence to suggest', he claims, 'that language learning after puberty frequently proceeds in a way that seems to involve two distinct and independent types of mental activity' (p. 157).

To express our concerns in Felix's terminology: we have already seen that for L1 acquisition there is good evidence for an LS-system. In this chapter we shall seek evidence to: (a) confirm our expectation of a PS-system in L2 mastery, and (b) suggest the existence of some LS-system pathway for L2 acquisition. The evidence we shall be considering centres very much around the notion of Universal Grammar (UG). Therefore we need to spend time on some concepts related to this notion before considering the issue in detail. As will soon become apparent to the reader, the nature of the subject matter in this chapter necessitates a more detailed and more 'technical' treatment than in other chapters.

Universal Grammar and Second-language Acquisition

Central to the Chomskyan position on language acquisition which we out-lined in chapter 1 is the view that (in the words of Wode 1984) 'the kind of cognition required to be able to learn languages must be different from the kind of cognition or the capacities underlying problem solving or the kind of operations crucial in Piagetian types of developmental psychology'. In chapter 1 we discussed the arguments put forward in support of the idea that general cognitive structures cannot account for language acquisition. These arguments, particularly the 'poverty of stimulus' one (part of Plato's problem), are now commonly rehearsed in the introductions to discussions of L2 acquisition in the Chomskyan tradition, in White (1986) and Cook (1988), for example. The arguments suggests an innate component to lan-guage acquisition, and this component is said to have the form of a universal grammar – viewed as a set of abstract principles which limits the way in which the child can conceive of language. Until recently it was assumed that UG consisted of a set of linguistic universals found in invariant form in all the world's languages. But as we shall see below, it is now believed that UG principles vary somewhat from language to language, suggesting that 'there are certain restricted options, or open parameters, associated with a number of principles of UG' (White 1986, p. 56).

Before we look specifically at work done to relate UG to L2 acquisition, we need to consider three ideas which have played important roles in the field (at slightly different times in its development).

Implicational universals

Many UG studies base themselves on an in-depth study of one language, but some have been typological in nature, considering a number of world languages and seeking common elements. Three types of universals have been described. *Substantive* universals are actual fixed features (e.g. pho-netic or syntactic) that are found in all languages; *formal* universals are more abstract, dealing with underlying principles (for example, of word order constraints governing the construction of interrogatives). The third sort of universal is the one which needs further explication. *Implicational* universals relate one feature to the presence of some other one. An example of implication was given in chapter 1 from Greenberg, who relates the existence of SVO word orders to the presence of other phenomena. Ellis' (1985a) example is from the work of Comrie and Keenan (1978), and will be

Table 3.1   Types of relative clause

Symbol	Relative pronoun function	English example
SU	Subject	The man that kicked the dog . . .
DO	Direct object	The tree that the man cut down . . .
IO	Indirect object	The man that she cooked the cake for . . .
OBL	Oblique (in English = object of preposition)	The house that she lives in . . .
GEN	Genitive	The dog whose owner has died . . .
O COMP	Object of comparative	The man that I am richer than . . .

Source: Ellis (1985a, after Comrie and Keenan 1978)

SU > DO > IO > OBL > GEN > O COMP

Figure 3.1   Comrie and Keenan's (1978) relative clause accessibility hierarchy

given here in detail since we wish to refer to it later. Table 3.1 lists types of relative clause.

Comrie and Keenan are able to order these clause types in a hierarchy such that the presence in one language of one property implies the presence of all properties above but not below it on this list. This they refer to as an *accessibility hierarchy*, and it is as listed in figure 3.1.

Hence, in a language which has OBL, for example, you will find IO, DO, and SU, but not necessarily GEN or O COMP.

Markedness

The second concept is that of markedness/unmarkedness. Informal characterizations of the notion *unmarked* use terms like 'more natural', 'frequent,' 'basic', with *marked* being associated with 'the exception', 'less common'. Cook's (1988) non-linguistic example is that black sheep are marked, white sheep unmarked. Lyons' (1968) linguistic example is that singular nouns in English are unmarked, while the plural is marked by an 's'. Eckman (1977) provides a more rigorous definition which brings out two essential characteristics of the notions – their relational nature (principles are not marked or unmarked so much as *more* or *less* marked) and the involvement of implications: 'A phenomenon A in some language is more marked than B if the presence of A in a language implies the presence of B; but the presence of B does *not* imply the presence of A' (p. 320).

One of two examples which Eckman provides is syntactic and relates to passives. There are languages (e.g. Arabic, Greek, Serbo-Croat, Persian) which have passives without expressed agents but no passives with expressed agents. In other words, they permit sentences like 3.1, but not like 3.2:

(3.1) The door was closed.
(3.2) The door was closed by the janitor.

There are languages which have both passive types, but none which have passives with agents without having passives without agents. Therefore the presence of passives with agents implies the presence of passives without agents, but the reverse is not true. Hence sentences like 3.2 are more marked than sentences like 3.1 (For further examples related to English, see Rutherford 1982.) Although the marked/unmarked distinction is a relative rather than absolute one, it has been related to the issue of universals, with unmarked forms being the more common and hence the more universal. Indeed, around the beginning of the 1980s, linguistic theory introduced the notions of 'core' and 'peripheral' grammar (Chomsky 1980, 1981), with unmarkedness becoming associated with the former, markedness with the latter. Generative phonology has particularly exploited this notion, with Chomsky and Halle (1968) noting, for example, that /p, t, k, s, n/ are the least marked (most 'core') consonants, occurring in most languages. Other consonants, such as /v/ and /z/, are more highly marked and less 'common' or 'core' (Richards et al. 1985).

In the field of L1 acquisition it is usually assumed that unmarked forms are acquired before marked, White's (1983) references for this being Chomsky (1969), Kiparsky (1974) and Phinney (1981). In White's own words (1983): 'the child's initial hypothesis constitutes the unmarked case, the assumption that he or she will make in the absence of counter-evidence, whereas a marked option requires specific evidence and will not be considered without such evidence' (p. 310).

Markedness and cognitive complexity

It is important for us to be clear how the notions of cognitive simplicity/complexity and unmarkedness/markedness are related. We might expect unmarkedness to imply cognitive simplicity, and Eckman (1977) says as much when he observes that 'languages, and hence language universals, are a reflection of the structure of human cognition . . . if one makes the . . . assumption that humans learn to do things which are less complex before they learn to do things which are more complex, and, further, that no human being learns to do things which are more complex without also *a fortiori* learning to do related things which are less complex (Sanders 1977), then typological markedness is an accurate reflection of difficulty' (p. 329).

But although 'unmarked' *usually* means 'cognitively simple', need this *necessarily* be so? It is surely theoretically possible (in spite of what Eckman says above) to differentiate the two: constructs considered unmarked according to a definition like the one given earlier may not necessarily be those that a measure of cognitive simplicity would identify as 'easy'. Indeed, we shall see in a moment that it is possible to distinguish the ideas, finding cases where an unmarked form is not necessarily the 'simplest' one available. The relevance of such evidence will become obvious as our consideration of the UG literature unfolds.

The concept of markedness was prevalent in the 1970s and early 1980s, when (as mentioned earlier) the belief was that UG comprised some set of 'core' features. Since that time, the 'principles and parameters' model (first elaborated in Chomsky 1981) has come to the fore. This model is outlined below. In it, markedness does not play a central role, and indeed for many the concept now has no useful place in L2 acquisition theory.[1] It is, however, the case that much of the work we need to refer to makes use of the markedness concept, precisely because discussion of the concept often entails discussion of cognitive simplicity, a notion which is central to our concerns. For this reason we need to work with the concept.

Principles and parameters

The essence of the principles and parameters model is that there are certain universal design features (or *principles*) which all human languages share. These principles are invariant, but within them, a degree of variation is permitted (the *parameters*). These usually entail some form of binary choice. Towell and Hawkins (1994) illustrate these concepts by means of an analogy and a linguistic example. The analogy is with car wheels. All car wheels are driven by a motor linked to the axle to which the wheels are attached. This universal feature is a 'principle'; but it is one which permits variation. Some cars have front-wheel drive; others, back-wheel drive; still others, four-wheel drive; these are the possible parameters. Their linguistic example relates to head–complement relations. 'Head' words are by definition the core of the phrase in which they occur. Hence, in phrases like 'books about second language acquisition' and 'keen on second language acquisition' (Towell and Hawkins' examples), the head words are 'books' and 'keen', respectively, with the remainder of each phrase being the complement. The head–complement relationship holds for a large number of phrase types, and has characteristics which may be regarded as universal principles. The associated parameter is whether the complement comes before or after the head. In languages like English, French and Italian, complements follow heads (*head complement*), as in the two examples given above. But in other languages (Towell and Hawkins cite Japanese, Turkish and Burmese), the order is *complement head*, yielding the equivalent of 'about second language acquisition books', and 'on second language acquisition keen'. For descriptions of the 'principles and parameters' model, see Chomsky (1981, 1986 or 1988).

UG and Second-language Acquisition: Three Positions

The review of the UG and L2 acquisition literature which we shall now undertake is a focused one and has fixed aims in mind – to ascertain the extent of evidence for PS- and LS- systems in L2 mastery. In order to find a path through the huge, complex and somewhat messy L2 acquisition literature, we shall adapt a version of a framework mentioned by White (1986), Schachter (1988) and Cook (1988). The framework identifies three positions regarding L2 acquisition. These positions are first outlined, then considered in detail. The names we give these positions, as well as the order in which we present them, differ from those found elsewhere.

Position 1: 'start with the simplest'

Cook (1988) uses the term 'no access to UG' to describe this position. According to it, L2 acquisition develops following quite different principles to L1 acquisition; UG has no part to play in the L2 acquisition process, which follows the path of general cognitive development. The label 'start with the simplest' is our own. It conveys the expectation that if general cognitive principles control L2 acquisition, we will find the learner following a progression in acquisition from cognitively easy to cognitively difficult; the learner, in other words, 'starts with the simplest'. Evidence for this position would be evidence for the existence of a PS-system of L2 learning. Evidence for this position *only* would suggest (but not prove) that perhaps no LS-system exists for L2 acquisition.

Position 2: 'back to UG'

This position claims that the learner returns to UG for his or her second language, showing unmarked, universal, core principles in his or her early interlanguage. The implication is that these principles will occur whatever the nature of the first language, from which there is no transfer.

This position can easily be associated with Krashen's concept of acquisition, and relates to notions of developmental 'creative construction' (the Dulay and Burt term we noted earlier), where we find universal acquisition orders irrespective of the learner's first language. Evidence for this position would therefore be evidence for the existence of an LS-system of L2 learning (and evidence for this position *only* would suggest – but not prove – that perhaps no PS-system exists for L2 acquisition).

The term 'back to UG' is Schachter's (1988), while Cook (1988) speaks of 'direct access to UG'. Associated with this position are attempts to find evidence of unmarked, core forms occurring first in interlanguage, particularly significant where the nature of the first language would expect transfer of marked forms.

Position 3: 'start with L1'

Again the phrase is Schachter's, with Cook having 'indirect access to UG'. This position predicts transfer effects from the first to the second language. In a model which involves markedness, we would therefore expect to find an influence on the second language of markedness in the first; while in terms of principles and parameters, we would expect transfer of parameter settings from the first language to the second. Different language groups would therefore experience different problems in learning the same second language. The position is akin to the contrastive analysis hypothesis found in earlier decades, although the underlying frameworks (both psychological and linguistic) are quite different. What evidence for position 3 would tell us regarding PS and LS is rather more complex than for the other two positions, and we take up this question when we come to consider the position in detail below.

The diagrams in figure 3.2 are adapted and reordered from Cook (1988) and summarize the three positions.

We shall now look at these positions in turn.

Position 1: 'Start with the Simplest'

One of the arenas in which the issue of L2 acquisition processing has been applied is that of German word order rules, particularly those relating to verb position, or *verb placement*, as it is called. A number of papers discuss this issue, particularly Clahsen and Muysken (1986), Clahsen (1988), Clahsen et al. (1983), Pienemann (1985, 1989), Ellis (1989), and Rogers (1994). In order to understand the issues involved, we need to consider the rules which govern German verb placement.

German verb placement

German permits verbs in two sentence positions (for declaratives). Finite verbs can appear in sentence second position in a main clause, and in sentence final position in a subordinate clause. Non-finite forms appear finally. Figure 3.3, which is slightly adapted from Rogers (1994, on which some of this discussion is based), illustrates these possibilities.

These possibilities may be described in the following terms. SVO is the 'normal' order, found in sentence 1. Sentence 2 displays (subject/verb) *inversion*; 3 and 4 have *verb separation*, and 5 has *verb-end*.

German verb placement in L2 learners

Rogers (1994) cites two papers which trace the development of these word order rules in German. The first is by Clahsen et al. (1983). They study 45 adult Romance learners of German acquiring German in a naturalistic or untutored way. In relation to the three features mentioned above they find an apparent acquisition order of

SVO → verb separation → inversion → verb-end

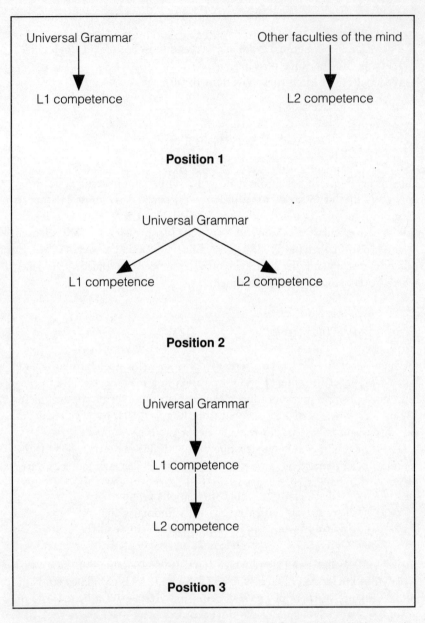

Figure 3.2 Three positions regarding Universal Grammar's role in language acquisition (adapted from Cook 1988)

Verb-second (tensed verb) in a declarative main clause

1   Die Kinder essen den Kuchen
    S   V   O
    The children eat the cake

2   Heute essen die Kinder den Kuchen
    Adv   V   S   O
    Today eat the children the cake

Verb-final (untensed verb) in a main clause

3   Die Kinder müssen den Kuchen essen
    S   Mod   O   V
    The children must the cake eat

4   Die Kinder haben den Kuchen gegessen
    S   Aux   O   V
    The children have the cake eaten

Verb-final (tensed verb) in subordinate clauses

5   Ich weiß, daß die Kinder den Kuchen essen
          conj. S   O   V

Figure 3.3 The position of the verb in German main and subordinate clauses (slightly adapted from Rogers 1994)

The second paper is by Ellis (1989). He is interested in the relationship between natural acquisition (as studied in the Clahsen et al. paper) and tutored learning in a classroom. Consequently, he compares the acquisition order of the Clahsen et al. subjects with that of a group of learners studying German in a formal classroom setting. His finding is that the acquisition order is as above, even though this order reflects neither the order in which the items were treated in class, nor the degree of emphasis they were given in teaching. This leads him towards the conclusion that acquisition order is not affected by formal instruction.

The importance of these findings for our concerns in this chapter lie in the explanation which Clahsen et al. (1983) and Pienemann (1989) put forward for the acquisition order. This involves general processing conditions determined by cognitive factors. Clahsen (1984) and Pienemann (1989) use the term *canonical order strategy* to describe the learners' strategies, which have much in common with the processing strategies described by Slobin (1973), Bever (1970) and Bever and Townsend (1979). These strategies posit a base, 'natural' order in which events and entities are perceived, and this is assumed to be SVO, reflecting 'actor–action–acted upon'. The 'natural' order is exemplified by sentence 1 in figure 3.3. At a later stage learners attend to the beginnings and ends of sentences, noting that non-finite verb forms may occur at sentence ends (sentences 3 and 4). Clahsen (1984) refers to this as the *initialisation–finalisation strategy*. Sentence 2 likewise involves a sentence extremity (an adverb is put at the beginning), but it also entails a sentence internal movement, and one which happens to disrupt the canonical SVO sequence. It is for this reason that inversion is felt to be acquired after verb separation. Finally, movements which occur in one sort of a clause but not others are permitted, and Clahsen's so-called *subordinate clause strategy* can account for the verb-end movement in sentence 5. In this way, Clahsen, Pienemann and others attempt to relate verb placement to general cognitive strategies.

The learners in Clahsen et al. (1983) were Italian, Spanish and Portuguese. These are all SVO languages. Consequently, although the explanation we have considered above involves a strategy of 'starting with the simplest', it is not the only one available. An alternative would be to postulate a degree of transfer, with the SVO order first occurring in interlanguage simply because it occurs in the first language (unlike the other constructions, which violate the first language's SVO order). To investigate the important issue of L1/L2 relationships, we now turn to a further paper which focuses more on these.

German verb placement in L1 and L2 learners compared

Clahsen (1988) argues, following Clahsen and Muysken (1986), that 'child first language (L1) acquisition and adult second language (L2) acquisition are guided by distinct sets of principles . . . adult L2 acquisition follows from general learning strategies, while child L1 acquisition primarily follows from principles of UG' (p. 47). His evidence relates to the verb placement data we have already considered, but also to the area of subject–verb agreement. This is signalled in German by various endings, such as 'e' for first singular present tense (*ich* liebe), 'st' for second singular (*du* liebst) present tense, and so on (the full details are not relevant here).

Clahsen's account of German verb placement is slightly different from others considered above, and is based on the assumption, following Thiersch

(1978) and Koster (1978), of an underlying structure which has the verb in sentence final position; thus, SOV is the unmarked, 'core' order in German. When the verb is finite, it is moved to sentence second position by a process known as *finfronting* (Finite-fronting), to create sentences like 1 and 5 earlier. A second movement, called topicalization, moves an element to the front – for example, the adverb in sentence 2.

Clahsen and Muysken (1986) detail the empirical studies which have been done on L1 acquisition of these two syntactic areas, which seem temporally related (i.e. they are acquired at roughly the same time). For verb placement, they postulate a number of developmental stages, which are seen to reflect the movements of finfronting and topicalization. Thus L1 children begin with verbs mostly in sentence final positions. Over time, finite verbs are moved into first and second positions: first all finite verbs are moved, then only those not occurring in embedded clauses. This development depends crucially on the concept of finiteness: for finfronting to occur, the child must have grasped the non-finite/finite distinction. This distinction is of course also relevant to subject–verb agreement, since it is only finite verbs which display the relevant morphemes. Clahsen is thus able to account for the temporal relationship between acquisition of verb placement and that of subject–verb inflections: it is only at the point where finite verbs are moved to non-final positions that the inflections are seen throughout the system. In Clahsen's words (1988), 'the availability of the agreement system implies that "finiteness" becomes accessible in the children's grammars as a distinctive feature of verbal elements. Therefore, as soon as this notion is available, the use of finfronting no longer causes the children much trouble' (p. 56).

Clahsen then turns to the L2 acquisition data which we have already seen, though he now makes mention of Turkish learners, along with the Romance learners (Italian, Spanish, Portuguese) already mentioned. As we have already seen, the development of verb placement in these learners is quite different to that of the L1 children. Most importantly, the acquisition order is apparently quite different (with SVO, not SOV, being the first acquired). But in addition, the relationship with subject–verb agreement is also different. Clahsen takes his data on L2 subject–verb agreement from Köpcke (1989). He attempts to correlate this with the stages of development just described in relation to verb placement, and finds two things. The first is that the concept of subject–verb agreement seems familiar to the learners from the beginning, and although there are considerable differences in the use of inflections from subject to subject, they in general appear at the earliest stage, suggesting that conceptually they pose no problems. Secondly (and partly following from the first point), there is no correlation between subject–verb agreement and verb placement, of the sort that was found in relation to L1 children. These pieces of grammar develop separately from each other, such that no implicational relationships can be set up.

Clahsen's processing strategies involve a cognitive simplicity order ('starting with the simplest'), and clearly exemplify position 1 in figure 3.2. Two further important points need noting. One is that Clahsen makes mention of some Turkish learners in the study. Turkish is an SOV language yet, like the other learners, the Turks acquired SVO first. It therefore appears that transfer from L1 cannot account for the data (as it might do for the Romance learners).[2] The second is that these data provide a clear example of where an L1 parameter setting (the German SOV) does not coincide with the 'cognitively simple' (the so-called canonical SVO). The relevance of this finding will be clarified later.

German word order and PS-/LS-systems

The data we have been considering provide useful evidence that one pathway exists in which cognitive mechanisms operate – Felix's PS-system. What the data do not, however, clarify is whether some other pathway can occur, in which a language-specific mechanism (Felix's LS-system) operates. Clahsen tells us that learners can start with the simplest, but not whether there is any other possible strategy. We need to continue the search for 'LS' elsewhere.

Position 2: 'Back to UG'

There are three hypotheses or ideas which may be associated with this position.

Interlanguage, like other natural languages, is subject to the constraints imposed by linguistic universals.

If L2 learners return to UG, we would expect the principles of UG to be respected in their interlanguage. If, however, they start with their L1, the result might be interlanguage forms not constrained by UG.

Ellis (1985a) cites Schmidt (1980) as evidence for how interlanguages conform to UG. She investigated how learners from five different language backgrounds deleted elements from co-ordinate structures in English, and found that no learners produced unnatural deletion patterns (i.e. patterns not found in a natural language). Hence acceptable orders such as those found in examples 3.3 (a) and (b) were attested, but not (c) or (d):

(3.3) (a)   John sang a song and played the guitar.
       (b)   John plays the guitar and Mary the piano.
       (c) * Sang song and John plays guitar.
       (d) * John the violin and Mary plays the piano.

The principle here is that only a second identical noun or verb may be omitted from the sentence. Cook (1985) reports further evidence from Ritchie (1978) relating to the appearance in interlanguage of sentences like 3.4 (a) but not (b):

(3.4) (a)   That a boat had sunk that John had built was obvious.
       (b) * That a boat had sunk was obvious that John had built.

But the Clahsen paper that we have just considered provides counter evidence to this hypothesis. On the basis of the adult L2 verb placement data which he considers, he is led to claim that 'adults . . . create syntactic rules which are more complex than the rules acquired by children and which cannot be defined in terms of "rules of grammar" at least in current frameworks of generative grammar' (p. 65); the adults' rule systems 'fall out of the range permitted by principles of UG' (p. 48).

Implicational universals can be used to predict the order in which properties of the second language appear in interlanguage.

It is clear that this is what one would expect if the 'back to UG' position were correct. Gass (1979) looks at the acquisition of relative clauses by adult L2 learners of English. She finds a close correlation (with one exception) between accuracy orders with these functions and Comrie and Keenan's accessibility hierarchy, which we looked at earlier. Hence, SU causes fewer problems than DO, than IO and so on. If we may assume that accuracy orders are the same as acquisition orders, then this study lends support to the above hypothesis.

L2 learners learn unmarked (or less marked) properties before marked (or more marked) properties of the target language.

According to this hypothesis, interlanguage will always show unmarked forms before marked, whatever occurs in the first and second languages. Table 3.2 is taken from Hyltenstam (1982); it is reproduced in White (1983) as well as Ellis (1985a). It well expresses the prediction that unmarked will first appear in interlanguage and, as we shall later see, it can also be modified in relation to position 3, thus illustrating how positions 2 and 3 differ.

Table 3.2 Markedness theory and interlanguage

Native language (L1)	*Target language (L2)*	*Interlanguage*
1 Unmarked	Unmarked	Unmarked
2 Unmarked	Marked	Unmarked
3 Marked	Unmarked	Unmarked
4 Marked	Marked	Unmarked

Source: White (1983, p. 311, based on Hyltenstam 1982)

Rutherford (1982) illustrates this hypothesis in relation to question forms. He cites Burt and Dulay's (1980) evidence for the following L2 acquisition order for Wh-questions:

(3.5)   (a)   What's that?
          (b)   What are those?
          (c)   I don't know what those are.
          (d)   I don't know what this is.

According to Rutherford, markedness theory can account for this. 9(a), as the singular, is unmarked in relation to the plural (b), and (a) and (b) are unmarked in relation to the embedded forms (c) and (d). The only mystery to solve is why the plural (c) is learned before the singular (d). According to Rutherford, this is through the influence of the 'latest learned' form (c) – the learner has just learned a plural, and continues with them! One may feel that this way of dismissing facts which get in the way of the theory is unfortunate, arguing that the consistent application of markedness theory implies the learning of (d) before (c). From this point of view, the reliance on some *deus ex machina* ('latest learned') severely damages the theory's credibility. Other evidence for the hypothesis, mentioned in Ellis (1985a), comes from Schmidt (1980), Gass (1984), Kellerman (1979) and Gass and Ard (1984).

Position 2 and an LS-system

That part of the Burt and Dulay Wh-data which markedness can easily explain – i.e. sentence 3.5 (a) above before (b); (a) and (b) before (c) and (d) – can also be explained in terms of a concept of propositional cognitive complexity. We have already noted that, *in general*, unmarked is the same as cognitively simple. Wherever this is the case, one might if one wished simply postulate general processing principles to account for unmarked before marked specifically, and in general for the early occurrence of UG forms in interlanguage. On the basis of this evidence, 'back to UG' is the same as 'start with the simplest'; it is impossible to distinguish the two positions.

But we also noted earlier that 'unmarked' need not *necessarily* be the same as 'cognitively simple'. If we are able to separate 'unmarked' and 'cognitively simple', then we would have the possibility of distinguishing the 'back to UG' and the 'start with the simplest' positions, the former predicting unmarked first in interlanguage, the latter cognitively simple first. If we could demonstrate instances where unmarked precedes cognitively simple in interlanguage, or vice versa, we would be able first to distinguish the two positions, then perhaps to falsify one or other of them.

We have already seen that Clahsen provides precisely the instance we seek, where German SVO is recognized as cognitively simpler, but the unmarked form is SOV. In this case, he shows that the adult L2 learner's interlanguage follows the cognitively simple to complex path, rather than beginning with a cognitively more complex but unmarked form. So in this one 'test case' we have what may seem to be counter evidence to position 2, with marked as opposed to unmarked appearing first in interlanguage. In fact it is not true counterevidence at all because, as we have already noted, our framework allows for two pathways, in one of which there is uncontroversially 'starting with the simplest'. So Clahsen's evidence for position 1 does not tell us whether position 2 can or cannot occur. The most we can say is that when a test case has occurred, it provides no evidence for position 2. Evidence of LS continues to elude us.

To conclude regarding position 2: in general we might expect unmarked forms also to be the simplest, and where this is the case position 2 ('back to UG') is not differentiated from position 1 ('start with the simplest'). In order to differentiate these two positions, we need 'test cases' where unmarked and simplest do not coincide. In the Clahsen data, the evidence is for a 'start with the simplest' strategy, rather than for a 'back to UG' one.

Position 3: 'Start with L1'

In relation to this position we shall cover selected attempts made in the literature to utilize the concept of UG to make predictions about where L1 transfer will occur. Once again we shall be using the concept of markedness, because the papers we refer to do so. Those who consider the concept unuseful will at least in general terms be able to 'translate' findings into principles and parameter terms (even though in the case of individual findings this may be difficult). Hence when we speak below about markedness differences in L1 and L2, this translates into parameter-setting differences between the two languages.

As with position 2, there are various hypotheses associated with position 3. We begin with a general one concerning L1 and L2 differences.

L1 unmarked forms are transferred into interlanguage.

Rutherford's account of Burt and Dulay's Wh-question data (reported earlier) illustrates how unmarked precedes marked in interlanguage. We suggested that there are in fact two possible explanations for this acquisition order: it may either be a case of 'start with the simplest' (position 1), or of 'back to UG' (position 2). Translating these possibilities into the terms of table 3.2, we are accounting for the 'unmarked' in column 3 of rows 1 and 2 by saying either that it reflects UG, or that unmarked is conceptually easier marked and hence to be expected in interlanguage. But we now note that a third explanation is possible, in terms of L1 transfer. Hence, unmarked in interlanguage may occur simply because the L1 (in rows 1 and 2) has unmarked, transfer being the process rather than anything directly to do with cognitive simplicity or the nature of UG. Rutherford's findings may hence be counted as an example of 'the transfer of unmarked forms'.

The above clarifies that all of our three positions make similar predictions regarding rows 1 and 2, and in relation to these rows it will be difficult to provide evidence for one position as against the other. White (1983) discusses the issue at length in relation to positions 2 and 3, quoting data from Mazurkewich (1984), but does in fact find it difficult to reach any conclusion. Unmarked forms in interlanguage are simply a poor test case in relation to the hypotheses we are considering.

Under this heading of 'transfer of unmarked forms' (p. 207), Ellis (1985a) also cites Eckman (1977). It is true that this study does provide indirect evidence regarding the transfer of L1 *unmarked* forms, but its real concern relates to L2 *marked* forms, so we now consider it under that heading.

L2 marked forms are particularly difficult.

L2 marked forms are found in rows 2 and 4 of table 3.2. Eckman's (1977) study of English, German and French phonology is important here and needs to be reported in some detail. The phonemic facts he discusses are as follows.

1 English has a voicing contrast in word-initial, -medial and -final positions ('tin'/'din'; 'betting'/'bedding'; 'bet'/'bed'). German has the contrast wordinitially and medially but not finally. In word-final position, German has only the voiceless obstruent.
2 French uses the phoneme /ž/ in initial, medial and final positions. English has it medially and finally ('azure' and 'garage'), but not initially.

Eckman is interested in learning difficulty in general, and also in what he calls 'directionality of difficulty' – cases where differences between languages A and B (for example) lead to the speaker of A learning B experiencing difficulties, which the speaker of B learning A does not have. Eckman makes two statements about learning difficulty and directionality. One is to observe, following Gradman (1971), that English-speaking learners of French experience no apparent difficulty with the second point listed above. The other is his own observation that German speakers learning English have more difficulty with the first point than English speakers learning German. He looks at how three theories – traditional contrastive analysis hypothesis (CA), generative phonology, and markedness in UG – can handle these insights regarding learning difficulty.

Although traditional CA generally makes no statements regarding directionality of difficulty, Eckman does find statements in Moulton (1962, a work concerned with comparative German–English phonology) which appear to make the assumption that it is more difficult to learn a new contrast, or new positions of contrast, than to learn to suppress a contrast. Applying this criterion to point 1 apparently correctly predicts that the German learner of English will have more problems learning the word-final contrast than the English learner of German will have suppressing the contrast. However, although the prediction is correct there, it does not handle the French–English example (point 2) so well, since it predicts difficulties for the English speaker which apparently do not occur.

Generative phonology handles the facts of point 1 by means of a rule in German phonology, called *terminal devoicing*, which makes obstruents voiceless in word-final positions. This rule does not operate in English. Although generative phonology (like CA) makes no specific claims about learning difficulty, Eckman argues that one is implied here: the English speaker of German has to acquire an extra rule, terminal devoicing, which the German speaker of English does not have to acquire. Hence the former, with more to learn, should experience more difficulty. But this does not happen.

Turning to UG and the concept of markedness, Eckman now proposes what he calls a *markedness differential hypothesis* (MDH). The basis of this is that 'those areas of the target language which differ from the native language and are more marked than the native language will be difficult' (p. 321). In order for the facts given above as points 1 and 2 to be accounted for by the MDH, it will have to be shown that: (a) the distribution of voiced and voiceless obstruents in English is more marked than in German; and (b) that the distribution of /ž/ in French is not more marked than in English.

In support of both these contentions, Eckman cites a study by Dinnsen and Eckman (1975) which shows an implicational relationship regarding voicing contrasts over a large number of languages. Final voicing contrast implies medial contrast which in turn implies initial contrast, and according to the definition of markedness we gave earlier, this leads one to conclude that initial and medial contrasts are less marked than final contrast – the most marked of the three. This interpretation suggests that both (a) and (b) above are correct: English word-final voice contrast is marked, and French word-initial voice contrast (involving /ž/) is unmarked. Eckman goes on to show that his MDH can also be made to apply to syntactic phenomena (Comrie and Keenan's relative clause implicational hierarchy which we considered earlier). Liceras' work (e.g. 1989) on pro-drop also suggests a notion of 'directionality' where English learners of Spanish find more difficulty with the construction than Spanish learners of English.[3]

It might be argued that the statements regarding directionality of difficulty which Eckman imputes to CA particularly, but also to generative phonology, are not in fact those which these two movements would have put forward, and that this weakens his attempt to show that UG – and only UG – would make the correct predictions concerning learning difficulty. However, the paper's conclusions do have an intuitive correctness; they are the conclusions a language teacher might reach regarding these particular instances of learner difficulty.

Though we have not entirely ignored rows 3 and 4 in table 3.2, we have not so far considered what happens when there are marked forms in the first language. The evidence here is mixed. According to some studies, transfer does not occur, while according to others it does. We now consider these contradictory claims.

L1 marked forms are not transferred into interlanguage.

Ellis here cites Zobl (1984) and 'combien extraction' in French. French permits extraction of a noun phrase modified by 'combien':

(3.6) (a)   Combien voulez–vous d'oranges?
        (b)   Combien d'oranges voulez–vous?

whereas English does not:

        (c) * How many do you want oranges?
        (d)   How many oranges do you want?

Zobl claims that non-extraction is unmarked, extraction marked (i.e. French has both marked and unmarked, English unmarked only). His low-level French learners of English used the non–extracted rule in English; that is, they avoided transfer of the marked form. Kellerman (1979) generalizes in a way which encompasses 'combien extraction'. His claim is that where the first language possesses both a marked and an unmarked form, it is the less marked form that will be transferred. His English example is:

(3.7) (a)   He claims that he knows it.
        (b)   He claims to know it.

where (a) is taken to be unmarked, and (b) marked. Sentence 3.7 (a) will hence be the form that will transfer if an English speaker is learning another language. Pollock (1989; see also Rizzi 1990) argue that these French–English differences are part of a larger set of differences involving among other things possible verb movement patterns.

L1 marked forms are transferred into interlanguage.

White (1983) reaches a different conclusion. Her evidence comes from the acquisition of dative questions in English. Two kinds of questions are permitted:

(3.8) (a)   To whom did John give the book?
        (b)   Who did John give the book to?

Table 3.3 White's predictions concerning markedness and L1 transfer

Native language (L1)	Target language (L2)	Interlanguage
1 Unmarked	Unmarked	Unmarked
2 Unmarked	Marked	Unmarked
3 Marked	Unmarked	*Marked*
4 Marked	Marked	*Marked*

Source: Abridged from White (1983, p. 312)

Sentence 3.8 (a) involves what is known as 'pied-piping' – that is, moving the entire prepositional phrase to the front of the sentence. Sentence 3.8 (b) has 'preposition-stranding', with only the Wh-pronoun being moved; the preposition remains in place, and is hence 'stranded'. White cites claims by van Riemsdijk (1978) and Hornstein and Weinberg (1981) that pied-piping is unmarked, and preposition-stranding marked.

French does not permit preposition-stranding; hence forms like 3.9 do not occur:

(3.9)   * Qui as-tu donné le livre à?

Despite the fact that French permits the unmarked form only, White predicts that English learners will persist with the marked (stranding) form in their French interlanguage. The reason is related to the fact that although English permits both pied-piping and preposition-stranding, the latter is much more common than the former. 'In situations like these', White notes, 'the learner has had positive evidence in L1 for a marked setting' (p. 314). He or she has to 'notice the *absence* of some construction' in L2, which is difficult. White cites further evidence in support of her claim from Tarallo and Myhill (1983), and Muñoz-Liceras (1983). Similar arguments relate to row 4 in table 3.2 3.5: where evidence shows the learner the need for marked forms in both languages, use of an unmarked form in interlanguage would involve ignoring such positive evidence.

These considerations lead White to replace the paradigms shown in table 3.2 with her own (p. 312). Table 3.3 is a simplified version of this. The differences (in italic) from table 3.2 are that in column 3 of rows 3 and 4, we find 'marked' rather than 'unmarked'.

We noted earlier that one (but only one) possible explanation for the instance of unmarked in the interlanguage column of rows 1 and 2 is L1 transfer. If we accept that explanation, then it should be noted that figure

3.6 corresponds in all detail to what would be the 'traditional' CA transfer position, with interlanguage completely reflecting the nature of the first language.

Position 3 and an LS-system

There are four hypotheses associated with position 3, and these are evident from the subsection headings:

1 L1 unmarked forms are transferred into interlanguage.
2 L2 marked forms are particularly difficult.
3 L1 marked forms are not transferred into interlanguage
4 L1 marked forms are transferred into interlanguage.

We observed that if the first hypothesis were true, its consequences would be difficult to distinguish from those of position 2, which in turn was in most cases indistinguishable from position 1 – the 'start with the simplest' view. Note now that the same may be said for hypotheses 2 and 3 above. In other words, these hypotheses are precisely what one would expect from a learner proceeding from cognitively simpler to cognitively more difficult. But as in our earlier discussion, this is only true where the equations of 'unmarked = simple', 'marked = complex' hold true. Real test cases would occur where this equation is not true, and such test cases are difficult to come by.

We thus reach two conclusions. One is that there is an overlap of empirical consequences as regards three of position 3's four hypotheses; they are consequences which other positions would also predict. The other is that in relation to these three hypotheses there is nothing which is incompatible, on the basis of available evidence, with the 'start with the simplest' position.

The crucial hypotheses 4 remains to be considered. We need once again to remember that although marked usually means complex, it need not necessarily be so. The Clahsen data which we considered earlier provides a case where we find marked in interlanguage, as in column 3 of rows 3 and 4 of table 3.3. But Clahsen demonstrates that where his example is concerned, the marked case is the cognitively simple one. In this way marked in interlanguage may in fact be evidence for a 'start with the simplest' position. But since (as we have earlier argued) marked normally does indeed imply complex, Clahsen's data would seem to be the exception rather than the rule, and we would be misrepresenting the picture if we treated all the data relevant to hypothesis 4 in the same way.

UG and General Cognition: Some Conclusions

From these conclusions specific to position 3 we may now attempt to reach some general conclusions in relation to the rather messy picture that has been drawn. We began this chapter by accepting the possibility that there may be two distinct ways of mastering a second language. We expressed the view that one of these ways – the 'learning pathway' – is likely to be controlled by general cognitive mechanisms. The German verb placement evidence has been taken as support for this (position 1). But we have throughout been faced with a serious research problem – that it is difficult to find decisive 'test cases' where it can be shown whether or not 'start with the simplest' is the process at work. Hence, even with the German verb placement data we are unable to dismiss the possibility that parametric transfer is the process involved. This evidence is therefore only suggestive, not conclusive.

The same research problem has plagued our consideration of whether or not the other of those ways of mastering a language is language-specific. In many of the situations where L1 transfer may be hypothesized, 'start with the simplest' cannot be discounted. It is important that this research problem should not lead to a negative conclusion regarding the possibility of L1 transfer, and of an LS-system. We have *not* shown that L1 transfer does not happen, but merely that the research problems involved in providing firm evidence are difficult to overcome.

A further consideration muddies these already murky waters. One way of accounting for the position 3 data where L1 marked forms are transferred into interlanguage would be to take them as evidence for the existence of an LS-system at work in L2 acquisition. Given a choice of the cognitively simple or the cognitively more complex, the learner 'elects' to acquire the latter first, because language has its own 'problem space' (the phrase used in chapter 1) for the learner. But there is a complication with this conclusion. In our introductory comments on position 1, we said that the phrase 'start with the simplest' conveys the expectancy that if general cognitive principles control L2 acquisition, we will find the learner following a progression in acquisition from cognitively easy to cognitively difficult; the learner, in other words, starts with the simplest. But would a general learning theory account of L2 acquisition necessarily always imply starting with the simplest?

Although the UG stance on cross-linguistic comparisons distinguishes itself from traditional CA transfer studies, there are clear similarities. It is therefore relevant to be reminded that transfer studies were conceived as part of a general learning theory, dealing with all types of learning, linguistic and non-linguistic. The notion that a previously acquired behaviour will affect learning of a new skill – in positive or negative ways (positive/ negative transfer) – is born of a position that views language as non-unique, and is certainly no embarrassment to a cognition hypothesis of L2 learning. We speak of 'one sort of *behaviour*' because the behaviourist formulation of 'one sort of *habit*' would indeed no longer be acceptable; but this does not affect the general acceptability of the transfer concept. In other words, adoption of a general learning theory does not automatically imply a learning progression from cognitive 'primitives' to more complex, outlandish forms – 'starting with the simplest'. Transfer, which may result in acquisition of the cognitively complex before the cognitively simple, is admissible as well. If we were therefore to regard position 3's hypothesis 4 as evidence of transfer, this would be precisely what a general learning theory (not just a behaviourist one) would expect to occur.[4]

We do not, finally, find in UG studies much which falsifies – or even that is incompatible with a general learning theory account of second language by both pathways (learning and acquisition). But we avoid reaching anything like a firm a conclusion from this. Added to the complexity of the research problems is the fact that the application of UG to L2 acquisition is a relatively new phenomenon; positions are not yet truly established, and evidence is still often contradictory. With time, the case for LS is certain to become more persuasive.

In the following chapter we shall stay with L2 acquisition, and attempt to show that it is at least possible to utilize a general learning theory which will account for both learning and acquisition.

Notes

1 Cook (1991b) expresses the view that markedness is a largely otiose concept as employed in the language acquisition literature, with whatever is late learned being said to be marked. A similar view is shared by Towell and Hawkins (1994).

2 White (1991) and Towell and Hawkins (1994) offer an explanation for the Turkish speakers' behaviour which involves transfer.

3 Pro-drop is the phenomenon which allows some languages (like Italian and Spanish, but not English) to omit a subject pronoun; hence in English we say *He speaks*, but in Italian *Parla* is (in many contexts) sufficient.

4 In practice, of course, any theory which does allow both cognitive simplicity and transfer has to account for when one rather than the other occurs. But in theory there is no reason why these two criteria should not both be contained in a general learning theory account of L2 acquisition.

4 A Model for Second-language Learning and Acquisition

Cognitive Approaches: An Overview

There are a very large number of recent second language (L2) acquisition theories which either specifically make claims regarding the comparability of language with other skills, or which imply that comparability by utilizing concepts and mechanisms taken from cognitive psychology. In this chapter we shall consider these theories and the concepts underlying them, paying particular attention to the skill-learning model of the cognitive psychologist Anderson. We shall attempt to show how an extension of the Anderson model may stand as a model for L2 learning and acquisition.

Two recent sources which provide overviews of these theories are L. N. Chaudhry (unpublished observations) and Cook (1993). Chaudhry reviews 'seven models for second language acquisition that either profess to be based on trends evidenced in cognitive psychology, or incorporate a "cognitive" component'. Her synopsis precludes those views which we considered in the last chapter – 'explanations or theoretical models put forward by the strict adherents of UG and other schools of thought who take the extreme position that linguistic faculties and other human faculties exhibit no similarities whatsoever'. Chapter 7 of Cook (1993) is similarly devoted to a consideration of cognitive approaches to L2 acquisition research. He lists six approaches, and there is naturally overlap with Chaudhry's list. The following list covers the main approaches mentioned by Chaudhry (unpublished observations) and Cook (1993). It is intended to provide an overview of these cognitive-based models, and to relate them to issues we have discussed or will be discussing here.

1   **The experiential approach.** Associated with Hatch and Hawkins (1985), this approach uses script theory, as developed in Schank and Abelson (1977). Mention was made of scripts in chapter 2. The approach is based on the view that 'language grows out of experience', a view which relates directly to Piaget's own; as we saw in chapter 1, in Piaget it is assimilation of and accommodation to experience which leads to change.

2   **McLaughlin's cognitive theory.** Developed in McLaughlin (1987, chapter 6; and 1990), with the two central planks being automization and restructuring. McLaughlin uses the three-phase model of Karmiloff-Smith (1986), a model which is close to, though not identical to, that of Fitts and Posner (1967). We draw on McLaughlin's work later (mentioning the Fitts and Posner model), and the automization principle will be central to our discussion.

3   **Anderson based.** O'Malley et al. (1987), and O'Malley and Chamot (1990) are associated with this approach. We develop the Anderson model in detail later in this chapter.

4   **Raupach (1987) and the Kassel group.** As we shall see later in this chapter, the Anderson model relies heavily on the distinction between declarative and procedural knowledge. A group of scholars working at the University of Kassel have discussed this distinction in relation to applied linguistics in a number of papers. We discuss their work below.

5   **Bialystok's bidimensional model.** The references are Bialystok (1982, 1988, 1990), and Bialystok and Sharwood Smith (1985). The two dimensions to the model are 'analysis' and 'control'. In the Bialystok (1990) paper, analysis refers to: 'the process of restructuring mental representations organised at the level of meanings (knowledge of the world) into explicit representations of structures organised at the level of symbols' (p. 9). Her use of the word 'restructuring' here makes the clear conceptual connection with McLaughlin (see 2 above). Control is 'the ability to attend to only relevant information when solving a problem' forming the 'basis for the emergent phenomenon of fluency or automaticity' (Bialystok 1990, p. 9). We develop the analysis/control distinction below.

Hulstijn (1990) argues that the Bialystok analysis/control model is highly similar to the 'information-processing approach' associated with the Anderson model, and claims that 'it is impossible to choose between them on empirical grounds', the only difference being one of focus (p. 30).

6   **Schmidt's 'consciousness' hypothesis.** The reference here is Schmidt (1990). In this paper he explores different uses of the term

'consciousness' and argues that 'taking notice' must occur if input is to become intake. In this paper's appeal to attention theory (c.f. Kahnemann 1973), it relates to others utilizing the concept of automization, where the value of automization is seen as that of freeing the conscious attention for high level skills – a position which we shall be following. Schmidt's work will also be mentioned in chapter 5 where we deal with the role of conscious knowledge in language teaching.

7 **Plans and goals**. Faerch and Kasper (1983) are concerned with communication strategies, and their paper discusses at length where such strategies would fit within a general model of speech production. Their cognitively oriented model places emphasis on plans and goals (following Miller et al. 1960). Mention was made of Miller et al. (1960) in chapter 2, when we were discussing the hierarchical and goal-directed nature of skills.

8 **Gasser's connectionism model of transfer process**. Colley and Beech (1989) distinguish two types of cognitive model. 'Product systems approaches' include the Anderson model, and it is on these that we shall be concentrating. The other major type of approach is 'connectionist' and these are based on the concept of parallel distributed processing. Bechtel and Abrahamsen (1991) provides an overview of connectionism. Both Chaudhry (unpublished observations) and Cook (1993) mention Gasser's (1990) paper, which views L2 acquisition in connectionist terms. We shall not be considering connectionist models further here.

Some Basic Information-processing Concepts

In chapter 2 we emphasized the importance of the information-processing notion in cognitive approaches, and the skill-learning model which we shall outline later in this chapter makes central use of processing concepts. Before presenting this model, we shall therefore now outline the three most important of concepts, making mention of research which has been done in relation to each of them. By doing this we shall in effect be drawing attention to the core features of many of the approaches listed above.

1 Knowledge and control: the processing dimension

The terms 'knowledge' and 'control' are used by Bialystok, whose model is developed in a number of sources (1982, 1988, 1990, Bialystok and Sharwood Smith 1985). These terms describe 'two separate components' – knowledge is 'the way in which the language system is represented in the mind of the learner', and control is 'the processing system for controlling that knowledge during actual performance' (Bialystok and Sharwood Smith 1985, p. 104). Similar distinctions are found in one form or another in many information-processing models, though the terminology differs. By recognizing the importance of control, these models in effect identify an information-processing dimension to language learning (and teaching). The distinction is therefore at the very centre of information-processing approaches.

The distinction is easiest to demonstrate in relation to language testing, as Bialystok (1982) does. She observes that we have tended to assess language mastery quantitatively, providing statements that 'the learner simply knows more or less of the language, or knows some of the formal properties and not others' (p. 181). In this formulation, degree of mastery is assessed in terms of amount of knowledge. But we should also, she argues, ask qualitative questions, about the *conditions* under which these formal properties can be correctly manipulated. Mastery involves degree of control as well as degree of knowledge.

Two examples, one from a non-linguistic context and one from language use, will illustrate. A footballer may, in normal circumstances, be a good goal scorer. But when we assess his mastery, we will need to take into account circumstances which are far from normal. Can he, for example, score in a World Cup Final, in a foreign country with a difficult climate, against a good side, knowing that spectators at home will bay for the blood of the defeated? Similarly, when we come to judge students' linguistic ability, we would be foolish to pronounce that they have mastered the present perfect tense simply on the grounds that they have managed to use it correctly in a gap-filling task, done under 'ideal' conditions. They may 'know' the rules for forming the present perfect, but can they put that knowledge into practice? Can they, one would need to ask, use the tense correctly over a bad intercontinental telephone line, with all attention focused on getting the message across in the shortest possible space of time? These examples well exemplify the point: it is not 'what you know', but 'in what circumstances you can use what you know'. Bialystok's discussion of it is related to language testing, but there are clear implications for language teaching in general, and we shall explore some of these in chapters 6 and 7.

Evidence for a distinct processing dimension

There has been a good deal of research related to this distinction, and in the case of one seminal paper, Hulstijn and Hulstijn (1984), one of the aims is simply to demonstrate that the distinction has some reality. The terms they use are 'metalinguistic-knowledge' and 'executive-control', and they are concerned to show that this second dimension has separate, discernible existence. They have three hypotheses regarding executive-control.

4.1 If an 'executive control' dimension has reality, we would expect more errors in performance when time constraints are imposed on the task.

4.2 We would similarly expect more errors when there is message (as opposed to form) focus.

4.3 Supposing that such variations in performance as are explored under hypotheses 1 and 2 above do indeed exist, they will occur irrespective of degree of metalinguistic-knowledge, if indeed the knowledge/control distinction has reality.

Their experiment relating to these hypotheses involves learners of Dutch as a second language given a series of story-retelling tasks. Two linguistic structures were focused on: Dutch inversion of subject and verb in main clauses, and the placement of the finite verb in final position in subordinate clauses (a structure well familiar to us through the German verb placement work considered in the last chapter). Two variables were manipulated: whether the learner's attention was on form or message, and the speed at which retelling was required (fast or slow). After the story-retelling tasks, the subjects were interviewed to ascertain the degree of metalinguistic know-ledge they possessed (whether, that is, they 'knew the rules' or not); this knowledge is relevant to hypothesis 4.3 above.

The finding regarding the variable of time was that requiring fast per-formance really made no difference in terms of errors made. But the form/message focus did make a difference, with much more accuracy achieved when focus was on form (it was also noted that where the focus was on form, the tasks naturally took more time). As regards metalinguistic-knowledge, it was found that subjects who possessed it did do better overall; it was an important factor in performance. But there was no significant gain for those with knowledge in relation to either time or focus. That is, control is a different, distinct variable from knowledge.

A principal reason for the importance of this paper is that it establishes that there is indeed an identifiable processing dimension to language learn-ing – a claim of clear centrality to information-processing approaches. The paper also explores the effects of two factors – time and attention focus – which may be said to make a task involving language use more or less difficult. In chapter 7, we shall consider in more detail what other factors might contribute to 'task complexity' – an issue of obvious relevance to language teaching.

2 The declarative/procedural distinction

In the past two decades there has been a great deal of discussion in the cognitive psychology literature about how knowledge is best represented in memory, and a number of theories to account for this have been developed. A central issue in these discussions has been concerned with the old philosophical distinction between 'knowing that' and 'knowing how'; between what is termed declarative knowledge (associated with 'knowing that') and procedural knowledge (associated with 'knowing how'). This distinction will cause no problems to most language teachers, who have long accepted that knowing about English grammar is quite a different proposition from being able to use it.

There are, one might say, two 'paths' for the production of a piece of behaviour, the 'declarative path' and the 'procedural path', and indeed theories of knowledge representation have tended to be either 'declarativist' or 'proceduralist', according to which of these paths they advocate. Following the declarativist path, knowledge is represented in memory as a data base which has the form of a set of semantic networks. When parts of the data base are required to perform some operation, a general set of interpretative procedures ('rules') is used, to apply the data to some chosen end. To exemplify by means of a language-learning illustration – the rules for formation of the present perfect in English are roughly as follows: you use a part of the verb 'have' followed by the past participle, and the past participle of regular verbs is formed by adding 'ed' to the stem form. Learners following the declarative path of forming the present perfect would hold all the above knowledge in memory, and would apply it each time they were required to form the tense. When, for example, the present perfect of 'he works' was required, they would refer to memory on how to form the third singular of 'have', and would follow 'he has' with the participle of 'work' formed by adding 'ed'.

In the proceduralist path, on the other hand, knowledge is embedded in procedures for action, and not kept in some separate store. In computing terms, learners have a 'program' which tells them that the present perfect of 'work' (third singular) is 'he has worked'. Whenever the form is required, there it is readily to hand. To express the issue further in computing terms: declarativists have two components – a store of data and a general program for applying the data. The proceduralists have a set of specific programs which incorporate required data within them. For general discussion of the declarative/procedural distinction, see Winograd (1975).

'Declarativists' and 'proceduralists' argue in favour of one or the other pathway, and it is important to realize that both do have advantages and disadvantages (as discussed, for example, in Neves and Anderson 1981).

There are three main advantages of the declarative path. One is *generativity*. Once a fact is stored in data base it is available for use in any operation where it may be required, since all operations make use of the same data base store. To pursue our earlier language example: once learners know how the present perfect is formed, they have the 'generative capacity' to use that knowledge in whatever circumstance presents itself – specifically, with verbs they have never seen before.[1] The second advantage is *economy*. Data in a declarative system are stored once only in a form that makes them available for all necessary operations. Compare this to the state of affairs with a procedural system, where each single present perfect is stored as a separate piece of information – learners know 'he worked', 'he changed', 'he loved', 'he waited', and so on. The third advantage of the declarative path is that it is *low risk*. If new information is encoded in declarative form, conscious attention is devoted to it before operations using it are undertaken. As Anderson (1982) notes, 'one can be circumspect about the behavioural implications of declarative knowledge' (p. 381). This is because consciously known rules are relatively easy to abandon if they should prove faulty; information stored as facts can relatively easily be replaced by modified information. Imagine, for example, that learners wrongly learn that 'be' rather than 'have' is the auxiliary used in the formation of the present perfect (perhaps following some such practice in their first language). Since they refer consciously to the rule every time they use it, they can easily modify their behaviour when it is pointed out to them that their rule is wrong. Unconsciously applied rules are less easy to change: it is easy to imagine that if the learner persists with the wrong auxiliary for too long, and it becomes ingrained, it will become proportionally more difficult to alter.

The declarative path has two main disadvantages. The first is that it is *slow*. Each time an operation is done, the relevant information must be sought in long-term memory, brought into working memory, and held there while the operation is undertaken. Every time learners wish to produce a present perfect, they have to remember the rule consciously, and go through the steps one by one. Their interactants can be forgiven for losing interest in any conversation where this process continues for long! The second disadvantage is that declarative processing is *heavy on channel capacity*. Humans are only able to concentrate conscious attention on a few things at a time; indeed, Bobrow and Norman (1975) state that 'one does not err much by assuming that only a single high-level cognitive task can be performed at any given time' (p. 139). Working memory space is utilized while an operation is consciously undertaken on the data in it. In terms, once again, of the language example: if the learner has to devote conscious attention to forming the present perfect, less attention is available for doing other things – a point which we shall develop at length in chapter 7.

The procedural path has the corresponding advantages and disadvantages. With knowledge already incorporated into programs for action, no search in long-term memory is required, and little space in working memory is filled while the operation is done. The system has the great advantage of being fast (interactants do not lose interest); and it is also light on channel capacity. But (as we have already hinted) knowledge is not necessarily available to the system in a generative form, since data stored in one program for action will not automatically be available for other programs. Storage is also uneconomical because the same data may need to be retained in many programs. It is also high risk. If faulty data become stored in a plan for action, the entire program has to be abandoned or reassembled (rather than simply modifying the data base, as in the declarative system). If the program is not abandoned or reassembled, and is combined with other programs, the results can be disastrous. Anderson's (1982) analogy is with computing; 'anyone who incrementally augments computer programs will be aware of . . . [how] . . . a single erroneous statement can destroy the behaviour of a previously fine program'. In more human terms: if a musician learns to play a note wrongly, or a language learner to form a tense badly, it will be the devil's own task to eradicate this behaviour.

We have seen that both paths for skilled production have advantages and disadvantages, and these are summarized in table 4.1, using the terms declarative knowledge to mean 'knowledge about' (stored in memory), and procedural knowledge to be 'knowledge how to' (stored in programs for action).

The importance of both declarative and procedural knowledge to language use

What is the role of declarative and procedural knowledge in language use? Bialystok (1982) discusses this issue, although her paper uses different

Table 4.1 Advantages and disadvantages of declarative and procedural processing

Path/ knowledge type	Advantages	Disadvantages
Declarative	'Generative' Economical Low risk	Slow High on channel capacity
Procedural	Fast Low on channel capacity	'Non-generative' Uneconomical High risk

terms and has a slightly different conceptual framework from the one being developed here. Using our, not her, terms, she argues that the specific role of these two sorts of knowledge depends on the language task being considered. Hence, for tasks such as spontaneous conversation where immediate access to knowledge is required, procedural knowledge is important. But it will be less so in tasks like writing, where speed of production (and hence rapid access to knowledge) is often not required. While declarative knowledge, on the other hand, may have little part to play in spontaneous conversation, it will be crucial in many writing tasks, for example, where having a declarative knowledge data base of rules to refer to and manipulate will be an advantage.

It is essential to recognize that, apart from these task-related differences, both procedural and declarative knowledge are necessary for overall language mastery. Thus, in overall terms, the learner must have ready access to language knowledge, in procedural form; and, as we shall note later, it is important that scarce channel capacity should be made available for high-level language skills (not low-level manipulative ones). The generativity of declarative knowledge is also crucial. The student who has a series of specific rules (e.g. for the production of the present perfect of various specific verbs), but no generalized ones (for forming the 'present perfect' in general), cannot generatively create present perfect tenses for verbs not met before. There is no data base in the form of a set of rules for generating the tense, and hence the system cannot easily go beyond data already met. One might add to this a point not so far discussed but raised in chapter 5: the apparent utility for learning of declarative knowledge. There is some evidence (mentioned in chapter 5) from the general skills literature that having declarative *knowledge about* is a useful first step to developing procedural knowledge.

Dechert (1984) outlines the computational (information-processing) paradigm, and interprets six hypotheses for L2 acquisition in terms of it. The models include the *monitor hypothesis*, and the *procedural knowledge hypothesis*.

Möhle (1984) uses pausological analysis to compare L1 and L2 spoken productions in French and German. She notes considerable differences, and extrapolates different planning strategies from these.

Möhle and Raupach (1987) discuss of the declarative/procedural distinction in relation to L2 acquisition. They clarify the relationship between these concepts and other similar ones, such as explicit/implicit (Bialystok 1978); analysed/unanalysed (Bialystok 1984); controlled/automatic (Schneider and Shiffrin (1977); knowledge/control (Bialystok and Sharwood Smith 1985).

Dechert (1989) looks at cognitive transfer in relation to a story-telling task. 'Transfer in language production first of all reveals itself to be a cognitive activity, consisting of various interacting procedures of analogical reasoning' (p. 261). Analogical reasoning is important in the Anderson model, where analogy is one of the processes involved in generalizing knowledge. Other papers looking at production in story telling are Dechert (1987), Lennon (1984) and Appel and Goldberg (1984).

Möhle and Raupach (1989) consider what role can be seen for L1 transfer in the model. Anderson (particularly 1980, pp. 176ff.) discusses transfer of declarative knowledge in general (i.e. in non-language-related terms). But Möhle and Raupach argue that it is unclear how L1 transfer would be handled in the model; there are various mechanisms for doing so, but they are not clearly differentiated. Further discussion of transfer in such models is found in Faerch and Kasper (1985, 1986).

Dechert (1992) explores the notion of 'being good at something', where the 'something' involves some form of procedural knowledge, and emphasizes the role of flexibility – mental models of how to cope with problems, and procedures to overcome them.

Figure 4.1   Some Kassel papers on language production in the information-processing model

Since both procedural and declarative knowledge are important for language use, it is necessary for any adequate learning model to provide for both.

Evidence for a declarative/procedural distinction

There has been a certain amount of research geared to show the existence of declarative and procedural knowledge, and ways of processing utilizing them. Much of it is associated with the 'Kassel group', mentioned earlier. The general paradigm which such research follows is to show that there are faster and slower types of processing at work, the conclusion being that the faster utilizes procedural knowledge, and the slower, declarative. The characteristic research methodology employs 'pausology'. This technique is based on the claim, in Raupach's (1987) words, that 'an analysis of speech production can yield insight into some of the speaker's mental processes' (p. 133). As a consequence, Raupach and others use measures like pause/time ratio (the percentage of overall time spent pausing); mean pause length; mean length of runs (uninterrupted stretches of speech); number of hesitations. It is O'Connell and Kowal (1980) who refer to this methodology as 'pausology', defining it as 'the behavioural investigation of temporal dimensions of . . . speech' (p. 8). In a persuasive paper on the topic, Griffiths (1991) argues that it can be relied on to produce valid findings. He also notes its particular association with the Kassel group, of which Raupach is a leading member.

Figure 4.1 illustrates the scope of the Kassel group's work on language production in the information-processing paradigm. In order to exemplify this work in more detail, we shall here describe one of Raupach's papers (1987) which utilizes the declarative/procedural distinction as its starting point.

Raupach's data in his 1987 paper are from adult German learners of French as a foreign language, at university level, and he compares their performance in a conversational task before and after a term's visit to France. He also provides information from data collected by himself and others (Möhle and Raupach 1983, and elsewhere) on mean length of runs (measured in syllables) before and after the French visit. He uses pausology for his analysis (already noted as a favoured technique of the Kassel group), and the details of his findings are provided in table 4.2. The first language of all subjects is German.

Raupach uses his temporal variable findings to argue that procedural learning may be identified by smooth production without hesitation, while

Table 4.2 Mean length of runs (measured in syllables) of six German learners of French before and after a visit to France

	Length of runs	
Subject no.	*Before visit*	*After visit*
1	5.51	7.54
2	6.30	10.73
3	6.00	7.87
4	4.56	7.92
5	5.55	8.70
6	7.48	7.85

Source: Raupach (1987)

hesitations are one of the signs that the learner is having to utilize declarative knowledge (slower on processing). Interpreted in this way, his data suggest a progression from declarative to procedural.

O'Malley and Chamot (1990 and elsewhere) also provide evidence for declarative and procedural processing, and for a progression over time from one to the other. Their main concern is with the identification and analysis of learning strategies, building on earlier strategy studies such as those within the 'Good Language Learner' tradition, (e.g. Rubin 1975, Naiman et al. 1978). In the course of their strategy studies, they find a good deal of evidence to suggest that on occasion learners use declarative knowledge in language use and understanding, 'tapping into schemata related to the language topic, and calling upon that information to assist in their comprehension or production' (O'Malley and Chamot 1990, p. 145). In fact, they refer to language comprehension as a kind of 'problem-solving activity' utilizing information consciously brought to mind from memory store. At the same time, however, they evidence the kind of information-processing consistent with the use of procedural knowledge. One of the aspects of such processing that they draw attention to is adaptability; it is a characteristic of the better students that they evidence adaptability in their processing; recall the 'Wood Chopper's Ball' in chapter 2, and how flexibility won the day.

O'Malley and Chamot also have some contentious evidence for a progression from declarative to procedural processing over time. They note (1990) that beginner learners do seem to rely more on transfer from their first language than more advanced learners, using it as 'a major strategy' (p. 148). They claim that it is an implication of Bialystok and Ryan (1985) that 'analysed' (i.e. declarative) L1 information is more available for transfer than non-analysed information. On the basis of this claimed implication, they argue that beginner L2 learners are utilizing more declarative knowledge (from the first language) than more advanced learners. The evidence is contentious because, as we shall see later, the claim that L1 knowledge that is transferred is in fact in declarative form is questioned by Raupach (1987).

3 Automization

Automization is the process of 'making automatic', and it is a central concept within the study of cognitive skills acquisition; indeed, Shiffrin and Dumais (1981) call it 'a fundamental component of skill development' (p. 111). We need to be clear precisely why it is important, both to the development of skills in general, and to the development of language in particular. What function does the process of automization fulfil?

When a skill is newly learned, its performance takes up a great deal of conscious attention, or channel capacity. To use a commonly found illustration: novice drivers recently taught how to change gear will only be able to do so if they concentrate on this and nothing else. This state of affairs is unsatisfactory, because there are higher-level skills which require available channel capacity – drivers need to be anticipating the movement of other traffic, of pedestrians, and generally to be attending to what is happening around them. Channel capacity can only be made available for these activities if 'lower-order' skills like changing gear have been automated to the extent that they take up no 'room in the mind'. When novice drivers have automated gear changing, they will be able to perform the action without even being aware that they are doing it. The role of automization in skill learning is therefore to free important channel capacity for tasks which require it.

In general terms, the role of automization in language learning will be as just described; learners automate use of the tenses (for example) so that they can concentrate effort where it is needed – in comprehending and conveying meanings clearly. Though this will be important in all areas of language use, we might, again following Bialystok (1982), expect it to be more important in some areas of language use than in others. Hence in writing, where the learner may have much time to ponder, automized language performance will be less important than in conversational exchanges, where more store is put on rapid response.

Bialystok's point about different areas of language use was made earlier regarding declarative and procedural knowledge, and it is important to understand how these notions relate to the concept of automization. In effect, automization may be seen as the process of converting declarative knowledge into procedural knowledge, bringing with it all the advantages of the procedural, and eliminating all the disadvantages of the declarative. Given the central role this process has, we would expect a model of skill learning to account for how it occurs.

Evidence for automization

If automization is indeed the process of 'making procedural', as suggested above, then research which attempts to find evidence of automization at work will be research showing how declarative knowledge becomes procedural. It is hence likely to be comparative in nature: taking different groups of individuals, or the same individuals doing different tasks, or the same individuals at different times – and seeking differences in performance which can be accounted for by the process of automization. Also, it is likely to be very much within the same paradigm as the Raupach paper considered earlier, using pausology to identify declarative and procedural. Indeed, one might easily cite all the research mentioned above in relation to the declarative/procedural distinction as research identifying the process of automisation.

The above expectations are correct, and well exemplified in a paper by Towell (1987). His data is taken from a large corpus supplied by five students of French at undergraduate level, collected over a four-year period. He concentrates on specific grammatical structures, one of them being the choice of preposition (*à, de* or zero) following the French adjective '*difficile*'. He notes that there is a large amount of persistent variability over the entire period he studies. In order to account for this variability, he (like Hulstijn and Hulstijn) utilizes the concept of 'control' There is, he says, a 'diachronic' dimension to control, meaning that a learner's mastery of the 'control factors' in processing improves over time; automization, that is, does take place.

Towell uses four pausological measures on his data, with measurements taken at two points in time – years 1 and 3 of his study. *Speaking rate*, the first measurement, is calculated by dividing the total number of syllables produced by total time taken to produce the utterance (including pause time), and multiplying the result by 60 = syll/min. *Articulation rate* is arrived at by dividing the number of syllables produced by the number of seconds taken to produce them, not including pause time = syll/sec. The other measures he uses are *pause/time ratio* (the percentage of time spent pausing) and *length of runs* (uninterrupted stretches of speech). Here are the results for one of his subjects, who may be taken as representative: her speaking rate increased by 65%, her pause/time ratio by 37%, her articulation rate by 20%, and the length of runs between pauses by 95%. In addition: 'the number of utterances between 1–4 syllables fell by 30.4%, the number of utterances between 5–10 syllables increased by 3.79% and the number of utterances of 11 syllables and above increased by 19.91%' (Towell 1987, p. 125). It is clear from these figures that this one student (as well as others Towell considers) improves her performance on the control dimension considerably over time. This is taken to evidence the existence of automization.

Towell's paper is representative of a large amount of research geared to identify aspects of information processing at work, and McLaughlin (1987) contains a useful summary of such work which, as noted earlier, is often comparative in nature. McLaughlin lists his research overview under three headings: *lexical retrieval, syntactic processing*, and *reading*. Figure 4.2 selects examples of this research where something akin to the process of automisation may be said to be involved. The figure well illustrates the extent of the interest in automization in the field of L2 acquisition.

In this section we have considered some central information-processing concepts. We shall now go on to consider one particular model which incorporates these concepts.

The Anderson Model

Much of the work in this area of cognitive psychology has been concerned with the identification of types of human processing and with attempting to develop models to account for them. But (as Langley and Simon 1981 note), at the beginning of the eighties attention began to switch to attempts to develop learning theories which take account of these issues. One such attempt is the model developed by the cognitive psychologist Anderson, together with colleagues. What we shall refer to as the 'Anderson model' for convenience exists in various slightly differing versions; we shall here principally draw on Anderson (1982) but shall also include elements from Neves and Anderson (1981). A more accessible account of the model is found in Anderson (1983), and it is based on early work by Fitts (1964) and Fitts and Posner (1967).

Henning (1979) studied errors in lexical processing, and suggests that more-advanced learners group lexical items using semantic criteria, unlike less-advanced learners who seem to cluster acoustically, not having fully automized the items.

Dornic (1979) found that even with balanced bilinguals, encoding was slower in the second language than in the first, the explanatory factor thought to be extent of automization. Dornic also found that factors such as noise interfered with processing significantly more in the second language than in the first, a finding that together with work such as Hulstijn and Hulstijn's (considered earlier) suggests that task complexity is indeed a viable concept in language teaching.

Hatch et al. (1970) asked native and non-native speakers to cross out certain letters in a text (e.g. all letter 'e's). They found that native speakers ignored the letters more often in function than in content words, which was not the case for non-natives. This suggests to them that native speakers do not focus so much attention on function words, having automized their use, concentrating channel capacity on content words.

Rossman (1981) compared memory of semantic and syntactic features of a text, with native and non-native speakers. Native speakers showed better recognition than non-natives for semantic rather than syntactic changes. Non-natives showed better recognition than natives for syntactic features. This is because, Rossman hypothesized, native speakers have automized syntactic features and concentrate on the semantic, unlike non-natives.

Wolfe (1981) studied English-speaking children learning French as a second language. The task was to read a paragraph then to identify given sentences as the same or different from those seen in the passage, similarity or difference being to do either with language or content. The more proficient L2 speakers identified more different sentences correctly where the difference was semantic, while the less proficient had higher scores in identifying syntactic differences. This suggests a lesser degree of automaticity for the less proficient speakers, together with more concentration on form as opposed to content.

Segalowitz (1986) found 'reduced automaticity in word recognition and slowed second-language reading in otherwise fluent bilinguals' (McLaughlin 1987, p. 143).

Figure 4.2 Some examples of information-processing research (selected and summarized from McLaughlin 1987)

The model uses production systems. Productions are formal representations of 'programs' or 'plans for action'. They contain a statement of goal plus any relevant conditions, followed by an action, to form an IF . . . THEN sequence. P1 and P2 illustrate possible productions for generating part of the English present perfect (the example we used in earlier discussion of the declarative and procedural paths).

P1   IF the goal is to form the present perfect of a verb
and the person is 3rd singular
THEN form the 3rd singular of 'have'

P2   IF the goal is to form the present perfect of a verb
and the appropriate form of 'have' has just been formed
THEN form the past participle of the verb.

The model, developed partly as a consequence of research on the acquisition of skills in geometry, has three stages (closely resembling Fitts and Posner's 1967 three stages).

1 Declarative stage

Learners store knowledge they are given in long-term memory as a data base. When required to use this knowledge to perform, they use general interpretative procedures (procedures used to solve problems in general). Hence, if learners have to use new knowledge in geometry to work out a theorem, they apply general problem-solving procedures to the knowledge they have been given. The learners' encoding is hence declarative, and consists of the two separate components associated with declarative models: (a) a data base and (b) a set of general procedures. As Neves and Anderson (1981) note, these declarative encodings have the expected disadvantages and advantages which we outlined earlier. In P1 and P2 the data base would contain information about the third singular of 'have', and formation of the past participle.

2 Knowledge compilation stage

'With practice the knowledge is converted into a procedural form in which it is directly applied without the intercession of other interpretative procedures' (Anderson 1982, p. 370). Knowledge compilation in Anderson (1982) involves two processes. The first process is *proceduralization*. This eliminates clauses in the condition of a production that require information to be retrieved from long-term memory and held in working memory. That is, the data base specific to the task becomes incorporated in the production. P1, for example, would become P3:

> P3　IF the goal is to form the present perfect of a verb
> and the person is 3rd singular
> THEN form 'has'

The second process, *composition*, combines pairs of productions in sequence to form 'macroproductions'. The result combining P1 and P2 above would be:

> P4　IF the goal is to form the present perfect of a verb
> and the person is 3rd singular
> THEN form the 3rd singular of 'have'
> and then form the past participle of the verb

By continued composition and proceduralization, a production can be built that forms the present perfect of a given verb in one operation. Hence:

> P5　IF the goal is to form the 3rd singular of the verb 'change'
> THEN form 'has changed'.

The procedural encoding thus consists of one, not two, parts and has the form of a production which incorporates relevant information from the data base. Again, the encodings have the expected advantages and disadvantages of a procedural system, discussed earlier.

3 Procedural stage

At this stage three learning mechanisms operate. These are *generalization*, 'by which production rules become broader in their range of applicability' (Anderson 1982, p. 390); *discrimination*, where rules become narrower; and a *strengthening* process by which better rules are strengthened and poorer rules weakened. These processes have clear correlates in other learning theories, though Anderson indicates differences. These mechanisms together constitute a process of tuning.

It is important to note that the movement from declarative to procedural is a change in the way knowledge is stored; it has nothing to do with the nature of knowledge stored or the scope that knowledge covers. Scope of knowledge is extended by generalization and narrowed by discrimination. Anderson's (1982) example of generalization is from language acquisition, and indicates how P6 and P7 become P8:

P6   IF the goal is to indicate that a coat belongs to me
       THEN say 'My coat'.

P7   IF the goal is to indicate that a ball belongs to me
       THEN say 'My ball'.

P8   IF the goal is to indicate that object X belongs to me
       THEN say 'My X'.

The Anderson model as a framework for learning

The Anderson model is intended as a model of learning. That is, it was developed to handle skills (like those in geometry) where instruction is given, and it is explicitly acknowledged (Anderson 1982) that information is provided through instruction at the declarative stage. The strength of this model is that it provides a specification of how automization takes place, through the processes of composition and proceduralization. Composition speeds up action because a combination of two productions takes less time to perform than the two productions performed sequentially (Neves and Anderson 1981). Proceduralization diminishes required memory space because the relevant parts of the data base are incorporated into the production. The production encoding is then tuned.

The sequence which the model provides is a learning sequence:

declarative encoding → procedural encoding → tuning

In what follows, we shall have little to say about the model's third stage, although there is some relevant discussion in the L2 acquisition literature – Ellis (1985b), for example, has an equivalent to this stage, but his has one mechanism only (discrimination, operating according to an economy principle), while Anderson has three mechanisms (generalization, discrimination and strengthening). But we shall have plenty to say about the declarative to procedural sequence, and will henceforth refer to it by use of the abbreviation DECPRO. DECPRO is a learning sequence; indeed, one might even be tempted to think of it as the cognitive skills embodiment of Krashen's 'learning'.

This is the place to introduce a terminological issue. We have seen that in the Anderson model, the term 'proceduralization' is used to refer to one of two processes that occur at the second, knowledge compilation stage. He also (perhaps rather confusingly) uses the term 'procedural' to refer to the third stage of the model. We need a convenient term to refer to the entire process whereby declarative knowledge becomes procedural knowledge; at the risk of compounding the confusion, we shall henceforth use the term 'proceduralization' for this.

Disappearance of declarative encodings

There is a criticism of the Anderson model which is found both in L. N. Chaudhry (unpublished observations) and in a paper much concerned with issues being raised here, Bialystok and Sharwood Smith (1985). The latter take pains to dissociate themselves (p. 116, note 2) from the model, pointing out that in it declarative representations fall away, being replaced by procedural encodings; the former are hence no longer available for tasks requiring the use of declarative knowledge. This is a problem because, as we have already noted, there are occasions when declarative knowledge is important in language use; it must somehow be retained. Anderson certainly admits that this falling-away can occur. The example in Anderson (1980) is of the expert driver unable to explain to a novice how to change gear, and in Anderson (1982) the further example is of the person who has no access to a phone number except through dialling it.

There are three points to be made in relation to this criticism. Firstly, it is recognized by Anderson, as by others concerned with the declarative/procedural distinction, that it is important to find ways of maintaining declarative representation. He makes the point several times, and indeed a section of Neves and Anderson (1981) is entitled 'Getting the Best of Both Encodings.' The falling-away, when it occurs, is seen as detrimental. Secondly, although Anderson (1982) concedes that the falling-away *may* occur, it is not certain that it will. 'It should be emphasised', he states, 'that forming this [procedural] production does not imply the necessary loss of the declarative representation of the knowledge' (p. 383). Thirdly, it is clear that the machinery by which the model operates does permit knowledge to remain in data base after it becomes embedded in procedural productions.

Stated in the computerese which the model finds amenable, what is involved is a process of knowledge *copying*, not knowledge *moving*. What Anderson does not of course consider (because it is beyond his immediate concerns) is what preventative action to take when a declarative encoding does disappear. Because we are ultimately interested in language teaching, this issue is of concern to us – we must develop teaching strategies for maintaining declarative representations when they are in danger of disappearing, and we touch on this issue in chapter 5.

The Anderson model as a framework for acquisition

Anderson (1983) argues that procedural productions cannot be directly acquired, claiming that preventing procedural knowledge from entering the system too easily is 'an adaptive design feature' (p. 215), necessary because it is very difficult to change knowledge once proceduralized. The model therefore involves a progression from declarative to procedural (DECPRO) for all learning (non-linguistic skills, L1 and L2) and all learners. One learns declaratively first, then automizes over time.

But perhaps this formulation is too rigid as a model for the mastery of skills in general, and for both L1 and L2 acquisition. Starting with skills in general, we saw in chapter 1 that Karmiloff-Smith spoke of early 'procedural representations' in relationship to piano playing; the novice pianist acquires configurations of notes as a first stage. A similar point is made by the Kassel group's favoured philosopher, Ryle (1949, cited in Raupach 1987), who is talking about the learning of chess when he says: 'we learn *how* by practice . . . often quite unaided by any lessons in the theory' (p. 41). In short, in the mastery of skills in general, we may directly proceduralize knowledge, without going through the declarative. We also saw in chapter 1 that the same process may be said to occur in L1 acquisition. Anderson (1981, 1983) attempts to impose a DECPRO sequence on L1 acquisition. But it is difficult to see any sense in which the L1 child first develops declarative knowledge, and although Karmiloff-Smith's comments about 'early proceduralization' happen to occur in the context of piano playing, she herself generalizes the point to apply to the acquisition of the first language and other skills as well.

Turning now to L2 acquisition, we have also argued (in chapter 3) the need to recognize the existence of a second process, associated with what Krashen calls 'acquisition'. As further evidence of a process at work in L2 that cannot be described by the DECPRO formula, we may return to the Raupach paper (1987) cited earlier. In one of the strategies he observes, the

learner imports productions from the first language in already proceduralized form. Raupach's example relates to stress, when the learner produces
the following:

je ne *veux* pas euh devenir professeur   ['euh' = hesitation
                                                   phenomenon]

Here the learner wants, by placing stress on *veux*, to emphasize her not
being willing to become a teacher. Raupach points out that this kind of
syllable stress is not common in spoken French, but is quite usual in
German. In this case the learner has neither learned the wrong means of
expressing stress in French, nor was it initially *learned* in her first language,
German. It was *acquired* procedurally in the first language and is now
imported in procedural form into French. Raupach's conclusion is here
at odds with the O'Malley and Chamot finding noted earlier – that L1
knowledge is imported in declarative form. For Raupach, what we are
witnessing is the direct importation of proceduralized knowledge from the
first language.

It follows from these observations that if the Anderson model is to have
credibility as a model for the mastery of the first and second languages (as
well indeed as for skills in general), it needs to be extended. The necessary
extension is a comparatively simple matter because although the model as it
stands cannot handle 'acquisition'; its central concepts of declarative and
procedural knowledge may be used to account for that process. We may
regard acquisition as a process whereby direct procedural encodings are
formed. In these encodings knowledge is already proceduralized. Hence an
encoding like the P5 one given earlier might enter the system in that form.
In this formulation what we are witnessing is not DECPRO but simply
PRO – the direct proceduralization of knowledge.

Characteristics of PRO

We might expect this way of processing to have the advantages and disadvantages of all procedural systems, discussed earlier. The major advantages
are speed and lightness on channel capacity, and there are some language
users for whom these advantages are particularly attractive. Recent immigrants, for example, will have urgent communicative needs best met by
speedily assembled knowledge. The less channel capacity consumed on
linguistic matters, the better, enabling the user to concentrate on getting
messages across. Mention of recent immigrants perhaps brings to mind the

development of types of pidgins, where forms are quickly developed to satisfy urgent communicative needs – there is immediate availability for use.

It may further be argued that the formulation predicts that acquired output is more likely to occur with certain language tasks than with others. As we noted earlier, for Bialystok different tasks place different demands in terms of degree of automaticity required. In fluent conversation, for example, the user needs high automaticity while in writing tasks this will often not be the case. Because in the Anderson model it is the processes of proceduralization which lead to automization, it follows that encodings entering the system in proceduralized form will quickly become highly automized. It is therefore to be expected that these encodings should occur most often in tasks requiring high automaticity; one would predict, in other words, that there would be more acquired output in fluent conversation than in writing. This prediction seems to fit what researchers like Tarone (1983) have found. Her 'casual' style is the one associated with fluent conversation, and it is in this that most 'acquired output' occurs.

Acquired encodings, which come into the system in an already proceduralized form, quickly become highly automized and impermeable to change. It is this characteristic which makes them high risk. Earlier in this chapter we made the point that if a production is in some way faulty, a great deal of effort will be needed to eradicate it – just as when the learner of a musical instrument automizes some faulty procedure and has to undergo elaborate remediation to rectify it. One way of characterizing the fossilization of interlanguage is to view it as the fast automization of faulty productions. One would then predict that a factor determining fossilization (alongside those listed in Schumann 1978 – a book which, incidentally, links fossilization with pidgins, about which we have just spoken) is the speed with which, and extent to which, automization has taken place.

Proceduralized encodings are *inflexible* and *non-generative* because the relevant knowledge is contained in the production itself. This knowledge is not part of a data base and will hence not be available for other encodings. If acquisition is characterized by directly proceduralized encodings, then we would predict acquired knowledge to be inflexible or non-generative in this sense.

From PRO to PRODEC

PRO's problems of inflexibility and non-generativity are very serious indeed, and they are real ones that manifest themselves in real learners who develop early fossilized pidgins. These problems point once again to the necessity for formation of a declarative encoding. In the DECPRO sequence, the issue regarding DEC is to ensure that declarative remains when the procedural is developed. In the case of PRO it is a question of ensuring that the declarative encoding DEC is somehow added on to an already formed PRO.

How might this be achieved? It is possible that the DEC may form itself, and as we saw in chapter 1, Karmiloff-Smith sees it as a characteristic of humans to proceed beyond mastery, so that the child's initial linguistic I-representations become E-representations over time. But she also makes the point that DEC need not necessarily be formed from an initial PRO; many pianists (Karmiloff-Smith notes) do not go beyond the procedural, just as with language some pidgin speakers fossilize permanently (Schumann's 1978 Alberto being a celebrated case in point). In chapter 5 we shall consider ways in which the declarative knowledge may be developed. But the important point here is to realize that an initial PRO needs somehow or other to gain a subsequent DEC.

One way of stating the matter is to say that many acquisition approaches to L2 mastery may in fact be represented as being PRO only. But if we concern ourselves not just with what occurs, but with what should occur, then the only acceptable alternative to DECPRO is not PRO but PRODEC.

DECPRO and PRODEC

What we have in effect proposed above is an extension to the Anderson model. This extension achieves two related things. One is that it enables the model to account for a means of processing whereby procedural precedes declarative (PRODEC), something which was not the case with the original model. Secondly, it enables us to speak about 'acquisition' and 'acquisition-based approaches to teaching' within a framework based around the general cognitive concepts of procedural and declarative knowledge.

But what precisely are the relationships between DECPRO/PRODEC and learning/acquisition? It would be convenient to state that DECPRO is learning, and PRODEC acquisition; but this is not really the case. We can say with certainty that DECPRO is *a* learning strategy, and a common one which many teaching methods in one or another facet follow. In language teaching terms, for example, there is the grammar translation method, where grammatical explanations provide DEC as the starting point for teaching, from which PRO is supposed to flow. But there are other teaching methods, like audiolingualism, where the issue is not so simple. In this method, rules and generalizations are avoided at the first stage of teaching; any rules which may be given would come later – as Politzer (1961), a strong advocate of audiolingualism, has it: 'rules ought to be summaries of behaviours' (pp. 5–6). So, where a DEC is explicitly provided, it might be said to *follow* the PRO. But is what the student gets at the outset really PRO? Audiolingual lessons characteristically begin with the presentation of key sentences, immediately followed by controlled practice. As we shall argue at length in chapter 9, controlled practice of the audiolingual sort leaves much to be desired as a mode of proceduralization. Also, the key sentences are clearly intended to provide some sort of initial form of DEC. Arguably, what one finds in audiolingualism is DECPRODEC; it is certainly not a 'clean' version either of DECPRO nor of PRODEC.

If one considers learning as opposed to teaching there are other reasons why DECPRO and PRODEC cannot be presented as the only versions of what occurs. It may certainly be argued that the language learner does not exclusively follow either one or the other of these sequences, but mixes the two. There is no doubt that this is the case, and the word O'Malley and Chamot use to describe learners – 'opportunistic' – springs to mind here; sometimes they will be forming 'rules' after 'practice', and sometimes vice versa.

If not all learning is DECPRO, and PRODEC not always acquisition, then what is the utility of these formulations for discussion about language learning and teaching? The main value of conceptualizing language learning and teaching in terms of DEC and PRO is that it identifies declarativization and proceduralization as central to both processes, and hence provides a framework within which to locate the various tasks and problems a learner is likely to meet. We shall continue to talk in terms of DECPRO and PRODEC also because, despite the caveats we have just made, they do characterize two main strategies for learning and teaching.

Note

1   Vivian Cook (personal communication) points out that the word 'generative' is here (and throughout the chapter) being used in its non-linguistic sense of 'productive'. In linguistics the term has a different and very precise meaning (as in the phrase 'generative grammar').

5 Declarative Knowledge: Developing and Maintaining It

Declarativization and Proceduralization

So far in this book we have been concentrating on the nature of language as behaviour, and on language learning. Now is the time for the important change of focus – from now on language teaching will receive our prime attention. In the most general terms, the question is how we may assist mastery of a second language by means of some form of facilitation. We refer to 'facilitation' rather than 'instruction' in order to leave open the possibility that the best means of furthering language learning may involve activities – like simply letting the students talk freely to each other – which are not generally associated with the notion of instruction.

As a first step within our new focus on pedagogy, we might begin by taking our two models, DECPRO and PRODEC, and considering their implications in terms of pedagogic procedure.

In the light of what was said in chapter 4 regarding what is necessary for mastery to be achieved, we might say that the DECPRO model sets the following three tasks:

1   **Developing initial declarative representation**. How may we assist learners to develop a declarative representation in the first place? How best may declarative knowledge be imparted?

2   **Proceduralizing**. Once the declarative representation has been developed, it needs to be 'converted' into procedural knowledge. This is essentially the issue of automization, and how to assist the learner to achieve it.

3   **Maintaining declarative representation**. We have noted that there is a tendency for declarative representations to fall away when procedural knowledge is developed. We have also noted that this should be avoided,

because for most learners declarative knowledge always remains important. How may we help to maintain it?

In the case of PRODEC we may identify the following two tasks:

4 Developing initial procedural knowledge. This is an issue which 'acquisition' or 'naturalistic' approaches to teaching have concentrated on – developing activities which will help the learner to 'acquire' – in the classroom (or wherever else the language teaching is taking place).

5 Developing a declarative representation from a procedural one. Given that a declarative representation is important, by far the greatest problem that 'acquisition' approaches face is how to facilitate its development from the procedural knowledge that the learners have acquired in a more or less naturalistic way.

It will be clear that underlying these five tasks are two general processes which, given the approach we are taking, are seen as central to the language-teaching operation. These we may call *declarativization* and *proceduralization*; these involve the development/maintenance of declarative and procedural knowledge, respectively. We shall consider these central processes in this and the next chapters, starting with declarativization here. As noted at the end of the last chapter, we regard it as insightful to formulate language-teaching issues in terms of these two processes.

At this stage it is convenient to introduce into the discussion terms which are very often used in language teaching to describe a common teaching strategy (see particularly Byrne 1976). These terms are *presentation, practice* and *production*. In the conventional 'PPP' teaching model, new language is first *presented* to students; it is then *practised* (*drilled, manipulated* are also common terms), and students are then allowed to *produce* in a more or less 'free' way. We shall have reason to refer to the PPP model a lot, and note here that the first P (presentation) is largely concerned with the process of declarativization, while the other two (practice and production) are associated with proceduralization.

Declarative Knowledge: Some General Issues

Two roles for declarative knowledge

It is clear from the above characterization of the pedagogic issues (and from points made in earlier chapters) that we are claiming two roles for declarative knowledge in language teaching. In the first place, declarative knowledge may be used as the initial point for a process of proceduralization. This role is specific to the DECPRO sequence (as exemplified for example by the original Anderson model), because in that sequence procedural knowledge is developed out of the declarative base. The second role for declarative knowledge is relevant whichever sequence, DECPRO or PRODEC, one is dealing with. It is that this form of knowledge stands as a data base of knowledge, useful for language use in general, and for certain tasks such as many forms of writing in particular.

These two roles make quite different, even conflicting, requirements on the form declarative knowledge might best have. Declarative knowledge as the basis for proceduralization needs to be simple, uncluttered, concrete, and easily convertible into a 'plan for action'. Declarative knowledge as a data base for language use, on the other hand, needs to be accurate (which will often imply complexity), and as generalizable as possible (which may imply a good degree of abstraction). These differing requirements will become clearer as we discuss them in more detail below.

Because these roles are so different, they may need to be treated quite separately by the language teacher, and it may well be appropriate to address them at different points in the teaching process. Declarative knowledge as the starting point for proceduralization is naturally associated with an initial position in the teaching sequence – it is the DEC which precedes the PRO in DECPRO, and the first P in the PPP sequence. But it may well be that declarative knowledge as data base occurs best after proceduralization has occurred – at a point when complexities may be presented to the learner without fear of obstructing the proceduralization process. This is of course what happens in PRODEC (where DEC comes after PRO); to permit it to happen in the other model we would have to add a final DEC to DECPRO, thus making it DECPRODEC![1]

Declarative knowledge as conscious knowledge

Declarative knowledge need not be conscious knowledge, and is of the kind which Carroll (1973) is describing when he says: 'although it is often said that linguistic "competence" . . . involves some kind of "knowledge" of the grammatical rules of the language, this "knowledge" is ordinarily out of conscious awareness . . .' (pp. 7–8). But if we wish to convey declarative information to students, one of the most obvious ways of doing so is by means of conscious knowledge. Is this the best way of imparting declarative information? The history of language teaching reveals positions for and against the role of conscious knowledge. Rutherford (1987) provides a historical survey of what he, along with many others, calls consciousness raising (CR) – defined in his glossary as 'the drawing of the learner's attention to features of the target language' (p. 189). Rutherford's survey goes back to the Middle Ages, where grammatical study was regarded as a central discipline. He claims that approaches giving no importance to language study are, within the broad historical perspective, relatively recent. Audiolingualism, with its behaviourist base, shows the clearest example of a view that learning is a question of habit formation, and where consciousness either has no role at all, or simply works to summarize already proceduralized behaviour (in chapter 4 we cited Politzer's dictum that 'rules ought to be summaries of behaviour').

It is well known that in the 1960s one finds direct confrontation between audiolingualism and the 'cognitive code' approach supported by people such as Carroll (1966). Cognitive code is a kind of 'up-to-date grammar translation theory' (p. 102), and involves grammatical explanations: it entails the 'process of acquiring conscious control of . . . the patterns of a second language, largely through study and analysis of these patterns as a body of knowledge' (p. 102). As this quotation suggests, 'consciousness versus non-consciousness' is a central issue in the cognitive code versus audiolingualism debate. The 1960s was also a time when large-scale studies comparing language teaching methods were undertaken, and in Scherer and Wertheimer's celebrated study (1964) an attempt was made to assess the comparative success of audiolingualism and cognitive code. Unfortunately, the results of this study were somewhat inconclusive.

In even more recent times, the 'no role for consciousness' school has gained increasing support, largely as a result of the emphasis placed on acquisition (where consciousness plays no obvious part) as opposed to learning, and this has become very much the spirit of the age. Schmidt (1990) sees this as part of a more general trend, and is right to note, in his seminal consideration of the role of consciousness in language learning, that 'none of us have been isolated from the major intellectual trends of the 20th century, most of which until recently have been hostile to serious consideration of the role of consciousness in behaviour' (p. 130).

Schmidt cites Rutherford & Sharwood Smith (1985) among those who 'have argued that CR facilitates language learning' (p. 129). Their 'pedagogic grammar hypothesis' claims that form-focused tuition may 'under certain conditions significantly increase the rate of acquisition over and above the rate expected from learners acquiring that language under natural circumstances where attention to form may be minimal and sporadic' (p. 275). The CR they have in mind involves contrastive L1/L2 information. Schmidt also has his own evidence, reported in Schmidt and Frota (1986). This is research into Schmidt's own learning of Portuguese. He keeps a diary of his own learning, together with tapes of input and output. Diary and taped data were compared at intervals, and the conclusion is that he and his fellow researcher 'found a remarkable correspondence between my reports of what I had noticed when Brazilians talked to me and the linguistic forms I used myself' (p. 140). This leads him to conclude that 'noticing is the necessary and sufficient condition for converting input into intake' (p. 129); and later: 'conscious processing is a necessary condition for one step in the language learning process, and is facilitative for other aspects of learning' (p. 131).

Ellis (1990) is yet another who is convinced that there is a role for conscious knowledge. 'Learners who receive formal instruction', Ellis says, 'outperform those who do not' (p. 171). For him, as for many others, formal instruction is virtually synonymous with the presence of conscious knowledge; Krashen (1982), for example, has one of the defining characteristics of the learning pathway that it involves 'conscious knowledge of a second language, knowing the rules, being aware of them' (p. 10). Ellis (1990) also relates instruction most clearly to providing declarative knowledge: 'instruction's greatest effect', he observes, 'is perhaps on the development of declarative knowledge, as opposed to procedural knowledge' (p. 171).

Following our earlier comments regarding the considerable differences between the two roles for declarative knowledge, we shall here consider them separately in turn.

Declarative Knowledge as the Starting Point for Proceduralization

Conventional presentation techniques

It is in relation to this role for declarative knowledge that we are most obviously speaking about the presentation stage, the first P in the PPP model. Figure 5.1 lists the most common techniques language teaching has used at this stage. Mackey (1965) has a longer list, and standard teacher-training books like Matthews et al. (1985) contain similar ones, with discussions on the relative merits of these different methods.

Explanation. Common in grammar translation. Often uses difficult metalanguage.

Key sentences. A small number of sentences focus on the point to be taught, sometimes with an accompanying visual. Broughton (1968) exemplifies.

Dialogues. These will vary in the extent to which they include a context. Traditional dialogues are often a series of key sentences, littered with exemplars of the language points being introduced. The result is often highly inauthentic interaction. Other books have highly contextualized dialogues, with plenty of language introduced not because it is to be exploited, but precisely to help provide context. After the dialogue, chosen language points are focused down onto (see Abbs et al. 1975, for example).

Passage. What is said above about dialogues also applies here. Passages rather than dialogues tend to appear in courses where the emphasis is on the written language.

Teacher action. Particularly associated with certain structures where actions can clarify particularly well. An example might be the use of the present continuous to describe contiguous action – 'I am holding a pencil' etc.

Figure 5.1 Some conventional presentation techniques

Explanation, demonstration and proceduralization

The inclusion in the figure 5.1 list of 'explanation', rightly suggests that the conscious vs. non-conscious issue raises its head when considering declarative knowledge as the starting point for proceduralization. Our earlier discussion about the role of conscious knowledge is conducted in general terms, but there is much to say about it in relation to this specific role for declarative knowledge. Thus, the claim in Schmidt and Frota (1986) that noticing is necessary for the conversion of input into intake more than suggests that the role of declarative knowledge is as a starting point for proceduralization. A similar suggestion lies behind Ellis' (1990) claim that learners who receive formal instruction outperform those who do not. Elsewhere he is explicit about the process by which this occurs: 'instruction', he says, can help the learner to 'know' – in some declarative sense – that the third person singular verb requires -s. Initially, however, she [the learner] is unable to process this form. But because she 'knows' about -s, she is better equipped to perceive it in the input. When the prerequisite processing operations for -s have been developed, it is acquired. In this way, declarative knowledge serves as a platform for the acquisition of subsequent procedural knowledge. (p. 169)

The conclusion that learners who receive initial instruction outperform those who do not also finds support in the general skills literature. Keele (1973), for example, shows how important it is for the learner to develop an internal model (or 'cognitive map') of the subskill to be acquired, and there is evidence that training can facilitate this. Thus Fitts and Posner (1967) report how the time taken to lead a novice pilot to first solo flight can be reduced from 10 hours for a control group to 3 hours for an experimental group where the manoeuvres were discussed and explained beforehand. There is a role for initial explanation.

The actual nature of such explanation is, however, important. Some trainers tend to give elaborate, abstract and precise explanations. One of Gallwey's reasons for developing the distinctive approach to instruction which he describes in his book *The Inner Game of Tennis* (Gallwey 1974) is the inhibiting effect that elaborate explanation may have on those learning tennis. He notes, for example, how the coach often introduces a new stroke by a long description of arm movements, racket position, and all kinds of technical information – a common approach in much instruction for skills of all sorts. The result of this elaborate, abstract and precise explanation may be to develop a form of declarative knowledge which is difficult to convert into procedural knowledge. 'It is possible', Holding (1965) notes regarding elaborateness, 'to disrupt the operator's performance in a quite lasting way by the over-elaboration of instructions' (p. 74). He also cites work by Judd (1908) and Colville (1957) where instruction on the laws of refraction was given to groups throwing darts at submerged targets. This kind of abstract tuition was of limited value. Holding further notes that the best forms of guidance may well be figurative or emotive, rather than scientifically de-tailed and precise, explanation. He gives a number of examples, one being the advice given to young boxers to 'aim your punch through the oppo-nent's backbone'. This advice may have the effect of lessening the normal deceleration of a controlled movement which results in a pulled punch. Holding does, however, have to concede that what characteristics constitute useful 'figurative' or 'emotive' explanation is uncertain. The science of hints is, he has to admit, still rudimentary. It is easy to convert the tennis example, and Holding's general points, into language-teaching terms. The kinds of intellectually challenging explanations found in grammar translation teaching (where intellectual challenge was actually viewed as a benefit and indeed even a reason for learning a foreign language) are likely to inhibit rather than facilitate some important areas of language performance. Many teachers will also be able to relate to the notion that grammatical hints of various sorts may ease the learning task infinitely more than precise explanation.[2]

The skills literature also discusses ways of providing declarative knowledge that do not involve explanation. There is extensive discussion (for example, in Holding 1965) on the relative merits of explanation and demonstration, and it is possible to develop a coherent argument that the most valuable contribution of training as a starting point for proceduralization is to provide examples. These give the learner a model as the basis for initial imitation and with which to compare his or her own efforts; at the same time they draw attention to important perceptual cues (Holding 1965). Gallwey's (1974) conclusion is indeed to advocate demonstration above explanation. Noting how elaborate description of tennis strokes inhibits rather than facilitates, his answer is to 'cut down the quantity of verbal instructions' and give the learner a 'visual image' of the stroke by demonstrating it. Certainly a look at the techniques used by trainers of non-linguistic skills is likely to offer the language teacher exciting and fresh perspectives. There is, for example, the Suzuki method of violin playing where the learner is at an early age saturated with violin music, providing an internal representation of the behaviour which can be 'proceduralized' later. A further method is discussed in Gallwey (1974), where it is suggested that learning to become a good tennis player may be helped by mimicking the movements and even the idiosyncrasies of a great player. 'Pretending to be Jimmy Connors' may in part help one to play tennis like Jimmy Connors. One is left to speculate what the language-teaching equivalent of this might be.[3]

Simplicity, and quantity of declarative knowledge

The condition that initial declarative knowledge must be easily convertible into procedural knowledge affects not just how the information is conveyed, but also what may be conveyed. Where one is dealing with declarative knowledge in its second role – as data base – it may well be possible to deal with underlying, rather abstract language points, perhaps associated with

Universal Grammar (UG), and we shall illustrate this later. But linguistic complexities cannot possibly stand as the basis of proceduralization. For this purpose we have to deal with the simple, and it may well be that a condition similar to one of those which Krashen (1982) sets up concerning the occurrence of monitoring applies here – that the student should be able easily to 'know the rule' – a condition that is not easily met. It has for a long time been accepted that the role of the applied linguist involves a process of simplification, particularly of the linguistic information that linguists provide, for pedagogic purposes. Yet despite this acceptance it often happens that when an applied linguist looks at language-teaching materials, these are criticized as being oversimplified – distorting to the point of lying about how a certain structure is formed or used, for example. But when simplification is deliberately undertaken (that is, not by accident, because the materials designers do not know their grammar properly!), then there seems little reason to be defensive about it. There may, however, well be the necessity for some remedial 'complexification' at a subsequent stage, and this is clearly a potential role for subsequent declarative knowledge. So materials designers may deliberately simplify in order to aid the process of procedural knowledge formation; but may at a later stage introduce some language awareness activity which will rectify the simplification. Observations like these might lead one to suggest that this implies two language syllabuses – one specifying points which will stand as initial declarative knowledge, others for subsequent declarative knowledge.

How much initial instruction should be given? Trainers in all fields have often fallen foul of the mistaken assumption that lengthy instruction is, because detailed, good instruction. But there is evidence (e.g. in Carr 1930) that more than a small amount of guidance at the initial stage will result in a decrease of efficiency. In the following chapter we shall explore at length the notion that much of the information useful for learning will come from feedback – after, not before 'the event'.

The 'psycholinguistic status' of declarative knowledge

An issue of recent applied linguistic interest is the 'psycholinguistic status' of any initial declarative representation given to the learner, and the relationship of this to the internal one which a learner eventually develops. Here is Rutherford (1987): 'although we are still a long way from truly understanding the language-acquisition process, it is perhaps not unreasonable to speculate that the ultimately most desirable means for raising consciousness will come as close as possible to replicating in some general sense the nature of acquisition itself (p. 61). For many (e.g. Pienemann 1985 and elsewhere, and his 'teachability hypothesis'), 'replication' relates specifically to sequence of exposure (to grammatical items). But others, like Prabhu (1985), claim that if the teacher's initial declarative representation cannot resemble the learner's internal one, this is argument for not offering an external representation.

But it is the case that externally supplied rules can be internalized and change form (by a process like McLaughlin's 1990 'restructuring'). An anecdotal example: my car cassette player has complex rules regarding how to rewind/fast forward according to which side is uppermost in the machine. My initial set of (learned rules) came from the instruction booklet, and follow the familiar pattern for such sets of instructions. My final representation, which I now use, is quite different, and involves such personal instructions as 'press the button near the fire extinguisher to rewind side A' and 'to fast forward side B press the button on my wife's side'. If one accepts Rutherford's (1987) point that 'pedagogic descriptions are *aids* to learning, not the *object* of learning' (p. 18), then there is no necessity that such descriptions should initially relate in any direct way to the ultimate internal representation.

Declarative Knowledge as Data Base

Declarativization as a natural process

We have already argued that the learner with acquired knowledge needs somehow to obtain a declarative data base. One way in which this might happen is through some form of instruction whereby the learner's attention is explicitly drawn to linguistic facts. But instruction is not always necessary. For Karmiloff-Smith (1992) it is the potential to analyse (and thereby to develop declarative representations of) behaviour that separates humans from animals. One of the two quotations she places at the beginning of her chapter 'The Child as Linguist' is from Gleitman et al. (1972): 'young children know something about language that the spider does not know about web-weaving' (p. 160) – and that something is precisely the ability to analyse the behaviour, and by doing so making it available for further learning. The other quotation at the beginning of the same chapter reports an exchange between 4-year-old Yara and her mother:

Yara: What's that?
Mother: A typewriter.
Yara: No, you're the typewriter, that's a typewrite.

In the chapter itself Karmiloff-Smith concludes that there is ample evidence for the innateness of language structures. But this is only part of her conclusion. The child, she argues, is able to analyse the language it is using, understand its structure, to draw (in our terms) declarative knowledge from it. It is this ability which, again, separates child from animal. This leads her to speculate that even if the chimpanzee were to have an innately specified linguistic base, it would still not go as far as the normal human child: 'it would never wonder why "typewriter" isn't used to refer to people' (1992, p. 63). All this suggests that a degree of declarative knowledge will, for the first language, occur naturally; humans will speculate, attempt to analyse. It is reasonable to suggest that the same process will occur for a second language – declarative knowledge will to a certain extent form itself.

Facilitating declarativization through instructional tasks

But it is also reasonable to suggest that a degree of help may be given. To continue with Karmiloff-Smith's example: it may well be that a task in which an L1 child (or an L2 adult) were invited to consider morphological endings like 'er' and ponder their use would both support and even accelerate the natural human 'urge to analyse'. The task might even be 'fun', and in this respect Cook (1994) makes a general point which might well have interesting practical classroom implications. His paper is concerned with language play in advertisements, and he notes that 'ads are one of many discourses which provide evidence that the exuberant meaningless introspective play with language which is usually assumed to be the domain of the child is a feature of adult discourse too' (p. 114). Could there not, he asks, 'be room in second language learning for play, a focus on the code away from the demands of immediate social and ideational skills?' Using ads which involve language play for listening or reading comprehension might be one way of doing this in class, and there will be many others. Cook is in effect proposing to tap the 'urge to analyse' Karmiloff Smith describes.

The judicious selection of tasks may be enough to ensure that learners do their own analysis as occasions demand, simply by going though a procedural encoding and extracting knowledge from it. Rumelhart and Norman (1981) describe this as a process of 'using knowledge how to derive knowledge that' (p. 341), and exemplify it by noting the behaviour of people

asked how many windows their house has: 'most people report systematically "going though" the rooms in their house and "counting the windows".
Clearly, in these cases, our knowledge of windows is implicit in another
body of knowledge. We can, however, derive this implicit knowledge by
using our ability to imagine the rooms of our house systematically' (p. 341).

Some sorts of general task are likely to facilitate analysis more than
others. The process which Rumelhart and Norman describe seems to be
just the sort which native speakers might follow when faced with a linguistic
task requiring analysis. Writers, for example, may be forced by the demands
of their task to bring to consciousness differences in word meanings, use of
various syntactic structures etc.; they create declarative encodings as they
go along. Specific types of activities in relation to these tasks can facilitate
even more, and academic writing courses (particularly those produced after
the mid-seventies) very often contain many activities to stimulate language
analysis. Johnson (1983a) describes an approach to the teaching of writing
which involves sometimes elaborate exploration of the relationship between
the 'words on the page' and both their linguistic and non-linguistic context.
Learners are constantly asked questions like: 'why did the writer say X (and
not Y)?', 'what difference would it have made if he or she had written Y and
not X?', 'what would the writer have said if he or she had wanted to
emphasize A instead of B?', 'if the reader misunderstands sentence X in a
certain way, how may it be changed to eliminate misunderstanding?' C. N.
Candlin (personal communication) has used the revealing phrase 'gutting
reality' to describe an approach of this sort, and although it is most naturally
and easily applied to written texts, there is no reason why the reality of
spoken language should not be gutted in the same way. The transcript of a
role play exercise done the previous day in class could be subjected to the
kinds of questions given above, to great pedagogic advantage.

Language awareness and consciousness raising

Much recent methodological interest in this issue is associated with the
labels 'language awareness' (LA) and 'consciousness raising' (CR).[4] In
his discussion of CR, Rutherford (1987) identifies two sorts of technique.
The first asks the learner for a judgement or discrimination, and one of
Rutherford's examples is given in figure 5.2. The learner has to 'trace a
path' through a collection of sentences, each time selecting the one which
follows its predecessor in terms of the distribution of old and new
information. The exercise well illustrates how recent CR techniques relate

(E) Weathering and erosion of rock exposed to the atmosphere constantly remove particles from the rock.

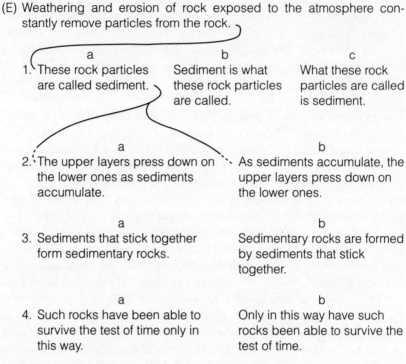

	a	b	c
1.	These rock particles are called sediment.	Sediment is what these rock particles are called.	What these rock particles are called is sediment.

	a	b
2.	The upper layers press down on the lower ones as sediments accumulate.	As sediments accumulate, the upper layers press down on the lower ones.

	a	b
3.	Sediments that stick together form sedimentary rocks.	Sedimentary rocks are formed by sediments that stick together.

	a	b
4.	Such rocks have been able to survive the test of time only in this way.	Only in this way have such rocks been able to survive the test of time.

Figure 5.2   Tracing a path (from Rutherford 1987)

closely to those found in the type of 'communicative' writing courses referred to in the paragraph above.

Rutherford's second sort of technique typically involves the learner in actual production. Figure 5.3 utilizes the notion of a 'propositional cluster' – a set of key content words which the learner has to use to create a sentence. Like the exercise in figure 5.2, the one in figure 5.3 involves the distribution of old and new information. In each pair of sentences, (a) provides a context for the sentence the learner produces from the propositional cluster in (b).

As this example suggests, Rutherford's work often involves exploration of quite complex and abstract linguistic points, including those related to UG. As a further example: he suggests ways of exploiting the internal grammatical relations of infinitival relative clauses of the sort 'the first bus to arrive', 'the best bus to take', where the head noun can bear either a subject or object relation to the infinitival (SV in *the bus – arrives* versus OV

```
1  (a)  On stage appeared a man and a child.
   (b)  sing – child – song
2  (a)  Last on the programme were a song and a piano piece.
   (b)  sing – child – song
```

Figure 5.3 Using propositional clusters (from Rutherford 1987)

```
 1  Data       (Data from dictionaries, grammar books; samples from
                authentic texts, learner language)

 2  Tasks      (Involving activities like analysing, evaluating, identi-
                fying, classifying, comparing)

 3  Processes  (Questioning, discussing, introspecting, analysing,
                visualizing)

 4  Modes      (Individual, pair/group, whole class)
```

Figure 5.4 Ingredients for 'good' language awareness activities
(abridged from Wright and Bolitho 1993)

in *takes – the bus*). Linguistic complexities of this sort are extremely difficult to teach through a DECPRO sequence, and awareness of them can really only be developed as they are met in use; in this sense they are more obviously suitable for what we earlier called 'subsequent declarative knowledge'.

Further techniques are exemplified in Wright and Bolitho (1993). Although their paper is concerned with teacher education, rather than straight language teaching, many of their suggestions are useful for anyone seeking to use LA with the language learner. The paper contains a useful list of 'ingredients for "good" language awareness activities', and figure 5.4. is an abridged version of this.

R. Bolitho (unpublished observations) has many interesting and imaginative examples of language awareness exercises. One productive technique rings certain language items in a text, and associated questions are designed to lead the learner, through discussion perhaps, to discovery and awareness. Although the conception of the technique is simplicity itself, the teacher or materials designer needs some considerable skill and experience to frame questions which will indeed lead to productive discovery and awareness. Figure 5.5 exemplifies this technique.

Shades of sunsets past

What date was this?

Roger A. Redfern

Some areas of the Earth, such as the Sahara and central Australia, receive over 90 per cent of the maximum amount of sunshine possible (more than 4,000 hours) due to a lack of cloud cover.

Other cloudy, stormy areas, such as Iceland and the Scottish Highlands, receive less than 2,000 hours a year, measured by a device called the Eppley pyrheliometer.

When the sun is high in the sky its rays come almost vertically to Earth, thus passing through fewer air molecules and dust particles than when at a low angle, as near sunrise or sunset. At those times the blue wavelengths are scattered, leaving the red wavelengths to colour the sky near Earth.

At this time of year in Britain, especially in dry weather when there's smoke and harvest dust in the air, gaudy sundowns are common.

But sunsets have never been better all around the world than in the few years following August 26, 1883, when the Indonesian volcano of Krakatoa exploded in the early afternoon, sending a black cloud of ash 17 miles into the sky. The climacteric explosion of August 27 was heard in Australia, 2,200 miles away and ash then reached a height of 50 miles.

The event propelled 3.6 cubic miles of broken rock into the heavens and ash fell on 1.5 million square miles of the Earth's surface. The whole of present-day Indonesia lay in darkness for 2½ days as the choking ash drifted down. When this ash had climbed to 50 miles the finer particles were blown westwards by

upper-atmosphere winds, so that by the afternoon after the final explosion the dust cloud was visible in Ceylon over 2,000 miles away. The next day it was seen over Natal, 6,000 miles away. Six days afterwards, the skies over Peru and Ecuador were darkened, and by September 9 the dust was blowing over the East Indies —an equatorial circuit in 13 days.

In Britain there were gorgeous sunsets in the autumn of 1883, and at the end of November some observers thought they were looking at the Northern Lights.

The eruption caused a 10–20 per cent fall in the amount of radiant energy reaching Earth for a long period, and the remarkable sunsets continued for several years.

Guardian 24 Aug '90

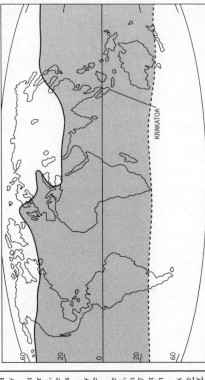

A map from a Royal Society report of 1888, showing the extent of the Earth covered by the Krakatoa ash cloud.

Could this have been the first word in the whole article?
Give a reason.

Which times?
How do you know?

Which time of year?
How do you know?

From where?

When?

Which event?

What does this imply?

Figure 5.5 'Shades of sunsets past' (from Wright and Bolitho 1993)

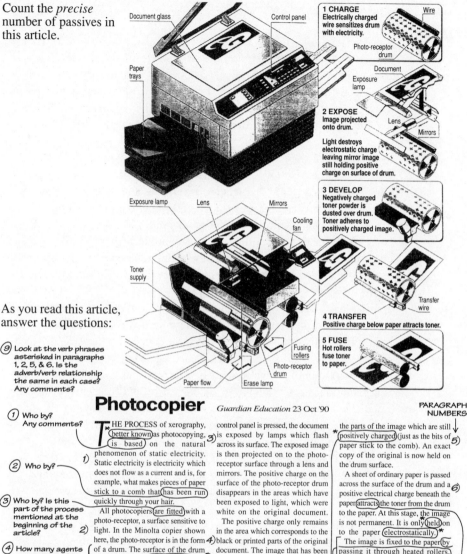

Count the *precise* number of passives in this article.

1 CHARGE Electrically charged wire sensitizes drum with electricity. Wire. Photo-receptor drum.

Document. Exposure lamp.

2 EXPOSE Image projected onto drum. Lens. Mirrors. Light destroys electrostatic charge leaving mirror image still holding positive charge on surface of drum.

3 DEVELOP Negatively charged toner powder is dusted over drum. Toner adheres to positively charged image.

4 TRANSFER Positive charge below paper attracts toner. Transfer wire.

5 FUSE Hot rollers fuse toner to paper.

Document glass · Control panel · Paper trays · Exposure lamp · Lens · Mirrors · Cooling fan · Toner supply · Fusing rollers · Photo-receptor drum · Paper flow · Erase lamp

As you read this article, answer the questions:

⑨ Look at the verb phrases asterisked in paragraphs 1, 2, 5, & 6. Is the adverb/verb relationship the same in each case? Any comments?

① Who by? Any comments?

② Who by?

③ Who by? Is this part of the process mentioned at the beginning of the article?

④ How many agents are mentioned in this sentence?

⑤ Why is 'becomes' used here? Is it a passive? Could it be replaced by another verb without changing the meaning?

⑥ Does the passive infinitive add anything which an active infinitive would not express here? Is the writer's choice grammatical or stylistic?

⑦ Are these two verbs passive or not? Explain your answer.

⑧ Why do you think the writer chose the active voice here? ... and here? ... and here?

⑩ Does this phrase contain an agent?

PARAGRAPH NUMBERS

Photocopier

Guardian Education 23 Oct '90

THE PROCESS of xerography, better known as photocopying, is based on the natural phenomenon of static electricity. Static electricity is electricity which does not flow as a current and is, for example, what makes pieces of paper stick to a comb that has been run quickly through your hair.

All photocopiers are fitted with a photo-receptor, a surface sensitive to light. In the Minolta copier shown here, the photo-receptor is in the form of a drum. The surface of the drum is sensitized by an electrically charged wire and the surface becomes charged with an electrostatic charge (positive).

The document to be photocopied is placed face down on the document glass. When the start button on the control panel is pressed, the document is exposed by lamps which flash across its surface. The exposed image is then projected on to the photo-receptor surface through a lens and mirrors. The positive charge on the surface of the photo-receptor drum disappears in the areas which have been exposed to light, which were white on the original document.

The positive charge only remains in the area which corresponds to the black or printed parts of the original document. The image that has been projected on to the surface of the drum is therefore a mirror image of the original.

A negatively charged developing powder (toner) is then dusted over the surface of the drum. It clings to the parts of the image which are still positively charged (just as the bits of paper stick to the comb). An exact copy of the original is now held on the drum surface.

A sheet of ordinary paper is passed across the surface of the drum and a positive electrical charge beneath the paper attracts the toner from the drum to the paper. At this stage, the image is not permanent. It is only held on to the paper electrostatically.

The image is fixed to the paper by passing it through heated rollers, which soften the toner and fuse it to the paper fibres. The result is an exact, permanent copy of the original document. The entire xerographic process can be repeated as many as 135 times per minute.

Figure 5.6 'Photocopier' (from Wright and Bolitho 1993)

As a final example, figure 5.6 shows an exercise where the learner task is simply to count the precise number of passives in the article. The task is geared to reveal various problems associated with the passive, including what constitutes a true passive. Learners can be expected to have to confront the problem, among others, of how to distinguish a 'true' passive from a BE + Adjective construction (like 'is based' in the first paragraph, perhaps?).

Techniques like the one illustrated in figure 5.6 suggest how potentially useful corpora may be for developing LA/CR. It is entirely feasible to envisage techniques where learners are given direct access to a corpus, are asked to find instances of a given structure, and are given some task to undertake with the resulting data. For example, learners might call up thirty examples of passive, and be asked to note how many times an agent is stated, and how many times not. They can then be asked to try and work out under what circumstances a writer or speaker will omit to state the agent of a passive.[5]

Mention has already been made of communicatively oriented writing materials which utilize techniques like these, and well-informed language teachers reading this section may well reach the conclusion that CR/LA techniques are already familiar in language teaching. They would be right; and this conclusion should be welcomed. It indicates that a wealth of already-existing techniques are available to be tapped by the teacher who has the time and the desire to adapt them to CR/LA ends. Introducing an added element of LA into foreign language classes need not involve basic and traumatic revamping of the existing language-teaching programme.

We began this chapter by identifying two processes – declarativization and proceduralization – as central to language-teaching concerns, and we have here concentrated on the first of these. We noted that there are two quite distinct roles for declarative knowledge: as the starting point for proceduralization and as a generative knowledge base. We have considered some practical ways in which we may facilitate the development of knowledge appropriate to these two rather different roles. In the next two chapters we turn attention onto the process of proceduralization.

Notes

1   As implied in the Introduction, it is not the aim of this book to put forward any particular 'approach', so much as to discuss language-teaching issues from a particular standpoint. The DECPRODEC sequence does, however, have

considerable appeal, a major advantage being precisely that it separates out the two roles of declarative knowledge.

2 Swan (1994) contains fascinating discussion regarding what makes a good pedagogic rule. He is in favour of 'rules of thumb', though not of the use of metaphor.

On the general issue of how analysis (involved, for example, in explanation) may impede proceduralization, Skehan (1994) has the following to say: 'excessive priority given to analysis will compromise the process of synthesis and the acquisition of a memory-based fluency in performance' (p. 187).

3 'Creative visualization' is a technique, described in Gawain (1978), in which individuals imagine they have achieved a desired state, in order to further the actual achievement of that state.

4 Some authors, e.g. Cook (1991a), distinguish language awareness and consciousness raising by making the former refer to language in general, including the learner's first language, while consciousness raising relates only to features of the second language. But this distinction is not widespread, and we here follow general usage in not distinguishing the terms.

5 This example was provided by Geoffrey Leech, who uses it as one example of how corpora may be employed to language learning ends.

6 The Processing Dimension: Errors and Mistakes

In the previous chapter we concentrated our attention on the formation of declarative knowledge. We now turn attention in this chapter and the next to procedural knowledge. In terms of PRODEC, the issue related to this kind of knowledge is to find activities which will stimulate the learner to active reception and production of language. As for DECPRO, the issue to consider is how declarative knowledge becomes converted into procedural knowledge, by the use of what might be called 'activation' techniques.

In language teaching the question of activation needs to be taken very seriously indeed. It has not always been in the past. Some methods, like grammar-translation, made the assumption that little more than presentation was required for learning to take place – the actual practice could be picked up outside the classroom. In terms of the presentation → practice → production (PPP) sequence we might dub such models as P_ _, the dashes signifying the absence of the second and third stages. Other approaches, like audiolingualism in all its countless and highly widespread manifestations, often has presentation and practice (PP _), but tends to omit free production. The assumption is again that this final stage is simply not required – learners who have drilled all the patterns of the language will be able to use that knowledge in natural ways outside the class. But not so! Two Ps are not enough, and very much more attention needs to be given to the activation procedure – very much a processing concern. A large amount of work needs to be done to convert good performance in the language laboratory drill (the second P) into good performance in a normal communicative situation.

We shall directly confront the issues of activation and participation in communicative activities in chapter 7. The task of the present chapter is to turn attention in a general way onto the processing dimension of language teaching. This we shall do by regarding it in relation to one single issue – the problem of what to do when learners get things wrong. From now on this chapter will concentrate on this question, but it should not be forgotten that our treatment of it is intended primarily to exemplify how important processing conditions are, the problems they raise, and how a skills orientation towards language teaching might tackle these problems.[1]

Feedback

We begin with a concept that is central to the skill acquisition literature – that of feedback. It is recognized that, as was suggested in the last chapter, though there is a place in training for initial guidance in skill learning, there is also an important place for feedback (viewed as the provider of information, rather than as a reinforcer). It seems at least intuitively true that a great deal of learning how to serve in tennis, for example, comes after any initial guidance the teacher might give, when the learner picks up the ball, serves and notes the outcome. The sequence of events, in this case, is not **learn →**
perform, but **learn → perform → learn**. This sequence correctly suggests that when we speak about feedback, we are speaking about something that potentially contributes to the learning process. For thorough discussion on the concept of feedback, see Annett(1969).

Though the situation is better today, much language teaching of the past exemplifies the **learn→perform** sequence. We teach, and the students learn; they then perform, exemplifying, we hope, the learning that has taken place. During or following performance, error correction is used to plug the holes. But feedback may have more of a role to play. A secondary aim of this chapter is to suggest that more attention should be given to the issue of how we can best provide feedback.

That more attention needs to be given to this issue is further suggested by what most teachers will see as the comparative failure of the feedback measures we employ. Students leave the 's' off the third person singular of the simple present; teachers put it back on for them, and at the next opportunity it is left off again. Parallel examples may be found in relation to almost any skill. A common mistake for novice horse riders is to lean forward on the horse; the teacher will tell novices to sit up straight; but a moment later they are leaning forward again. In these cases methods of feedback do not seem to meet with much success.

Errors and mistakes

To consider how things might be improved, we may utilize our declarative/procedural distinction to address the question of why it is that students get things wrong. There are at least two reasons. One is that they do not have the appropriate declarative knowledge, or have some false knowledge. They may either not know how a tense of English works, or have the wrong idea. In these cases we may say that their interlanguage knowledge is faulty. The result is what Corder (1981) calls an *error*.

There is, however, a further reason for a student getting something wrong. It may be a lack of procedural knowledge, of *processing ability*. Novice riders may well know that they should not lean forward on the horse, and when simply trotting round the paddock may well not do so. Their problem might emerge when approaching a small jump. Their feet may fall out of the stirrups, the horse may begin to get difficult, and one result (there may be other, more painful ones!) is that the novices lean forward. It is not their knowledge that is at fault here; it is their ability to 'perform their competence' (the phrase is taken from Ellis 1985a) in difficult operating conditions. The result is what Corder (1981) calls a *mistake*.

In earlier chapters we have come across distinctions which relate to the error/mistake one. In chapter 4 Bialystok's (1982) paper dealing with language testing was mentioned, and the general point made that the distinction between knowledge and processing ability indicates that it is not just 'what learners know' that is important, but also 'in what circumstances learners can use what they know'. Chapter 4 provided two examples. The non-linguistic one involved a footballer who may, in normal circumstances, be a good goal scorer. We noted that to have a complete picture of his skill we would need to ask questions about his performance in difficult circumstances. The second, linguistic, example concerned use of the present perfect in a gap-filling task as opposed to less-that-ideal conditions – over a bad intercontinental telephone line. We shall henceforth use the phrase *real operating conditions* (or ROCs for short) to refer to such 'difficult circumstances' and 'less-than-ideal conditions'. We shall argue that the incorporation of ROCs into language practice is a vital ingredient of an approach to language teaching which aims to have a processing dimension.

The error/mistake distinction is, then, one manifestation of the more general knowledge/processing ability distinction which we have already considered at some length. Focusing now on this one manifestation, one might justifiably claim that language teaching has paid more attention to errors than mistakes. What is certainly true is that techniques (like, perhaps, explanation) for handling errors spring more readily to mind than techniques for handling mistakes. It may further be the case that we have tended to treat mistakes as if they were errors – as we discuss later below, giving a grammatical explanation to someone who already knows the relevant grammatical point, but has failed to 'perform their competence', is unlikely to be helpful. Since errors and mistakes *are* different, it seems likely that they will need to be handled in different ways.

Corder (1981) argues that 'mistakes are of no significance to the process of language learning' (p. 10). But if we use the word 'mistake' to describe a malformation due to inability to process under difficult sets of ROCs, then it is likely that a good percentage of our students' malformations are mistakes and not errors. If this is the case, the subject of *mistake correction* becomes an important one in language teaching.

Mistake correction

How can mistakes be eradicated? One might propose that in order to achieve this, a student will need at least four things. These are:

1   The desire or need to eradicate the mistake. It is likely that a number of mistakes do not get eradicated simply because students know they can get by without eradicating them. The 's' on the third person simple present tense ('he like*s*') is a good example – it has little communicative value, and learners experience no trouble in getting their message across if they forget it.

2   A model of the correct form being used in the ROCs under which the mistake was made. The student needs, in other words, the 'knowledge' that makes the malformation a mistake and not an error.

3   A realization by students that their performance was flawed. The learner needs to know that a mistake has occurred. Some form of feedback will provide this.

4   An opportunity to repractise in ROCs.

In learning how to serve in tennis, then, the learner who has just served badly needs (1) a desire to serve properly, (2) to know what a good service looks and feels like, (3) a realization that the service was bad and (4) the chance to practise again.

We shall now look at these four points in turn.

Need to eradicate

There is one sense in which language skill is like ice skating[2]. In ice skating, learning the rudiments of survival – being able to stand up, move forward, turn, all without falling over – is a comparatively small part of becoming an accomplished performer. A large part of the task involves learning to conform to an accepted model, established over time by tradition, of what good skating looks like. In terms of pure survival, of 'getting by on ice', many details of the accepted model (how the legs and body should be held, for example) are mere frills. The same is true of language. The rudiments of linguistic survival can be met by a form of pidgin. Learners who say, 'please give me beer,' are unlikely to go thirsty, but they will have failed to conform to what might be called 'externally imposed norms' about language behaviour, norms which in pure survival terms are frills. The skill literature's distinction between intrinsic and extrinsic feedback (cf. Annett 1969) is relevant here. *Intrinsic feedback*, springing from the situation itself, is likely to provide information on whether the rudiments of survival have been met; it occurs when skaters fall over or learners fail to get their beer. The literature on pidginization and fossilization recognizes this point. Vigil and Oller (1976) argue that 'correct forms or any forms that elicit favourable feedback will tend to fossilise' (p. 285). 'Favourable feedback' in this case involves a listener response which indicates 'I understand' to the language user. Thus (to return to an earlier example), if the learner who constantly omits the third singular present tense final 's' is always understood, the incorrect version is likely to fossilize. Vigil and Oller's position has been comprehensively attacked, particularly in Selinker and Lamendella (1978), but the concept of 'stopping when needs are met' persists in fossilisation studies.

But intrinsic feedback is unlikely to provide information on whether 'externally imposed norms' have been adhered to; 'please give me beer' is likely to result in beer being given but without any information being provided on the well-formedness of the utterance. In recent years this has become a particular problem in language teaching, because of the development of a 'communicative' approach. Many communicative techniques place the emphasis on 'getting the message across', and sometimes this inevitably occurs at the expense of grammatical correctness. Often the result is that learners develop sophisticated communicative strategies for getting messages across in almost any situation, but in so doing they develop a form of pidgin (consisting of utterances like 'please give me beer') which many language teachers rightly find undesirable.

Skehan (1994, as well as Long 1985) discusses the way in which communicative production might lead to the development of reduction strategies resulting in pidginogenesis and fossilization. He cites Schmidt (1983) on the topic of the learner Wes, who progressed over time in conversational competence from being regarded as an unvalued interlocutor to becoming a valued one. But Wes achieved this largely by developing what Canale and Swain (1980) call strategic competence; his actual linguistic competence did not improve at all. One possible answer to this serious language-teaching problem would be to set tasks which in some way have built in a stage at which grammatical correctness is required – to attempt, that is, to build intrinsic motivation into the task. Although her paper is not specifically concerned with mistake correction, Johnson (1992) makes proposals for what she calls 'defossilisation' which are relevant here. She notes that 'communicative' activities very often develop communication skills but do not lead to new learning. She builds into her tasks a stage at which students must consult with the teacher, who introduces new, linguistically challenging dimensions to the task. A further, somewhat banal, solution in the mistake correction realm, is to introduce *extrinsic feedback* (from an outside source). The teacher simply corrects!

Providing a model

For a mistake to be a mistake and not an error, it is a *sine qua non* that the learner already possesses some internal representation of the correct form. This will probably have been provided by initial guidance, and how such guidance is best given has been discussed in the previous chapter where issues such as the relative merits of explanation and demonstration were discussed.

Though initial training may provide internal representation, it will essentially be an 'abstract' one, showing how the structure (or whatever it be) operates in a general way. But learners also need to have 'models in ROCs'. In chapter 2 we spoke about Aristotelian rhetoric, and illustrated in figure 2.2 the many parameters which have to be take into consideration when producing an utterance. Looking at the issue from a slightly different angle, the figure shows how the various contextual parameters control appropriate and correct linguistic use. The learner needs models of how context exerts its influence on rules. One of the best ways of providing this is 'after the event' – after, that is, the learners have performed the behaviour for themselves. One technique which 'models after the event' is *reformulation*. This technique, discussed by Levenston (1978), Cohen (1983) and Allwright et al. (1984), is usually used for the teaching of writing. There are several versions of reformulation, but the basis is that a native speaker (or someone with 'superior' linguistic knowledge) rewrites a student essay, as far as possible preserving the intended meaning. Reformulation is different from reconstruction, which is what most teachers do to student essays. In reconstruction, errors and mistakes are simply corrected. The result will be sentences free from gross malformations, but ones which may not remotely resemble sentences a native speaker would produce to express the same content. Because reconstruction focuses on errors and mistakes, it may well provide learners with information on where they went wrong. But what reformulation offers, and reconstruction fails to offer, is information on how a proficient speaker would have said the same thing. Reformulation provides, in other words, 'models in ROCs'. The clearest use of this technique is for the teaching of writing, but it is possible to imagine ways in which it may be adapted for use with spoken language, although the result may be rather time-consuming. A role play exercise may be taped, for example, and gone over with the class, discussing what might better have been said at appropriate points.[3]

Realization of flawed performance

In chapter 2 we noted that for Bartlett (1947), 'maybe the best single measure of mental skill lies in the speed with which errors are detected and thrown out . . .' (p. 879). Knowing what has been done wrong (and what to do about it) is something which, for example, distinguishes the skilled tennis player from the novice. Five points will be made about this stage.

1   It cannot automatically be assumed that the learner will be aware of having made a mistake. The very ROCs which produce the mistake may prevent its detection. The fact that the novice riders referred to earlier have so many things to attend to at the jump, on the difficult horse, with feet out of the stirrups, may make them lean forward; it may also prevent them from knowing that they have leaned forward. We have already discussed why intrinsic feedback may very well not provide the necessary information. Positive action needs to be taken to make learners aware, and the likelihood is that it will need to come from outside (i.e. be extrinsic).

2   The positive action of being told by the teacher is probably not enough. Learners seem to need to see for themselves what has gone wrong, in the ROCs under which they went wrong. There are various ways of achieving this. The riders' leaning forward on the horse may be brought home best when they see a video of themselves doing it. As a

second best it may be useful for them to see others making the same mistake in the same ROCs; and where others are not available, teachers often provide the information by mimicking the learners to indicate what is being done wrong. 'Monitoring oneself in difficult ROCs' suggests putting classroom language on tape or video.

3 Explanation is probably not the best way to give mistake feedback. It was noted in chapter 5 that explanation is a procedure to be used warily in all circumstances, and that performance can be positively harmed by elaborate explanation. One might further argue that any benefit that explanation might provide would be for errors rather than mistakes. The defining characteristic of a mistake is that the students know what should be done; explanation could therefore be seen as providing what they already have.

4 It may again be that the best way of providing the necessary realization is by confronting learners with the mismatch between flawed and model performance. This again points to reformulation. Novices may want to see what the teacher looks like going over the jump on a difficult horse (i.e. *in full operating conditions*), then to compare this with what they looked like, again *in full operating conditions*.

5 When reformulation takes place, it may be that the most useful feedback comes from those areas of mismatch which students are themselves able to identify, because those areas will accord with the stage of their skill (or interlanguage development). A further example from riding: a novice may be having problems doing a good trot, and the teacher might demonstrate what it should look like. It may be that during the demonstration the learner notices something about the position of the teacher's legs which had never been drawn attention to; it was not on the 'teaching programme'. Once the novice holds his or her legs in the same position, several of the things which he or she was getting wrong and which the teacher *had* drawn attention to might suddenly come right. In that situation the learner was learning something which the teacher had not set out to teach. Language teachers will find in their experience similar examples of where 'point learned' is at odds with 'intended teaching point'. One of the benefits of reformulation is that it creates the circumstances in which incidental learning may take place, and benefit may occur even if the teacher does no more than present learners with a model performance through reformulation, to be compared with their initial flawed performance. It may be left up to the students themselves to note and learn what they will from the comparison.[4]

Opportunity to practise again, in ROCs

The sequence we have been discussing here is one of **mistake occurrence** → **corrective action** → **retrial**. There is some evidence in the skill literature (e.g. Annett 1969) that the relationship between the second two is important. In terms of time, for example, it may be more important how soon retrial takes place after corrective action than how soon after mistake occurrence that action occurs. We therefore need to speak not just about 'feedback after performance', but also about 'feedback before retrial'.

It is vital that ROCs should be present in retrial. We shall exemplify this fundamental point by considering training in another non-linguistic skill – piloting an aircraft.

At a certain stage in their training, novice pilots may well be able to land in clear weather when the plane has no mechanical defects. But they may have problems landing the plane in fog (or when the flaps are not working correctly, or where there is some other complication). In this situation, to practise landing in clear skies in a perfect plane is clearly of restricted value; the trainees can do this already. What the novice pilots need to practise is, precisely, landing in fog. One learns to land in fog by landing in fog, not by landing in clear skies.

A parallel may be made with language learners who are able to form the present perfect correctly in gap-filling tasks but who have problems getting it right over that intercontinental telephone line mentioned in chapter 4. In this situation, simply giving more gap-filling tasks is of as restricted value to the language learner as landing in clear skies is to the trainee pilot. One learns to use the present perfect on intercontinental phone lines by phoning intercontinentally and using the present perfect – not by using it in gap-filling tasks.

For novice pilots, the machine known as a flight simulator is at hand. Essentially, this provides the trainer with various configurations of ROCs which can be activated by pressing buttons. One button on the console will miraculously 'create' fog, another will render the flaps faulty. It may be argued that the language learner needs something similar, some form of 'present perfect simulator' which will vary the ROCs – 'methodological buttons' that the teacher can 'press' to simulate just those types of ROCs which are presenting difficulties.

What might a present perfect simulator look like? It is clear that in important respects, free practice – the third P in the PPP sequence – offers a form of present perfect simulator. What free practice crucially provides is ready-made sets of ROCs; these will vary from moment to moment, and will place variable demands on the learners' ability to process. Sometimes the interaction will require speedy response, sometimes not; different inter-actions will involve different amounts of language; the demands of message (and hence the degree of attention learners must give to *what* they are saying rather that *how* they are saying it) will change. There will be other types of variation, not least in affective conditions (the degree of anxiety felt, attitude towards interactant etc.) which will affect the performer's processing efficiency. Bad conditions along parameters like these are the language user's equivalents to fog and faulty flaps. Free practice will go a long way towards simulating, over time, the ROCs in which mistakes occur. This is one reason why we made the point, at the beginning of this chapter, that the final P in the PPP sequence is so important. A very large amount of final P is needed for learners to be able to avoid processing mistakes in the variety of ROCs they are likely to meet in real life.

Retrial is, then, crucial to mistake eradication. Part of learning to use the present perfect on an intercontinental phone does indeed involve phoning intercontinentally and using the present perfect. But it is optimistic to suppose that retrial alone will efficiently eradicate mistakes. The kinds of corrective action we spoke about earlier are equally important. Both stages are seen as necessary but not, taken alone, sufficient for mistake eradication to occur.

Task grading

Because the previous section has dealt with 'language practice', its implica-tions go far beyond the mistake-correction issue, and the points made about processing conditions have relevance to our language-teaching strategy in general. Hence ROCs, and the final P, are important ingredients in lan-guage teaching even when no mistakes occur.

One important aspect of the flight simulator we spoke of earlier is that it can provide graded practice. Each button on the trainer's console controls a different operating difficulty (Button A for fog, Button B for flap malfunc-tion, Button C for undercarriage failure, and so on). These buttons give the trainer the possibility to grade the tasks the learners are given. When the novices can land in normal conditions, the buttons can be pressed in turn to simulate single difficulties. But as the novices become more experienced, combinations of buttons can be pressed, creating combinations of difficult ROCs – fog plus flap malfunction, and so on.

Although free practice in language teaching automatically provides configurations of ROCs, it would be highly useful for the teacher to be able to control which operation conditions he or she presents at different times. We here enter the realm of task grading, a topic which is taken up in the next chapter.

Notes

1   The remainder of this paper is closely based on Johnson (1988).
2   The similarity between language and ice skating was pointed out to me by Dick Allwright, whose comments on a number of points made in the paper on which this chapter is based are gratefully acknowledged.
3   A type of 'gutting reality' referred to earlier. The suggestion that reformulation might be used for spoken language does raise some practical, logistical problems which would need discussion.
4   Martin Bygate (personal communication) makes the point that although it may be useful for learners to observe the actual performances of teachers, there may be occasions when attention needs to be focused on process rather than on final product. For example, a tennis teacher might wish to say to a learner, 'All you are worrying about at the moment is whether the serve goes into the court. Forget about that for now and concentrate on how you hit the ball, irrespective for the moment of where it ends up.'

7   Making Automatic: 'ra-1'

This chapter is about procedural knowledge and how to facilitate its development in learners. At the beginning of chapter 5 we noted that in the PRODEC sequence the issue is how to develop initial procedural knowledge, while in DECPRO it is a question of proceduralizing from declarative knowledge. It will be convenient to consider these two procedures separately here.

Developing Procedural Knowledge in PRODEC

In PRODEC, the learner first internalizes language in a procedural form. This, as we argued in chapter 4, is the 'acquisition path'. For Krashen (1977), the essential requirement necessary for acquisition to take place is the learner's 'participation in natural communication situations'. Of course, the environment where this is most likely to occur is the target language country, where the learner comes across the language in natural situations, and at least a degree of participation is likely. The classroom is a less favourable environment for this requirement to be met. But where the teacher's aim is to help facilitate acquisition by bringing about initial procedural representations, the road to follow is clear – the teacher attempts as far as possible to simulate in the class the conditions under which natural acquisition will occur. The words 'as far as possible' are important here. Adherents of 'natural' approaches which attempt to make classrooms as much as possible like 'real life' are often attacked because 'the classroom never can be like real life'. This is undoubtedly true, but it is not the point. The issue is one of cost-effectiveness: how teachers may best spend the restricted class time available to them. If they believe that classes should attempt to simulate 'real life', then they must spend their restricted time in this attempt. They will not of course succeed entirely, and there will surely remain vast differences between class and real life. But their belief dictates that this will be the best way of spending the restricted, admittedly inadequate resources they do have.

The basic strategy involved in attempting to effect 'participation in natural communication situations' is clear – one tries to set up activities in which the students are involved in use of language. Language-teaching methodology has exerted a very great deal of creative effort in recent decades into developing banks of such activities, and any textbook of communicative methodology will illustrate the richness of these techniques, with their information transfer exercises, their jigsaw activities, their information gaps. These methodological tools are nowadays extremely widespread and do not need exemplification here.[1]

Similarly widespread today are approaches which attempt in one way or another to develop 'participation in natural communication situations' in systematic ways. We shall illustrate by describing just two of the many. Among those not here described but enjoying considerable interest is the Natural Approach of Krashen and Terrell (1983).

The procedural syllabus

One approach which results in simulation of acquisition processes within the confines of the classroom is the task-based teaching experiment which took place in Southern India in the late seventies and early eighties. This is described at length in Prabhu (1987), and is discussed also in Brumfit (1984b) and Johnson (1982b). Prabhu's central hypothesis, which forms the basis of his experimental teaching project, is that 'structure can best be learned when attention is focused on meaning'. This is an explicit formulation of what many communicatively oriented teachers practise, and of what is presumably the state of affairs in first language (L1) acquisition – the primary focus of attention on performance of a task rather than on the language needed to perform it.

There are for Prabhu two important consequences of this central hypothesis. The first involves the abolition of any kind of linguistic syllabus. He argues that if we permit classroom language to be truly derived from the exigencies of some communicative task, then the language will not be systematic in any of the ways by which we usually systematize language (e.g. in structural or notional/functional terms). If, in other words, we set the students some communicative task, and truly allow both teacher and them to say what they need and want to say in the performance of that task, then their language will not fit into the confines of any structural or notional/functional syllabus. Or, to state the issue the other way round, if we impose a semantic or structural syllabus on classroom language, we are taking away the teacher's and students' freedom to interact in a way natural to the task in hand. Linguistic syllabus specifications and free interaction naturally pull in different directions.

Prabhu replaces the linguistic syllabus by what he calls a 'procedural syllabus'. This is a 'syllabus of tasks' which are graded conceptually and grouped by similarity. The content of lessons is therefore planned in advance in terms of the task or activity it will involve, but no attempt is made to plan in terms of linguistic content. Figure 7.1 illustrates part of the Bangalore procedural syllabus, at a stage where it is concerned with maps and plans (RIE 1980):

Maps and plans

43 making the plan of a house (and labelling parts), following instructions; oral, then written, response.
44 task presented on paper.
45 charting movements from one part of the house to another; giving directions (first oral, then written).
46 competition between groups (house plans supplied; each group demands instructions from another).
47 map of a few streets, with places marked; giving directions from one place to another (oral, then written).
48 task presented on paper.
49 map of a district/state with different towns and roads marked; questions on possible routes from one town to another (oral, then written).
50 map of a district/state with distances indicated; choice of the shortest route and its distance.

Figure 7.1 Part of the (Draft) Bangalore Procedural Syllabus (slightly modified from RIE 1980)

The second consequence of the central hypothesis is the eschewing any of formal teaching procedures (such as drilling and error correction), where primary attention would be focused on 'form' rather than 'meaning'. Teachers control classroom language in the same way that adults control language in conversation with an L1 child. That is, they avoid items which will clearly be beyond their audience, and they freely gloss, rephrase, explain. Within these confines, teachers use whatever language is necessary for execution of the task. It is interesting to note that according to the experimenters, following such guidelines 'leads to an overall control in the teacher's language no lower than what one sees in "structural" teaching though, being more natural, it is less perceptible' (RIE 1980, p. 12).

Various rules of thumb are suggested for the avoidance of language practice (the second P in the PPP sequence, where the primary focus of attention would be on form rather than meaning). Here is one:

> occasional and explicit attention to language itself (e.g. 'do you know what X means? It means Y'; 'This is the way to say it, not that'; 'Be careful to spell this word correctly'; 'Try to write neatly') is legitimate, provided that: (1) it is incidental to – and seen by learners as necessary for – performing the task in hand; and (2) is done frankly and openly – as an adult does in talking to a child (or as a teacher of science or history does in teaching his subject), not as a hidden 'moral' of some pretended activity or communication. Similarly, errors in learners' expression are to be treated by a teacher in the way a child's errors are treated by an adult, e.g. rephrased more accurately or corrected explicitly (not, however, elaborately, through a drill) or simply accepted provisionally as being adequate for the occasion – all as a form of temporary digression from (or clearing the way to) more important business, viz. the activity/task in hand. (RIE 1980)

The approach also uses the concept of 'incubation'. The methodology eschews repetitive drills, and the syllabus (because it avoids specification of linguistic items) is unlikely to lead to regular and paced coverage of such items. It is therefore unlikely that the students will hear and practise items in a systematic or intense way. The result may be a long period of 'incubation' between the time that an item is first heard and its production by the student. Incubation is of course a phenomenon which occurs in L1 learning.

For a formal evaluation of the Bangalore experiment, see Beretta and Davies (1985). The evaluation does show areas (associated with 'natural communicative expression') where this type of teaching is particularly successful. But the teaching does result in a degree of pidginization – that undesirable and perhaps inevitable side-product of early proceduralization which we mentioned both in chapter 4 and in chapter 6: when students are required to communicate to do a task, but have not been provided with adequate linguistic means for the purpose, they develop communication strategies which over time result in a pidgin. It might be argued (as Prabhu

1986 in fact does) that in theory this pidgin should disappear with time, just as the L1 child's incorrect intermediate forms disappear in the process of acquisition. In practice there is a real danger that the pidgin will fossilize, at it often does in natural L2 acquisition (we have earlier mentioned Schumann's 1978 Alberto as a case in point).

Prabhu's experiment is not PRODEC, but PRO, and our standpoint (as argued in chapter 4) is that successful language teaching needs to make some provision for the development of declarative representations. One might certainly speculate how much more successful approaches like Prabhu's might be (in avoiding fossilization, for example) if they permitted instructional measures to provide a DEC subsequent to the PRO. But this would, of course, go quite against the grain of what Prabhu and like-minded applied linguists are proposing.

The procedural syllabus differs from traditional syllabuses in two important respects. One is that it is stated in other-than-linguistic terms (in terms, that is, of tasks), and in a way which does not attempt to map out linguistic content.[2] Secondly, it is a syllabus of *means* rather than *ends*. That is, the aim of the teaching is not the performance of the conceptual tasks specified in the syllabus; these are the means through which language is taught.

Time has been spent on the Bangalore project because it stands as such a coherent example of an 'acquisition approach' to language teaching. Since the initiation of the project, task-based approaches have proliferated, and it is difficult not to view these as owing a debt, albeit indirect, to Prabhu's work. There are of course differences, sometimes crucial; Long and Crookes (1993), for example, argue the case for the task as unit of analysis in syllabus design. The task for them is a unit in terms of which needs analysis may be done, while Prabhu seems to regard the whole concept of needs analysis as alien to his theoretical stance.[3]

A version of notional/functional

Among very many other similar tendencies nowadays is one which deserves mention simply because it is so widespread in areas where British applied linguistics has influence. It is a version of the functional syllabus. The type of notional/functional syllabus developed in Wilkins (1976) differs from the procedural syllabus in the two respects mentioned two paragraphs ago. It is true that Wilkins distinguishes the structural from the notional/functional in that the latter is made, initially at least, in behavioural (i.e.

other-than-linguistic) terms. But he clearly has the mapping out of linguistic content in mind, and indeed states that 'since it is language behaviour we are concerned with, it is possible, indeed desirable, that the linguistic content of any unit (in teaching materials) should also be stated' (p. 13). The Wilkins notional/functional syllabus is also a specification of ends; that is, it sets out to identify terminal uses of the language through the process of needs analysis.

But for many years now the practice of functional syllabuses appears to have moved away from both these positions. Detailed mapping of exponents has tended to diminish, and functional materials have become more and more sets of communicative activities loosely linked by a convenient functional label, during the use of which the teacher gives little thought to precise linguistic input and output. Secondly, the difficulties of stating terminal uses through needs analysis, especially for groups of general learners, have led some (e.g. Johnson 1983c, Morrow 1981) to argue that the important feature of the functional syllabus is the teaching of form in relation to some meaning categories, irrespective of whether the meaning categories one selects to teach form in relation to are ones which the student will ultimately find useful. So materials may include a unit on *invitations*, for example, not because a needs analysis has identified *invitations* as an important area of language use for the target audience, but because a wealth of activities involving opportunities for interaction and learning can be based on that the speech act area. In this formulation the functional syllabus becomes a specification of *means* rather than *ends*: a set of 'pegs to hang language on' rather than the result of elaborate needs analysis.

Conceived of in these terms there is not much difference between the functional and the procedural syllabus. In discussion of this issue, Prabhu (1986) defends the cognitive task (which his prodecural syllabus favours) as a basis for syllabus because it involves activities which are easily replicable – cognitive tasks can be repeated from class to class with similar results. The functional syllabus uses many tasks which involve a degree of affect that cognitive tasks, which are essentially 'emotionless', lack. For example, role play is a preferred technique in functional teaching, and in the process of a role-play exercise a learner may be expected to simulate anger, surprise, pleasure and various other affective states. Prabhu is right to point out that where affect is concerned, different reactions will be met from different learners. For example, in some cultures (but not others) the expression of emotion in a role-play exercise is simply not acceptable. On the other hand, because role play involves affect, it taps areas of language use which cognitive tasks do not touch.

Developing Procedural Knowledge in DECPRO

The issues discussed in the previous section, to do with proceduralization in PRODEC, have been well aired in the applied linguistic literature in recent years, because of the importance that has been placed on acquisition. Far less attention has been given to the question, relating to DECPRO, of how to turn declarative knowledge, once developed, into procedural knowledge. This is the question of automization. How can we help learners to make automatic language items which they have learned declaratively?

Automization

In chapter 4 we discussed the importance of automization to skill learning in general, citing Shiffrin and Dumais' (1981) statement that it is 'a fundamental component of skill development' (p. 111). We also considered the reason for this importance – automization frees conscious attention so that it becomes available for the high-level skills which require it. We exemplified this in relation to novice drivers learning how to change gear. In relation to language we considered Bialystok's (1982) claim that the role of automization depends on the exact nature of the task – with oral conversation, for example, demanding higher automization than writing tasks.

As a starting point to a consideration of the issue of how to facilitate this important skill, here is a characterization of automization worded in such a way that it will relate to a broad range of skills, not just linguistic ones:

The skill of automization is the ability to get things right when no attention is available for getting them right.

For this characterization to be useful, we would need to add to it some statement of what 'getting things right' means. In the case of language use, this would be based on our characterization of language in general skill terms, made in chapter 2. It is, stated in the most general way, understanding and expressing intentions in ways appropriate to various cognitive and contextual parameters (the ones exemplified in figure 2.2 of chapter 2).

We might illustrate this characterization by returning to two examples we have used earlier, adding a third for good measure. Two of the three examples are deliberately taken from non-linguistic realms, to illustrate the general applicability of the characterization.

1   A novice at a musical instrument will certainly find that he or she can play some notes and note sequences only when full attention is on them. When those notes and note sequences occur within a piece of music, where attention is required for many other things at the same time, mistakes may be made. This player has the ability to 'get the notes right when attention is available for getting them right', but not when this is not the case.

2   A novice horse rider may well be able to maintain a correct posture when walking round the riding school, with all attention focused on 'getting the posture right'. But as soon as attention is elsewhere (on negotiating a small jump, for example) posture may well be the first thing to go.

3   The learner of English may be able to 'perform' the present perfect correctly in a language laboratory drill (where there is form-focus). The skill of automization will ensure that the learner performs the present perfect correctly where there is full message-focus and where ROCs may be difficult – for example, over the poor intercontinental phone line mentioned earlier.

Armed with this characterization of what we wish to develop in learners, we now confront more directly the question of how to facilitate its development.

Facilitating automization by *'ra-1'*

The literature on skill acquisition has little to say on the issue of how automization might be facilitated, beyond that quantity of practice is relevant. In one often-quoted study of a factory worker rolling cigars (Crossman 1959), improvement in speed was shown over three million trials! As Huey (1968) notes (in a quotation that well summarizes the role of automization): 'repetition progressively frees the mind from attention to details . . . and reduces the extent to which consciousness must concern itself with the process'.

We shall here explore an idea which, though by no means unexplored within language teaching, has not been systematically developed. There are various ways in which a teacher has control over the amount of attention a learner can give to a language form, and we shall consider some of these in the following section. In order to develop the idea, let us for the purposes of exemplification focus on one way only: controlling the amount of language the student has to produce in a classroom activity. The teacher who sets up a classroom task can vary the length and number of utterances the learner is expected to produce. It is obvious that the more 'language' that is expected, the less attention is available for each 'individual piece of language'. Hence one might well predict (as indeed variability studies show) that at a certain stage of development, a learner will not make mistakes with (say) the present perfect when short utterances containing it are expected, but will make mistakes when long utterances (placing more load on the attention) are required.

The idea to be explored is that the teacher can exploit this control progressively to decrease the amount of attention available to a learner for performing a subskill. Thus, when learners are first introduced to the present perfect, they are given optimal conditions for its production, one of which will be the condition that short utterances containing no new, challenging language are expected from the learner. Progressively, over time, more and more language comes to be expected, and in this way we hope to develop the ability to 'get the present perfect right when no attention is available to get it right'.

One might represent this strategy by a formula. Let us say (speaking, of course, entirely metaphorically and in a highly simplified manner) that a learner possesses ten units of conscious attention; he or she has a channel capacity of ten. When the learner first learns the present perfect he or she requires all ten units to get it right, and the teacher introduces no element into the situation to prevent full use of those ten units on the present perfect. Quite soon, however, the teacher introduces an activity which requires use of more language; but only a small amount more – just enough (we might say) to consume one 'unit of attention'. The learner now has only nine units of attention available for the present perfect, which really needs ten. He or she is put under a small amount of pressure. Eventually, he or she will learn to give only nine units of attention to the present perfect. When the teacher perceives this, some further task is introduced requiring two units of attention, leaving only eight for the present perfect. Eventually, if the strategy is successful, the learner will produce the present perfect using zero units of attention. The behaviour will, in other words, be fully automated. Let **ra** stand for 'required attention'. The formula **ra-1** indicates the strategy where we consistently put learners in a position where they have less attention available (one unit less, as it were) than they actually need to perform a task with comfort. In these terms, the desired state of automisation may be defined as the condition in which the ra needed to undertake a given skill = 0.

Code complexity

linguistic complexity and variety
vocabulary load and variety
redundancy
density

Communicative stress

time limits and time pressure
speed of presentation
number of participants
length of texts used
type of response
opportunities to control interaction

Cognitive complexity

Cognitive processing

information organization
amount of 'computation'
clarity of information given
sufficiency of information given
information type

Cognitive familiarity

familiarity of topic and its predictability
familiarity of discourse genre
ease of relationship to background knowledge
familiarity of task

Figure 7.2   Skehan's (1994, p. 191) list of features involved in task complexity (based on Candlin 1987)

Factors contributing to task complexity

There have been a number of attempts to codify the factors which will contribute to task complexity. Johnson (1986) lists general task type, speed and clarity of language involved, amount of language required, and information focus (including whether an activity is predominantly form- or message-focused). Skehan's (1994) list is based on an earlier one of Candlin's (1987) (figure 7.2).

Bygate (1994) approaches the issue from a different angle. He identifies four intervention points at which the teacher is in a position to manipulate task complexity. The first is the *pre-task* stage, where the amount and type of preparation may be controlled. The second stage is that of *task selection*, where the teacher has control over which task is selected for classroom work. The third stage involves *on-task conditions*, such as the speed of response required from learners. Fourthly is the stage of *post-task follow-up*, and it involves the degree and nature of the feedback which teachers provide on performance in a given activity. Bygate illlustrates what kinds of intervention options are open to teachers at each of these stages, in relation to a picture differences task.

In order to clarify ways in which factors like these can affect tasks (and to a degree be manipulated by teachers/materials designers), four of those mentioned variously by Johnson (1986), Skehan (1994) and Bygate (1994) are now dicussed in more detail:

1   **Degree of form focus** To a large extent the teacher can, by the way an activity is set up, control the extent to which that activity is 'form-focused'. The communicative literature is full of techniques geared to make tasks more message-focused (and hence less form-focused), and the information-gap task is a good example. By definition, the more form-focused a task is, the less attention learners need to devote to *what* they are saying, and the more to *how* they are saying it.

2   **Time constraints** The teacher can require the learner to produce language at a more or less quick rate. One way of doing this is simply by making more or less time available overall to do a task. In certain circumstances another is to speed up the cues the learner is given, forcing the pace at which responses are expected.

3   **Affective factors** It is of course the case that both native and non-native speakers will experience processing difficulties when under stress or when nervous (as well as when tired or drunk!). Although the affective factors are not ones which most teachers would wish to manipulate, they do need to be born in mind. For example, earlier in this chapter we noted that some cultures find aspects of role-play activities unacceptable or difficult to handle, and these activities are hence likely to involve participants in stress. The teacher needs to bear this in mind as a factor which will introduce processing difficulties contributing to how difficult learners will perceive the activity.

4   **Cognitive and processing complexities** It is natural that certain sorts of task will, by their very nature, be more cognitively demanding

than others, and hence consume more conscious attention. The psycholinguistic literature is full of discussion on what makes information more or less difficult to process, as a glance at a textbook like Clark and Clark (1977) reveals. Brown et al. (1984) have in particular made a study of what factors contribute to cognitive/processing complexity in tasks set up for children.

Research into task effects

Works like Crookes and Gass (1993a and b), various contributions to Bygate et al. (1994) and Long (forthcoming) indicate that there is considerable current interest in task-based teaching. It is worth noting that interesting research has been done on task effects on learner performance, and one can imagine substantial future research projects in the area. We have already mentioned, in chapter 4, research by Hulstijn and Hulstijn (1984) which involved giving learners tasks in which degree of message focus and required speed of delivery were variables considered; differences were found in relation to learners' production of two linguistic structures. Although this work has a slightly different focus from ours here, it is in fact (like one or two other pieces of research discussed in chapter 4) research into task effects, and illuminates the issue of what makes tasks difficult. Skehan (1994) cites three more recent studies on task effect. Ellis (1987) looks at the variable of planning time and relates it to production of the simple past tense. Underwood (1990) extended this study by adding a longitudinal element plus some language instruction. Crookes (1989) also considers planning time, and reaches the interesting conclusion that although (in his study) this has no effect on accuracy, it does have an effect on the variety of lexis and degree of risk-taking the learners are prepared to engage in. Studies like these, Skehan concludes, 'hint that it may be possible to predict systematic influences of performance conditions on the nature of the language used' (p. 184).

Parking the attention

By manipulating factors such as those considered earlier, the teacher is able to exert influence on amount of attention a learner has available to concentrate on a particular language form. The amount of attention 'needed' by a form – its **ra** – will of course vary as learners increase the degree of procedural control they have over it. Hence, we may conceptualize what occurs as a constant tension in all situations of language use, both inside and outside the classroom. On one side of the equation there are the demands on the attention which all the contextual factors (such as those listed above) make. On the other (right-hand) side of the equation is the amount of attention a particular structure X needs to be got right. This equation predicts variability. When the contextual attention demands are small and the degree of attention structure X requires is high, we might expect the learner to get the structure right. But when the contextual attention demands are high, and structure X is not given the attention it requires to be got right, we can expect a mistake.

But how, in practice, may **ra-1** be achieved? One factor considered earlier was 'degree of form focus', and one obvious way of decreasing *form* focus is to increase degree of *message* focus. Much real communication outside the classroom is, of course, marked by a very high degree of message focus. So much so that we might almost modify our earlier formulation and define automization in language use as 'the ability to get "the how" (forms) right when full attention is focused on "the what" (messages)'.

Another way of conceptualizing this is to say that the principle underlying the strategy we are putting forward is one which involves the teacher in creating 'other things' for the learner's attention to focus on, such that less attention is available for form focus. A major 'other thing' in real communication is 'message'. This is one reason why the third P in the PPP sequence – the production stage – is so important, because at that stage most attention is likely to be focused on message, and on making the activities meaningful. Hence the 'present perfect simulator' we spoke about in the previous chapter is one which above all involves free practice.

While it is valuable to recognize the importance of message focus, there is a sense in which it does not matter onto what the attention is directed, as long as it is not on the form being practised. In the paragraph above we speak of creating 'other things' for the learner to focus on; the answer to the question 'what other things?' can therefore be 'anything'. If this is accepted, then one may begin to think in terms of 'artificial attention distractors'; that is, elements introduced into the practice with the sole and blatant aim of consuming the learner's conscious attention. The skill acquisition literature provides some interesting examples of this. Gallwey (1974), for example, speaking about the 'inner game of tennis', observes that 'to still the mind one must learn to put it somewhere . . . it must be "parked"'. He advises the learner to watch (and even listen to!) the ball, not principally because this highlights important perceptual cues, but simply as a 'parking procedure'. A second example, cited in Reed (1968), is of the rowing trainer Fairbairn, one of whose highly successful techniques was to ask the learner to 'concentrate his attention on his blade and leave Nature to work his body in unconscious response'. Concentrating on the blade does not give the rower any information; it simply keeps the conscious mind occupied. To add a personal anecdote: literally the most powerful aid in my giving up smoking was to give up peanuts at the same time! I deliberately decided to give up something else at the same time as stopping smoking, to 'park the attention'. All my emotional energy was channeled into the effort not to eat peanuts, and cigarettes slowly became forgotten.

In chapter 9 we illustrate how the language learner's attention may be 'parked' by providing tasks which contain 'distractors'. We shall argue there that one way of viewing many of the techniques associated with communicative methodology is in fact to regard them as providing 'parking procedures' for the attention, in order to facilitate automization.

Illustrations of task complexity: seven versions of an exercise

In order to give some flesh to the bones of this discussion, we shall consider different ways in which one simple language-teaching drill may be presented varying the degree of complexity involved in the task. The drill is intended for eight-year-old children, and is deliberately simple in order to illustrate that task complexity is not a concept that is applicable only at advanced levels (sometimes the case with proposed methodological innovations in language teaching).

Figure 7.3 illustrates the basic exercise. It may be done teacher–pupil, but we shall here assume pupil–pupil; pupils work in pairs and practise questions and short answers with the verb *be*. For example:

Student A: Number one. Is it a bicycle?
Student B: No, it isn't.

Student A: Number one. Is it a dog?
Student B: Yes, it is.

One reason why this version of the exercise is so tedious is that it is entirely form-focused. There is really very little for the pupils to focus attention on save correctly forming the utterances. With both pupils looking at the pictures, the utterances are not informative, and no challenge is

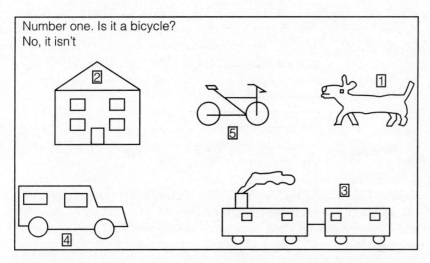

Figure 7.3 Version 1 of the number exercise (derived from Johnson 1982a)

involved: pupils are telling each other things they already know and can clearly see.

Version 2 of the exercise (figure 7.4) complicates it slightly (and makes it considerably less tedious) by introducing an information gap. Here student A covers the bottom of the page and concentrates on the top, while student B looks at the bottom and not the top. A asks the questions, B answers, and A writes in the appropriate words. It may take several questions before A finds the answer he or she is looking for at a given point (for example, to find out what Number one is, four questions may have to be asked).

The introduction of an information gap introduces a degree of message focus into the exercise: pupils are now not asking for the sake of practising grammar, but to find out the answers to questions and to write that information down. In addition, the task involves a degree of cognitive processing, and the alert pupil will be able to fill in all the words with fewer questions than the less alert pupil; indeed, this makes it possible to do the exercise as a 'competition' in the class, with each pair trying to fill in the words with the least number of questions.

Similar points may be made about version 3 of the exercise (figure 7.5), which has the form of a 'Find the Difference' game. Presenting the exercise as a game is likely to increase pupil perception of it as a message-focused activity and, as with version 2, a degree of processing is involved.

Version 4 (figure 7.6) differs minimally in appearance from version 1, but

Student A. Find out:
Number one. Is it a bicycle?

1. _____
2. _____
3. _____
4. _____
5. _____

bicycle   car   train
        dog   house

Student B. Answer the questions:
Yes, it is. No, it isn't.

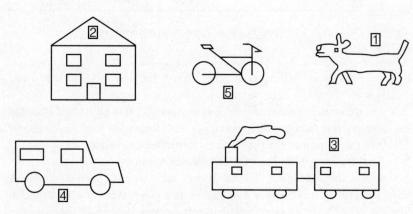

Figure 7.4   Version 2 of the number exercise

the result is a dramatic increase in the complexity of the task. The drill is
now presented as a memory game. Pupils may look at the pictures only for
a minute, then have to close their books. The teacher (or one chosen pupil)
then asks the questions. It is likely that all conscious attention will be put
into the process of remembering, as opposed to the process of 'getting the
short answer form right'.

   In version 5 (figure 7.7) a reading comprehension dimension is added
to the task. The boxes at the top represent parcels for Christmas presents,
and the text indicates what presents have been bought for whom. Pupils
read the text and draw lines from presents to parcels. This version of the
exercise introduces language which is almost certainly unknown to the

Find the differences

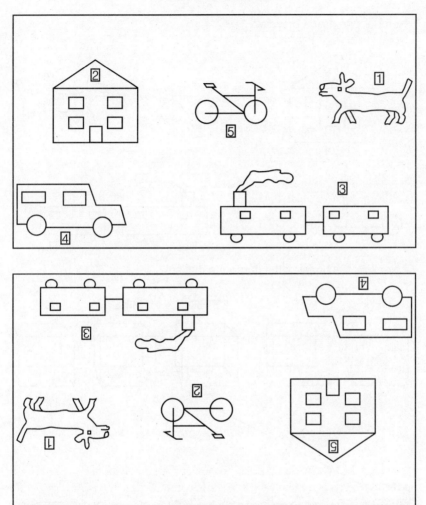

Figure 7.5 Version 3 of the number exercise

pupils at their learning stage – 'would like', 'going to', 'I've bought' being three such untaught structures. The exercise therefore now involves the ability to process information in the presence of unknown language items (a skill required in very many communicative situations, yet rarely practised in class).

Look for one minute. Then answer the questions.

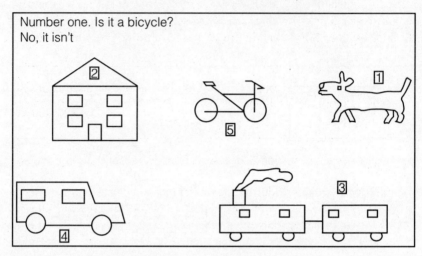

Figure 7.6 Version 4 of the number exercise

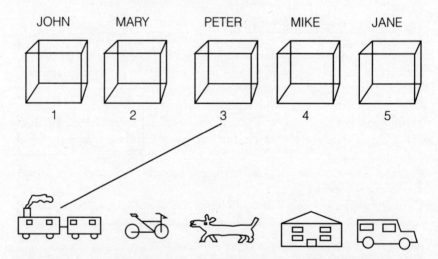

The train is for Peter. He likes trains a lot. Mary would like a dolls house. Jane doesn't have a bicycle; I'm going to give her one. I've bought a dog for John and Mike can have the car.

Now check: Number one. Is it a bicycle?

Figure 7.7 Version 5 of the number exercise

Further versions of the exercise could of course be added, with yet more difficulties introduced. A sixth version, for example, might follow the pattern of version 5, but introduce a problem-solving element. Figure 7.8 gives the pupils all the information they need to work out who gets which present:

The train is for a boy, but it isn't for John or Mike. The dolls house is for a girl, but not for Jane. The bicycle isn't for a boy, and the car isn't for John

---

Figure 7.8 Text for version 6 of the number exercise

Once the notion of introducing the relevant information in different ways has been introduced, many other versions become possible. Figure 7.9 also follows the pattern of version 5, with the information this time being introduced by a grid of the sort commonly found in puzzle books. The names outside the box give clues as to where the objects in it can be found.

Task complexity and the present perfect simulator

In chapter 6 we spoke about the possibility of having a 'present perfect simulator': a device which would give the operator/teacher control over the introduction of different processing conditions. The point was made that free practice naturally introduced real operating conditions (ROCs) in various configurations, this being a prime motivation for including a great deal of the final P in language teaching. But task grading of the sort we have been examining here gives the possibility of much more control – more sophisticated, touch-sensitive 'buttons' perhaps, whereby ROCs can be introduced in a graded way.

Task complexity offers a new and important dimension to the grading of language-teaching materials. In the past, grading has generally been in terms of language content. An exercise was considered more or less difficult than another one largely in terms of what language items it included. So exercises expecting the present perfect passive would, for example, be regarded as more complex than those expecting the simple present. It is central to a processing approach to language teaching, however, that what learners are expected to do with language is as important as the actual content of that language. From this standpoint, it is perfectly feasible to have a challenging, difficult exercise that uses relatively simple structures –

B	L	S	R	A	T	M	E
K	I	W	S	R	G	M	P
T	A	C	A	R	N	X	L
F	S	I	Y	Q	W	S	A
A	N	O	I	C	D	G	E
Z	P	E	D	V	L	J	I
O	U	H	O	U	S	E	W
M	P	Q	G	V	G	K	N

JANE   JOHN   PETER

MIKE (row 3)   MARY (row 7)

Figure 7.9 Grid for version 7 of the number exercise

and an 'easier' exercise which uses more complex language; processing conditions and task complexity are crucial factors in what make exercises easy or difficult.[4]

In this chapter the **ra-1** principle has largely been discussed in relation to the second P of the PPP sequence. The principle was initially illustrated in relation to the practice of one structure, the present perfect tense, and the versions of the number exercise all practise the same discrete structural items. The point therefore needs making that **ra-1** should have a more general effect on the teaching programme overall. Learners need to be able to handle ROCs in all areas of language use, and practice in this needs to be provided. Task grading should therefore be a concern in all learning activities, not just at the practice stage where discrete items are drilled.

The taxonomies of operating conditions we considered earlier in this chapter may be seen as the essential prerequisite for any **ra-1** strategy. Essentially such taxonomies will define the 'buttons to press' on the 'present perfect simulator'.

We shall return to **ra-1** again in chapter 9 where we argue that techniques for practising processing skills are already found in so-called communicative methodology in language teaching.

Notes

1 The reader who wishes to know more about these standard communicative techniques will find descriptions of them in books such as Johnson and Morrow (1981).
2 Long's (1985) characterization of tasks well captures their other-than-linguistic nature: ' "tasks" are the things people will tell you they do if you ask them and they are not applied linguists' (p. 89).
3 Long himself (1985) identifies this difference between his stance and Krashen and Terrell's natural method.
4 Long (1985) makes the point in these words:

> *Grading* is determined by the degree of difficulty of the pedagogical tasks themselves (from simple to complex), as well as such normal considerations as variety, pace and duration. 'Difficulty' here, however, does not mean difficulty in terms of the linguistic demands . . . rather it refers to the difficulty of pedagogical tasks in such aspects as the number of steps involved in their execution, the number of parties involved, the assumptions they make about presupposed knowledge, the intellectual challenge they pose . . . and so on. (p. 93)

8 Towards a Skill Framework for Language Teaching

Our discussion of language teaching has so far focused on two issues, the declarativization and proceduralization of knowledge. This narrow focus has been deliberate, because it is indeed our belief that a reading of the skills literature does place central importance on these two processes.

But this literature has much else to say of relevance to language teaching. Anyone who picks up a book such as Holding's (1965) *Principles of Training* is likely to be amazed at how much of it is relevant to language teaching, even though that topic is not directly addressed at any point. In this chapter we shall consider some issues other than declarativization and proceduralization where the skills literature may be felt to have something to say to the applied linguist. A consideration of these issues will, it is hoped, move us a little closer to a framework for language teaching which will be beginning to have its own distinctive characteristics.

The Part/Whole Issue

Whether or not to divide

One of the initial sets of issues one faces when discussing the role of instruction for a complex skill concerns the division of the required behaviour into parts for teaching. There are two problems: one is whether or not we should attempt to divide the behaviour up into pieces for instructional purposes. This is the issue of whole versus part training, and it is one that is discussed in the skills literature at length. If the answer to this question is that we should indeed divide, then the second question becomes: 'what sort of parts should one divide into?' This question has received much attention in language teaching, and we shall deal with it in a later section (the one on content specifications). We begin our discussion of the first issue by considering how the part/whole debate has been conducted in language teaching. Then we turn to what has been said about the same issue in the skills literature.

In language teaching the part/whole debate has tended to be argued in terms of extreme positions – either entirely 'part' or entirely 'whole'. On the 'part' side we have the behaviourist model (or, at least, one partial and distorted version of it – see McDonough 1981 on how language teaching espoused a somewhat peripheral version of behaviourism from the psychological literature). This learning theory clearly advocates division of large-scale behaviours up into pieces, each piece being taught in isolation until it can be performed without error, before proceeding to the next. This process of dividing a large-scale behaviour into manageable pieces, incrementally teaching them one by one, is known in behaviourism as 'shaping', and has given proponents like Skinner considerable success in teaching animals like pigeons to perform relatively complex sequences of action, such as playing table tennis. The language-teaching manifestation of shaping is the structural syllabus with its division of language into structural patterns – characteristic configurations of structure, each minimally different from the others. In behaviourist-influenced language teaching, language behaviour is 'shaped' by teaching structural patterns one by one. Wilkins (1976) uses the term 'synthetic' to describe this 'step by step instruction . . . based on the identification of . . . the components of the terminal behaviour . . .' (the quote is from Newmark 1979, p. 160); it is synthetic because the learner's task is one of synthesizing the component parts as taught, into a unified whole. The learner synthesizes.

Wilkins uses the term 'analytic' to describe the alternative to 'synthetic' (the 'whole' side of the part/whole distinction). In an 'analytic' approach, the language is fed to students in a more or less undigested form, rather than being broken down in advance into digestible chunks. Newmark, the applied linguist cited above, supports an analytic approach to teaching because 'acquisition cannot be simply additive; complex bits of language are learned a whole chunk at a time', with the learner being able to exploit what he calls the 'exponential power available in learning in natural chunks'. This type of approach would be 'analytic' because in it the learner's task is one of analysis, breaking down the component parts of the 'whole chunks' to work out how the language operates. The learner analyses.

It is important to identify the kind of evidence Newmark appeals to in defence of analytic teaching, and this is clearly exemplified in a seminal paper he wrote with Reibel (Newmark and Reibel 1968). Working within a

Chomskyan tradition, they point to the similarities between first and second language (L1 and L2) learning. It may be (they argue) that the language acquisition device – the mechanism utilized by the child for L1 learning – becomes 'rusty' by adolescence. But it can be 'oiled' back into the service of learning a second language, the message for instructors being that they should model their behaviour on what parents do in the L1 situation. It is clear how this position of Newmark and Reibel is linked to the more recent 'acquisitional' approaches of Krashen, Prabhu and others. Such approaches (related to our PRODEC) equally clearly fall on the 'whole' side of the part/whole debate.

So much for the language-teaching discussion on the issue. Skill psychology provides a rather different perspective – one which offers the possibility of less extreme positions, and which meaningfully differentiates approaches according to the nature of the skills concerned. It is recognized that for some skills, division into component parts for practice is well-nigh impossible. High diving is a skill sometimes mentioned in this respect. There are obvious reasons why you cannot divide this skill into component actions, practising each in isolation. So if the teacher wishes to introduce some type of 'grading' into the practice of high diving, then one is really faced with keeping the behaviour as a whole, but varying the height dived from. Thus the beginner's dive is from a low height, and this is increased as the practice continues. We might say that in this case we have 'whole practice' right from the beginning, with the practice made simpler by control over such parameters as height. At the other end of the spectrum are skills where 'part practice' – dividing the behaviour up into small parts which are practised one by one – is both perfectly feasible, and the obvious training strategy. Computer programming is an example; the component parts – learning how to loop, how to handle dimensions etc. – can be taught separately, and in the case of this skill we can predict that once each subskill is mastered, joining them together to create complex programmes is a relatively simple operation. In the case of a third category of skills, division into components is both possible and highly desirable, but the components are not so isolated and discrete as they are for computer programming. The skill of piloting an aircraft is an example. The sheer size and complexity of the skill argues against whole training from the start – some kind of initial part practice is necessary. It is also feasible; unlike with high diving, one can find ways of dividing piloting into subskills. But piloting is also an example of a skill where, although division is possible, much of the eventual skill involves 'doing various things at the same time' – simultaneous and interdependent use of subskills. In the case of such skills, the 'sooner the skill can be performed as a whole, the better will be the results' (Peterson 1975, p. 94). In other words, when a skill involves a high element of 'doing various things at the same time' – what we called in chapter 2 'combinatorial skill' – then there is the need for early whole practice – 'combinatorial practice'.

In the respects that we have been discussing, language behaviour has something in common with piloting an aircraft. Firstly, it is such a large-scale behaviour that some sort of dividing might be felt to be necessary; for many, simply leaving the learner to cope would be like leaving trainee pilots to work out how to fly an aircraft by themselves. Secondly, division into parts is indeed a feasibility. For centuries, language teachers have divided languages into component syntactic structures, which are taught one by one. Other linguistic areas, like the phonological, also lend themselves to division into discrete parts, although yet other areas (like speech acts) are not so easily or usefully divisible (an issue discussed later in this chapter). Thirdly, as we have already explored in chapter 2, language does indeed involve a good deal of combinatorial skill, and the word 'fluency' is often used to describe mastery of this skill. The suggestion is clearly that part practice has a role, but that whole practice should be introduced early on. This is our conclusion, and it strengthens the argument, made earlier at various points in this book, of the importance of free practice in language teaching – because free practice is whole practice.

Combining part and whole practice

The part/whole issue is a good example of one where a skills approach provides a principled consideration of a concern relevant to language teaching. As soon as we cease to think in terms of *either* part *or* whole practice, and allow a place for both (as in the above formulation) then we can begin to think about how best to combine these two elements. Little thought appears to have been given to this question in applied linguistics. To give some idea of the complexity of issues involved (and the wealth of possible approaches available), we shall now spend a few paragraphs focusing on just a few of the relevant variables, identifying various possible part/whole combinations. Although some judgmental points are incidentally made regarding these various approaches, our aim here is not really to reach conclusions, but the lesser one of illustrating the kinds of issues involved and the range of solutions available. What we are here discussing has relevance to chapter 4's consideration of DECPRO and PRODEC. The concepts of PRO and whole practice on the one hand, and DEC and part practice on the

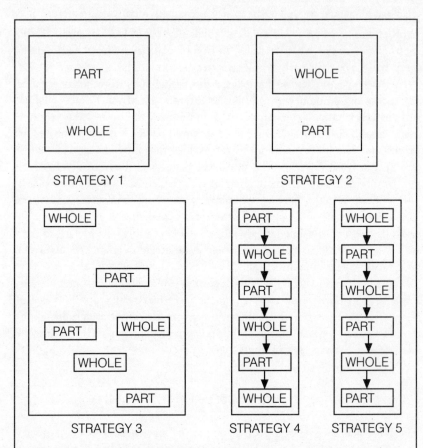

STRATEGY 1 has a long period of part practice (perhaps several years), followed by whole practice.

STRATEGY 2 has a long period of whole practice followed by part practice.

STRATEGY 3 has lessons of whole practice and lessons of part practice each week (not necessarily connected in terms of content).

STRATEGY 4 has part practice followed by whole practice, e.g. in each lesson.

STRATEGY 5 has whole practice followed by part practice, e.g. in each lesson.

Figure 8.1 Possible part/whole configurations

other are related, though they are by no means identical. Therefore it is inevitable that discussion of possible part/whole sequential relationships will bring up issues relating to whether DEC should come before PRO or vice versa.

One major variable is the possible time relations between whole practice and part practice components. To consider the role of this variable it needs to be clear just what we mean by 'part practice component' and 'whole practice component'. The former would consist of a period of drill-like activities practising chosen parts of the language in isolation – they might be structures, phonological distinctions, semantic 'notions', or speech acts. In a 'whole practice component' the activities would be of the 'combinatorial' type – like role plays, discussions, simulations or communicative games, where a main aim of the activity would be to practise 'doing more than one thing at the same time'. Bearing this difference in mind, let us now further distinguish sequential and simultaneous approaches. A *sequential* approach is one where a period of one type of practice (i.e. part or whole) is followed by a period of another; for example, one might envisage several years of part practice followed by an amount of time spent on whole practice. In a *simultaneous* approach, the two types of practice would proceed side by side, with (say) part practice every Monday, Wednesday and Friday, and whole practice on the other class days. Of course, the sequential/simultaneous difference is a relative one – when the time spans involved in a sequential approach become very short, it in effect becomes a simultaneous one.

Figure 8.1 exemplifies types of solution available, and gives short characterizations of five strategies. We shall have observations to make on each of these strategies in turn.

Strategy 1 is very common in a type of classroom mentioned at the beginning of chapter 6 – audiolingual ones where the third P of the PPP sequence is often omitted (P P__), or put off until a very late stage. There may even be a period of, say, five years in which the patterns of the language are systematically and comprehensively covered, and where the only sort of practice given is part practice. At the very end of the course (perhaps in year 6!) some attention might be given to 'activating' the learned structures, through a freer sort of (whole) practice. The most obvious problem associated with this strategy is that it unacceptably delays communicative practice. Students are learning for a very long time before they can *do anything* with the language; it is not until extremely late in the proceedings that learners reap any benefit, in terms of communicative ability, from the investment they have put into learning.[1] A second problem is likely to occur in any sort of sequential solution: it is that tedium will build up in any situation where there is a great deal of any one thing to the exclusion of other things.

There is a third problem involved with strategy 1 as it is actually practised in many situations. This involves a further time variable: the relative length of components. We have just noted the tendency in much audiolingual teaching to de-emphasize whole practice (quite often to the extent that it cannot really be said to exist). Where one has 'long part practice' followed by 'short whole practice' we find a failure to recognize the degree of attention which needs to be given to the activation process. We have earlier made the point at some length (at the beginning of chapter 6, for example) that there is the world of difference between, on the one hand, the ability to practise language in small segments, in restricted conditions and, on the other, using language in ROCs. We have also noted that practice with real operating conditions to a large extent means whole practice; hence what we are advocating is a lengthy whole practice component. One solution which recognizes the need for lengthy activation involves a version of strategy 1 rather different from the one conventionally used. It is illustrated in figure 8.2.

In this solution, the teacher might spend the first two months of (say) a year-long course providing an overview of grammar, and drilling it pattern by pattern. This would be followed by eight months of whole practice in which the DEC just formed would be proceduralized.

Strategy 2 is a second sort of logically possible sequential solution which involves beginning with whole and moving to part practice. To the restricted extent that we may legitimately associate whole practice with PRO and part practice with (part of the procedure involved in mastering) DEC, then this strategy is one version of PRODEC. Like various 'acquisitional' or 'naturalistic' approaches, it would involve acquiring through using. We noted in chapter 4 that such approaches provide PRO, but need to find some way of adding the essential DEC. Strategy 2 does this by including a period of more formal teaching – it would be something akin to Krashen's 'acquisition' bolstered up by some 'learning'; an interesting proposition, and one rarely followed to any serious degree.

Discussion of the simultaneous solutions only really becomes meaningful if we introduce another variable: how the two components might relate in terms of actual content. *Strategy 4* is arguably the most common of all the strategies we present here. It is the conventional PPP, and usually there is a rather strong content relationship between part and whole practice. So we may introduce the present perfect tense in our part practice, then set up

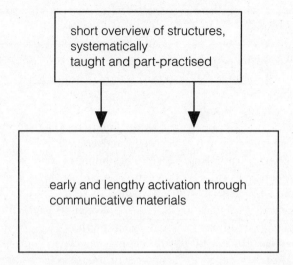

Figure 8.2   An uncommon version of strategy 1

tasks in which we predict its use in whole practice. In the terminology
which our framework here employs, we would call this a 'simultaneous part
to whole solution with a strong content link between the components'. A
valid objection to this strategy is voiced by Prabhu (1986 – we shall discuss
his point further in chapter 9). He points out that the free production in this
strategy is in fact *reproduction* – that is, the free practice is not in fact free
at all, but a thinly veiled invitation to the students to continue practising
certain identified linguistic items.

Strategy 3 is an interesting alternative in which there is no content relationship between the components. So no attempt would be made to ensure
that the structures which appeared in the part practice on Mondays, Wednes-
days and Fridays (for example) also made an appearance in the whole
practice on (say) Tuesdays and Thurdays. This problem is also avoided
in the corresponding whole to part alternative (*Strategy 5*). This is the so-
called 'deep-end strategy' introduced in Brumfit (1979) and discussed in
Johnson (1980a). It involves the sequence shown in figure 8.3.[2]

This is not the place for full discussion of these strategies, and there
are certainly many factors not touched on here which need consideration.
Important in this context is to illustrate the complexity of the issues, and
the richness of possibilities, which come to the fore when we take seriously
a suggestion made in the skills literature.

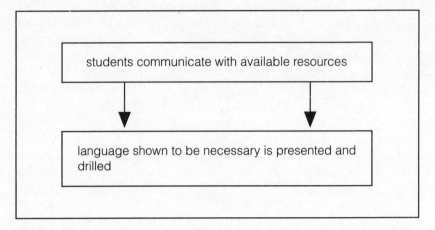

Figure 8.3 The 'deep-end' strategy

A minimum condition for part practice?

We have already noted that where division of a behaviour into subskills is possible but the task involves simultaneous and interdependent use of subskills, the 'sooner the skill can be performed as a whole, the better will be the results' (Peterson 1975, p. 94). We have observed that language is this type of behaviour.

There is a danger which any part practice potentially entails, but which is particularly a risk with the type of behaviour just described. It is the danger that the strategies the learner develops to handle the subskill in isolation may be at odds with those the subskill requires in the full behaviour (a point discussed in Crossman 1960). Holding (1965) gives a clear example of this from the teaching of swimming: 'Practising the arm movements of the breast stroke on land', he notes, 'may not be the same thing as using them to swim in co-ordination with the legs.' In other words, it is possible to make part practice so remote from the desired eventual behaviour that it becomes at best useless and at worst damaging. In the case of the swimming example, practising movements on land may be so different from practising them in water as to be useless; or (in the worse case) it may develop muscle movements which actually have to be 'unlearned' when the learner tries the strokes in water. To guard against this danger, we may need to impose 'minimum conditions' on the part practice – conditions which it must meet to preserve essential characteristics of the subskill. In the swimming example, a possible minimum condition might be that all part practice should at least take place in water!

There is one candidate for a possible minimum condition in language practice (the second P) which is discussed in the communicative literature (e.g. in Johnson 1979). The argument runs thus: in communication, central focus is on conveying a message; the desire to convey a message is the speaker's starting point and he or she selects language to fulfil this purpose. The procedure of language encoding is hence basically a procedure of seeking linguistic forms to express a desired message. It may be argued that where the prime focus in part practice is on *form* and where the starting point is not the desire to convey a message at all, but the intention to practise a grammatical item – that in these circumstances the basic process of encoding meaning into form is missing. It is certainly true that learners trained solely with this sort of form-focused practice will meet grave problems of transfer when they try to communicate outside the classroom. They will never have attempted the process of converting messages into forms, and hence will not be able to do it.

A possible methodological implication of this is to place a minimum condition on part practice, that it should contain an information gap. Johnson (1980b) argues this, and makes the point that it is possible to introduce such information gaps while maintaining the drill-like nature of the part practice; information-gap exercises may be drills.

In chapter 7 we compared a non-information-gap drill (version 1 of the number exercise) with its information-gapped equivalent (version 2). We made the point that in version 1 all students are looking at the same pictures, hence student A (the pupil who asks the questions) already possesses the information he or she is asking for – an odd communicative situation, although admittedly not an impossible one. Student B, who provides the answers, is also of course aware as he or she responds that student A already has the requested information. In version 2, on the other hand, student A is asking questions to which he does not already have the answers, and student B is supplying answers which he knows to be new information for his interlocutor.

For many teachers, one (if not *the*) major value of the information gap is motivational; providing information to those who already have it is likely to be seen as a pointless exercise and hence a tedious one. But it may be argued that by far the more important consequence of the information gap is that it introduces a degree of message focus, and hence simulates in this important aspect the essential process of converting messages into forms. It allows actual formulative processes to take place, along the same lines that they occur in 'real' communication.

The number exercise in figure 7.4 is not, of course, 'real' communication. It remains a drill, and a far cry from the kinds of interaction people have in the outside world. Yet, one may argue, it at least adheres to a minimum condition, achieved by the introduction of an information gap.

Cost-effectiveness in part/whole training

In the earlier section entitled 'whether or not to divide' it becomes clear that much of the part/whole debate in language teaching has been argued in theoretical terms – with grand issues like the nature of language behaviour being raised. It is of course important to have a theoretical dimension to such debates; but we need perhaps also to (have the humility to) remember that practical cost-effectiveness is a vital consideration. It may take ten hours to teach a subskill in isolation and a further ten hours to integrate it within the whole behaviour (eliminating any distortions introduced by the isolative practice). If an approach using whole practice from the start takes fifteen hours to achieve the same end, it is more cost-effective; if thirty hours, then it is less cost-effective. The same may be said about the minimum conditions argument, the question being whether practice starting with complete form focus and gradually moving to message focus is more or less efficient than practice which is message-focused from the start. In principle all these questions of cost-effectiveness can be investigated empirically, although the history of applied linguistics is littered with warnings of the research problems which such empirical investigations entail.

A Skills Syllabus

A conclusion to our earlier discussion on the part/whole debate was that there is indeed a role for part practice in language teaching (as there is also for whole practice, early on as well as late). Part practice implies 'dividing (the language) up', and this in turn implies a syllabus which states what the constituent parts are, and in what order they will be taught. What kind of syllabus do we then need? Is there such a thing as a 'skills syllabus', and if so what does it look like? Would it be substantially different from already existing types?

In this discussion we shall find it useful to make use of a distinction which is in fact relevant to consideration of any syllabus of whatever orientation – between a syllabus inventory and a syllabus. For detailed discussion of this distinction, see Johnson (1982b). The inventory is a set of lists of items to be covered, or 'taken into consideration' during the language-teaching programme. Precisely what the lists are will depend on the framework in which one is working; for the Council of Europe tradition (as outlined in Trim et al. 1980, for example), lists would commonly be of settings, topics, roles, notions, functions and structures. Syllabus designers would identify one of these lists as the 'unit of organization' of their actual programme. Thus, they might decide to make the programme a 'functional' one, arranging it so that each teaching unit covers one function. It is important to observe that items on the other inventory lists would not be ignored in this functional programme, but would simply not form the organizational base. Hence, in a functional syllabus, the settings list would determine the contexts in which the functions were introduced; the role list would determine who spoke to whom, and so on. In this model, the syllabus inventory is a set of unordered lists; the syllabus selects a unit of organization from the inventory lists, and orders items for teaching purposes. For most of this section we shall be speaking about syllabus inventories, turning in the final paragraph to consider how our inventories might become syllabuses.

Munby (1978) contains an initial attempt at a skill taxonomy. His skills are stated in terms of an 'operational element' (the 'action done') plus a statement of the domain over which it operates, which he calls 'communicative feature'. Hence the skill of 'understanding relations between different parts of a text' consists for Munby of the operational element *understanding* and the communicative feature *relations between different parts of a text*. In his recognition of these two elements, Munby places himself within the tradition of rigorous needs analysis and behavioural specification which owes much to the work of Bloom and other educationalists who attempted to specify objectives in rigidly behavioural terms. See Stern (1983) for an overview of attempts in language teaching to do this, including the work of Munby.

We shall here maintain Munby's distinction, though broadening his categories, and (for reasons given below) replacing his term 'communicative features' with the label 'content specifications'.

Content specifications

The approach we take here is to attempt to identify different levels of analysis at which skills identification may be made. This procedure of identifying different levels is common in syllabus design; see Stern (1983) for an overview of how this has been achieved in the past. When we follow this procedure, it becomes clear that our attempt to divide language behaviour into subskills is going to result in a list that has much in common with those found in conventional, traditional syllabuses, and this is one reason why we prefer a wide term like 'content specifications' to the narrower 'communicative feature' which implies certain specific areas of language that the so-called communicative movement chose to focus on. One level of analysis will of course be the syntactic – or, to put it another way, 'using syntactic structures' is a large skill area – and hence items like 'the present perfect' would have a place on a skills syllabus (as well as other traditional items, such as points of phonemic distinction). *Forming the present perfect correctly* and *contrasting /i/ with /i:/* are as much skills as Munby's own example, for a more communicative age: *understanding relations between different parts of a text.*

In our attempts to break language behaviour down into subskills, the general areas of phonetics/phonology and syntax would, then, follow traditional lines and would not pose any new difficulties for syllabus designers. A more problematic area is (as it has always been in language teaching) that of language use. There has been in the language-teaching literature considerable discussion as to whether categories of language use can be listed for the purposes of syllabus design at all, with discussion naturally revolving round what has been the most systematic attempt in the field to approach such teaching – the notional/functional (n/f) syllabus. The issue is partly the extent to which categories of language use can be isolated and presented in a pedagogically useful way; for discussion of this issue, see the short series of linked papers appearing in *Applied Linguistics* 2/1 – Brumfit (1981), Paulston (1981) and Wilkins (1981).

Would a skill-based syllabus contain notions and functions? It is certainly the case that we would wish to identify levels of analysis at which semantic and speech act categories would be relevant. In addition, there seems no reason why items like *invitation* and *expressing certainty* (a 'function' and a 'notion') should not be considered as skills, and ones furthermore that many students will need to master. But two points need to be made – as relevant to the development of any sort of syllabus as to a skill-based one. The first observation is that for an item to be really useful in syllabus terms it needs to be 'generalizable about' ('generative' in the use of this word we have been employing in this book). It may be said that a good number of the functions appearing in many syllabuses do not meet this criterion (for discussion of which see Brumfit 1981 and Johnson 1983b). Are there, for example, generalizations about how we invite in English which can be conveyed to learners? Is there a (pedagogically accessible) 'grammar of inviting'? If not, then any attempt in a n/f syllabus to teach 'inviting' will not involve conveying generalizable rules, but will degenerate into the presentation of lists of set phrases to be taught in parrot fashion – an outcome which Widdowson (1978) sees as occurring. How does this undesirable state of affairs come about? It happens because in the traditional Council of Europe model of n/f syllabus design, functions are arrived at by looking at learners' terminal needs, by a process of needs analysis. Hence 'inviting' (for example) may appear on a syllabus because it has been identified as 'something the learners will want to do in their foreign language'. But it does not follow from this that there are any generalizations to be made about how one invites in English. One may therefore say that n/f syllabus design has been dominated by the issue of whether or not something is done (the question asked being: do the students need to be able to invite in English?). But a more secure basis for syllabus design (with a skills or any other orientation) is whether or not useful generalizations can or cannot be made about the categories identified. So from this point of view a skill-based syllabus would contain notions and functions – but only those about which pedagogically accessible generalizations can be made.

The second observation follows on from the first. It is that skill specifications should go 'below the surface' in a way not always practised in the n/f syllabus. It has always been perceived as a major part of the appeal of the n/f syllabus that it has face validity. Learners should be able immediately to recognize the utility of the categories on their n/f syllabus. So individuals coming to study in Britain should recognize in their pre-sessional syllabus the validity of being taught how to ask for and give personal information, make requests, greet and invite. But the less acceptable side of face validity is superficiality. If one is seeking categories about which valid generalizations may be made, it is possible, indeed likely, that many of them will not have the kind of immediate face validity which a learner would instantly recognize. To continue the earlier example, a needs analysis might reveal that learners need to know how to invite, and the very fact that a needs analysis has identified this function should endow it with face validity for the learners – they should recognize their own need to invite. But following the line of thought developed earlier, the syllabus designer might decide that no useful generalizations can be made about inviting, and on this basis decide not to devote teaching time to it. The syllabus designer may, on the other hand, decide that useful generalizations – to do, for example, with being polite in English – can be made about such things as 'being circumspect and indirect in approach'. Hence this latter category may have a useful place on the skills syllabus. But it may be (and this is the point here) that this item, being somewhat abstract, has a good deal less face validity than the *invitation* category.

The result of these observations is to suggest that syllabus designers should ask rather different questions about the skills involved in language use than has been the norm. With different questions being asked it is inevitable that the results of a skill-based enquiry will differ considerably from that of the usual n/f syllabus – though it is certain that a skill syllabus will recognize these dimensions of language behaviour.

Recent years have seen the development of 'process approaches' to teaching, particularly of the writing skills. For general discussion of the process concept, see Breen (1987), and for concrete illustration of what this approach implies for the teaching of writing, see White and Arndt (1991). The word 'process' in this context reflects a distinction, found in the educational literature in general, between *process* and *product*. Process syllabuses are seen as ones which concentrate on how (that is, the processes by which) language is learned and used, rather than simply listing and teaching the product – language items. Some of the areas covered in White and Arndt (1991) for the learning of process writing will illustrate: they have sections on *generating ideas* for an essay, *drafting* essays, *structuring* and *evaluating* them.

Does such an approach have a place in skill-based teaching? One might wish to quibble with the process/product distinction, asking whether processes, when listed, do not become products. But quibbles aside, items like generating, drafting, structuring, evaluating are clearly skills, and it is certainly the case that a full skill-based approach would wish to deal in levels of analysis like the paragraph and the essay – the levels which White and Arndt (and similar approaches) most clearly relate to. Indeed, it seems that our two-element framework (with *content specifications* and *operational elements*) is capable of handling both processes and products. Hence White and Arndt's 'generating new ideas' would be analysed in terms of a content specification – 'new ideas'; and an operational element ('generating').

Work on listing processes is still in its infancy, and the categories covered by White and Arndt are large-scale, general (and important) ones. With time the specifications will doubtless become more detailed, and smaller-scale processes will be included. As I write this section, for example, I am aware of undertaking processes like the following: getting rid of word repetitions by employing synonyms; modifying sentences to change topic to comment, comment to topic; making paragraphs begin and end in different places in order to reflect small changes in what it is decided to emphasize.

Once one begins to look seriously at process, floodgates are opened wide. To consider how much fascinating work there is to be done involving the identification (and teaching) of a myriad of processes so far not considered, is indeed an exciting prospect for applied linguistics to contemplate.

To summarize this part of the chapter: we have considered how content will need to be specified on various levels. Some of these will be entirely traditional, because items like *using the present perfect*, like *distinguishing /i/ from /i:/* are important skills. We have also noted that on more semantic, pragmatic levels, skills specifications should consider generativity more and face validity perhaps less. We have also recognized a higher, organizational level related to what is nowadays called the process syllabus.

Operational elements

It is clear from the above that although there will be differences on the level of content specification between a so-called skills syllabus and a traditional one, there will also be substantial similarities. It is when one comes to consider Munby's 'operational elements' that the possibility of real innovation emerges. A recurring theme in this book has been that 'it's not *what* you can do, but *in what conditions* you can do it'. Processing conditions are important not just for teaching methodology (the sphere in which we have so far discussed them), but also for syllabus design. If a syllabus is a statement of what we decide to teach, and if our approach gives importance to the processing dimension, then we might expect the syllabus to make statements regarding processing conditions. We have already noted that there is a tradition of behavioural specification in syllabus design; Munby's work fits into this, and his 'operational elements' illustrate how this tradition does give a degree of consideration to processing conditions.

Important as it is to recognize the processing dimension; it is doubtful to what extent specific and detailed processing specifications can usefully be made in relation to individual items of content. We have several times illustrated processing problems by using the example of a learner who cannot use the present perfect on an intercontinental phone line. This might suggest 'the ability to use the present perfect on an intercontinental phone line' as a candidate item for our skills syllabus. But this degree of detailed mapping of content items (like 'the present perfect') with operational elements (the 'intercontinental phone line') is clearly absurd. What is required is a means of incorporating the processing dimension into syllabus design without resorting to the kind of ultimately vacuous detail which some past attempts have resulted in.

How may this be achieved? We have already noted that lists of the settings, topics and roles which learners will have to deal with have often made their way into syllabus inventories. Settings, topics and roles do of course imply different sorts of processing conditions. As one example, 'the intercontinental phone line' is a setting, so if it appeared on a syllabus, this would clearly imply focus at some point on certain operating conditions. As another example, the lists of both social and psychological role relations would carry many important implications regarding the affective dimension to processing, a dimension which occurred in our consideration of processing factors in chapter 7. We may therefore expect the syllabus inventory lists to carry with them certain sorts of processing constraints. However, settings, topics and roles are not really on the Council of Europe's lists principally because they imply processing conditions. More important for that framework is the fact that they entail the use of different exponents. For example, a Council of Europe syllabus may specify a 'boss to employee' role not because this may involve the learner in operating conditions which might be affectively troublesome (the employee could be scared of the boss). The role relationship is mentioned because associated with it are certain structural and semantic forms. For example, if the learner is learning French this role relationship implies certain consequences regarding the uses of *tu* and *vous*.

If we truly wish to provide coverage of processing conditions in a meaningful way, the coin we need to deal in is the task. In chapter 7 we discussed Prabhu's task-based work, and have considered at some length ways in which tasks may be specified in terms of complexity. It is taxonomies of tasks specified in terms of complexity which provide the syllabus designer with a real processing dimension for his syllabus. Task complexities *are* processing conditions, and for this reason we conclude that task specifications are an essential component for skills syllabuses which wish to incorporate a processing dimension.

From syllabus inventory to syllabus

A syllabus identifies one category type from the syllabus inventory, and makes it a unit of organization. It is a well-established principle of syllabus design that the unit of organization should change in the course of the language-teaching operation. This is clearly seen in Yalden's (1983) 'proportional syllabus', for example, where initial structurally based syllabuses become more communicatively oriented as the programme progresses. Our model identifies different levels of skills analysis, and we can similarly envisage such changes of focus. At one stage the focus might be on structures; later it may be the function that becomes the unit of organization, and yet later (in some situations) processes might become the organizing principle. With all these orientations, the task list will effectively act as specifications of methodology; providing substantial guidance as to the kinds of tasks the language practice will involve and the classroom activities learners will engage in. But it may very well be that in later stages of learning, tasks themselves become the unit of organization so that, superficially at least, one uses a task-based syllabus not dissimilar to that of Prabhu (1987).

Notes

1 Wilkins (e.g. 1976) and others utilize the insurance concept of 'surrender value' in discussion of this matter. The type of course being described here may be said to have low surrender value because if learners have to stop the course before its end, there is relatively little 'payoff' in terms of ability to communicate for all the effort ('investment') put into learning. Wilkins claims that notional/functional courses provide high surrender value.

2 One of the putative values of the 'deep-end strategy' is that it avoids Prabhu's *reproduction*; by placing the free practice first, learners will not be tempted to use structures that have just been taught. The strategy practises important skills associated with risk-taking, because initial free practice may well require them to use structures that that have not yet been taught.

9 Communicative Language Teaching and Information Processing

This final chapter will consider how the conceptualization of language teaching we have been discussing relates to other language-teaching approaches. We wish to clarify not just how our conceptualization is 'new'; but also how it is not – how it links with other traditions found in language teaching today. We shall focus on three language teaching approaches: a version of 'traditional' language teaching which we shall characterize below, recent 'acquisition' approaches, and a version of communicative methodology (CM). The title of this chapter reflects the fact that we shall spend a good deal more time of the last of these than on the other two.

'Traditional' Language Teaching

There is, of course, no one language-teaching approach which may be called 'traditional' – how the term is used will depend on the context of its use. But there is one approach which still has very much currency throughout the world, which has been affected little by recent communicative developments, and is generally perceived of as being 'traditional' (as opposed to innovative). It is a kind of diluted version of audiolingualism, and is well exemplified by textbooks like Broughton's (1968) *Success with English*. A carefully graded structural syllabus is used, presentation is through key sentences, there is a good deal of controlled practice, and the production stage is all but absent.

An important similarity between this traditional approach and the DECPRO pathway is that both are clearly learning models. It might further be thought that both demonstrate the PPP sequence. DECPRO certainly maintains something like it, with declarativization being the aim of the first P, and proceduralization the aim of the subsequent two. But the point was made in chapter 6 that this kind of 'traditional' teaching is in fact very much a two-P model. We argued there that although in recent decades language teaching has improved greatly in this respect, the idea predominated long that once a subskill had been thoroughly explained and drilled in isolation it was as good as mastered. The final P was considered all but unnecessary because something that had been explained and drilled in class would, it was believed, make its own way into the learner's use outside class – transfer from inside to outside class would occur. But, we claimed, presentation and practice are just small beginnings to the task of proceduralization; a great deal more effort is required for automization to be achieved. For us, the final P is seen as central to the operation, and our model is very much a three-P one. The point is vital because the imputed failure of traditional teaching is a major reason why some (see Prabhu 1984, for example) have abandoned it in favour of 'acquisition' approaches. But anyone who considers abandoning the traditional needs to be clear that the failed model is probably a PP__ rather than a PPP one. Where this is the case, restoring the final P is a viable alternative to replacing the entire strategy by some quite different model.

There is a second important different between our conceptualization and this version of the traditional. The concept of automization is central to the former. But did not the drilling procedures of audiolingualism aim to make structural patterns automatic? Carroll (1966) identifies as one of the 'principal ideas' of audiolingualism that 'habits must be automatized as much as possible so that they can be called forth without conscious attention' (p. 101). It might therefore be claimed that automization procedures have already been tried and found wanting (since applied linguists have for decades pronounced audiolingualism to be 'wanting'!). But there is a fundamental difference between automization in audiolingualism and the kind being proposed here. It relates to what exactly is being made automatic. In audiolingualism, patterns were largely drilled with a good degree of form focus. But, as we argued in the previous chapter, the essential skill of communication is getting structures right when there is message focus. Audiolingualism was, quite simply, automizing the wrong skill. 'Getting structures right when there is nothing else to focus attention on' is the skill audiolingualism develops, and this is neither what happens in real communication, nor is it a skill that transfers easily to real communication. To put the matter in terms of the 'minimum conditions' discussion we had in the previous chapter: audiolingual practice is like practising, and automating, the arm movements of the breast stroke on land – nothing whatsoever to do with executing these movements in water.

'Acquisition' Approaches

DECPRO is, as we have noted, a PPP model. Most 'naturalistic' acquisition approaches are, one might argue, exemplars of _ _ P. That is, they avoid formal presentation and practice, and rely on something like free production ('deployment' in Prabhu's 1983 terms) to achieve mastery. This is not to deny an important role for input in such approaches, as well as an incubation stage before production occurs; it could be said that the 'presentation' occurs naturally in input, and the 'practice' occurs silently during incubation.

The difference between 'acquisition' approaches and DECPRO is thus clear. But what about these approaches and PRODEC? We touched on the difference in chapter 4 in the following terms: 'acquisition' approaches are just PRO – that is, they concentrate on the development of procedural knowledge. PRODEC begins with the PRO; but we have argued the need for development of a declarative base out of the procedural knowledge, and although we concede that this may happen naturally, we do envisage pedagogic steps being taken to facilitate this, as discussed in chapter 5. In other words, we actively develop a DEC to follow the PRO. The difference is vital, and led us to speculate, in chapter 7, how much more successful 'acquisition' approaches might be if they permitted instructional measures to provide the DEC to follow the PRO.

At various points in this book we have made mention of Prabhu's experiment in Southern India, and the fact that we find a place for task-based learning in our own framework makes it necessary to specify how our conceptualization relates to his. It is important to note that although the task-based concept owes much to him, his version of task-based teaching is founded on a quite different set of premises. Prabhu's approach is truly acquisition-based: he does not use a linguistic syllabus, has no rule isolation, and largely avoids overt error correction. We have taken 'the task dimension' from Prabhu, but have totally divorced it from this acquisition framework. This is clearly exemplified in our discussion of task complexity, and the various versions of the number exercise developed in chapter 7. These exercises practise structures in isolation, and their complexity is measured in terms of the extent to which they deflect attention from the structure being taught. They are a very far cry indeed from the kind of task-based teaching described in Prabhu (1987).[1]

Communicative Language Teaching

Communicative methodology and its atheoreticality

The 'communicative approach' to language teaching has enjoyed great popularity in recent years, and as a consequence the word 'communicative' has unfortunately suffered the fate of words like 'democracy' and 'freedom' – through overuse they have come to mean whatever the user wants them to mean, usually referring to something generally considered (in some vague way) to be 'a good thing'. Anyone referring to CM therefore needs to clarify which version of 'communicative' is being referred to.

The version of CM we shall be considering here is a British-based one which has enjoyed great popularity throughout the world. It has the following three characteristics relevant to this discussion.

1   It places much importance on the role of message focus in language practice.

2   It attempts to simulate processes of language use by employing techniques like the 'information gap' (as exemplified in version 2 of the number exercise in chapter 7) and 'information transfer' (as in version 5 of the number exercise; see Johnson and Morrow 1981 for a description of this equally ubiquitous technique).

3   It is part of a learning, as opposed to an acquisition, model. It does not avoid one of the characteristics which, we noted at the beginning of chapter 3, Krashen associates with learning: rule isolation, and this is well exemplified by the information-gap exercise just referred to, which practises discrete structures. It is this characteristic in particular which delineates this version of CM from some others that had been put forward.

It is possible to level at this version of CM an accusation which Paulston (1981), among others, levels at the notional/functional syllabus – that it is 'atheoretical as regards learning theory'. The accuracy of this accusation regarding notional/functional is open to dispute; after all, Wilkins (1976) does attempt to associate these syllabus types with a particular view of learning. But it is true to say that the impetus for these kinds of syllabus comes from a view of 'what language and language activity is', rather than a view of 'how people learn'; the notional/functional pedigree lies with Hymes, speech act theory and sociolinguistics, rather than with second language acquisition studies and psychological learning theories.

Though some (notably Brumfit 1984a) do attempt to relate CM to views of learning, its pedigree too lies with a characterization of language rather than of language learning. Consider, for example, the characteristic of 'message focus' referred to above. It would of course be possible to justify this in terms of a view of learning. One might argue, for example, that for a methodology to work, meaningfulness is important; in Stevick's (1976) words, 'method should be the servant of meaning' (p. 160). The justification would then claim that message focus is a central precondition for meaningfulness.

Though such an argument is possible, this is not where this version of CM derives its notion of message focus from. The source here is in the work of linguists like Halliday who characterize language as, centrally, message-focused activity – a system developed for, and existing to, convey messages. Message focus is central to CM because it is central to language use, and communicative methodologists aim to simulate processes of language use in the classroom. So it is as a characteristic of *language* rather than of *language learning* that message focus finds its way into CM.

One might then, with some justice, note a certain atheoreticality as regards learning theory in this version of CM. This is potentially a very serious criticism; to say that any language teaching methodology is not based on a view of how people learn is clearly a potentially damning indictment.

CM and automization

We shall argue here that what this version of CM presents us with are in fact techniques for the proceduralization of language, and that the learning theories we saw in chapter 4 which were concerned with language processing therefore form the natural learning theory home for CM.

Consider the types of techniques we discussed in chapter 7 when attempting to find ways of facilitating the automization of language forms. One example, version 4 of the numbers exercise (figure 7.6) is a memory game. Pupils look at the pictures for a minute, trying to memorize the objects and their numbers. Then they turn the page over, and the teacher (or a partner) asks questions like 'Number one: is it a house?', or 'Number one: is it a bicycle'. Pupils reply, 'No, it isn't' or 'Yes, it is.' Version 3 of the same exercise (figure 7.5) is a 'find the differences' game. Learners working in pairs have pictures of the same scene, but with a small number of differences in the pictures. Pupils question each other in order to find out what the differences are.

Both these exercise types are commonly found in CM; memory games and 'find the difference' exercises are now extremely widespread in communicatively oriented textbooks. The very fact that the examples we elected to present in chapter 7 (to suggest ways of automizing) are central exercise types in CM suggests that what CM is attempting and what chapter 7 is about share something in common. But note how CM would justify these two exercise. Both may be said to involve a kind of information gap, and it would be argued that the existence of this creates the conditions under which basic communicative processes can occur (with communication seen as bridging of the information gap). Mention would also doubtless be made of motivation. Both activities are very controlled drills, yet they are felt to be more interesting and motivating when presented as 'games'; pupils are not mouthing things they all know – there has to be an effort to remember, to inform, to communicate. A term which encapsulates what these activities attempts is 'message focus'; what the information gap does is to make available a message for communication; the pupils' attention is focused on message.

But in chapter 7 we view these exercises from a rather different perspective. In them, we say, the pupils' attention is deflected *away from* the forms that are being practised. So in the memory game attention is engaged in trying to remember, lessening the amount of channel capacity available for concentration on form. The memory element is an artificial attention distractor; a 'parking procedure' precisely of the sort we discussed in relation to **ra-1**. Similarly, in the other exercise (version 3) the activity of trying to find differences may be seen as occupying channel capacity so there is no space left available for thinking about grammar. This characterization sees the same exercises not so much as message focus, but as *form defocus*. In them, a task is being introduced which will deflect the learner's attention from form, as part of a strategy for facilitating automization.

One might argue that this form defocus characterization, as opposed to the standard message focus CM one, is indeed more honest and more satisfactory in terms of what exercises like this actually achieve. In chapter 8, we noted Prabhu's criticism that often 'free practice' exercises in fact involve not real language production but language reproduction; that it, the learners correctly view them as carriers for language points rather than as true opportunities for communication. This criticism holds for many information-gap activities, which often involve a highly restricted amount of message focus. 'Find the differences' activities are a case in point. Unless one is dealing with very young children, it is unlikely that burning desire exists in the classroom to find differences in pictures; this is not what students would really like to talk about. It is not *real* communication, and it seems to be rather stretching the point to describe these exercises as message-focused! What they can more accurately be said to achieve is to direct attention away from form.

The form defocus characterization of these specific exercises can lead us to view the CM universe in general from a slightly different angle. To spell out the argument: the traditional justification for aspects of CM like its concentration on message focus is that language is 'like that' – by simulating message focus, we simulate important processes of communication. We are arguing for a rather different justification, made in terms of form defocus and related to a view of language as skill. It notes that an important characteristic of many skills is 'the ability to get things right when no attention is available for getting them right'. It therefore uses exercises like the ones we have been considering to deflect attention away from form. This ability is important so that higher-order behaviours can be given the attention they require. It just so happens that in the case of language, the 'higher-order behaviour' is often concentration on message: message focus; but the basic concept we are dealing with is a broader one, that of form defocus.

This argument constitutes a reformulation of the aims of CM. What in practical terms will be the result of this reformulation? In the most general sense, the answer is that our central concept now becomes form defocus. Message focus is seen as one brand of form defocus, and the one most developed in CM. But **ra-1** would permit any form of distractor, even very artificial ones. Our reformulation would lead to the development of 'distraction techniques', as discussed in chapter 7. There will also be particular implications. For example, with speed recognized as a factor which can increase or decrease available attention (it was one of the factors we identified in chapter 7 as contributing to task complexity), perhaps we should manipulate this variable more than at present. This might lead in the direction of computer-assisted language learning, where it is possible to set tasks with definite time specifications (and where it is relatively easy to control/vary amounts of time available for particular tasks).

Our reformulation of CM has benefits for CM. The major one is that it now relates to a learning theory, to a concept of automization and to a view of how this comes about. Hence the atheoreticality accusation loses its bite. The new formulation may also have the effect of breathing life into a methodology which, some argue, has lost its way. It is perhaps where the future of CM lies. But the benefits of the reformulation are not all one way. By linking our conceptualization with CM we are providing the former with a ready-made bank of techniques – much of the rich literature on CM becomes relevant to our efforts to facilitate automization. Secondly, and in more abstract terms, our conceptualization becomes part of a whole tradition, and one that has been in the mainstream of language teaching for the past few decades.

The End of the Beginning

The point we have reached is just the end of a beginning. We have done little more here than establish a number of principles, the main ones relating to the processes of declarativization and proceduralization. We have claimed that many applied linguistic problems may be stated in terms of these processes, arguing that both are important to language teaching. We acknowledge that there is more than one path to second language mastery, and that these various paths have their own problems and solutions for the provision of declarative and procedural knowledge.

One of the attractive aspects of the conceptualization we have been following is that it suggests rich agendas for further work. For one thing, the skills literature does indeed contain much interesting information that has not so far been considered in relation to language teaching in any real detail. The effect of our preparedness to take a 'new' orientation is to open a whole new area of literature to the applied linguist. Secondly, there are various other skill models to explore in relation to language teaching, and we have not really done this to any degree here. The day will perhaps dawn when the Suzuki method of violin playing is studied for its implications for language teaching (perhaps even becoming prescribed study for TESOL students!). And who knows – maybe one day someone will write a further volume in the *Inner Game* series entitled *The Inner Game of Language Learning*. Thirdly, as we have noted particularly in chapters 7 and 8, there are areas where a great deal of interesting research suggests itself. The two areas mentioned in those chapters were research into task complexity, and into the specification of processes involved in language use.

Note

1 It is also clearly distinguishable from other task-based approaches, such as Long's (1985 and forthcoming).

Bibliography

Abbs, B., Ayton, A. and Freebairn, I. 1975 *Strategies* Harlow: Longman

Allwright, R. L., Woodley, M.-P. and Allwright, J. M. 1984 'Investigating reformulation as a practical strategy for the teaching of academic writing'. Paper presented at the BAAL Annual Meeting, Bangor, September

Anderson, J. R. 1980 *Cognitive Psychology and Its Implications* San Francisco: W. H. Freeman

Anderson, J. R. 1981 'A theory of language acquisition based on general learning mechanisms'. *Proceedings of the Seventh International Joint Conference on Artificial Intelligence*, 97–103

Anderson, J. R. 1982 'Acquisition of cognitive skill'. *Psychological Review* 89/4: 369–406

Anderson, J. R. 1983 *The Architecture of Cognition* Cambridge, Mass.: Harvard University Press

Anderson, R. C. and Pearson, P. D. 1988 'A schema-theoretic view of basic processes in reading comprehension'. In Carrell, P. L., Devine, J. and Eskey, D. (eds) *Interactive Approaches to Second Language Reading* Cambridge: Cambridge University Press, pp. 37–55

Annett, J. 1969 *Feedback and Human Learning* Harmondsworth: Penguin

Appel, G. and Goldberg, M. 1984 'Referential choice in second language narrative production'. In Dechert, H. W., Möhle, D. and Raupach, M. (eds) *Second Language Productions* Tübingen: Gunter Narr, pp. 138–55

Bartlett, F. C. 1932 *Remembering* Cambridge: Cambridge University Press

Bartlett, F. C. 1947 'The measurement of human skill'. *British Medical Journal* 4510–11: 835–80

Bartsch, R. and Vennemann, T. 1972 *Semantic Structures: A Study in the Relation between Semantics and Syntax* Frankfurt: Athenäum Verlag

Bechtel, W. and Abrahamsen, A. 1991 *Connectionism and the Mind* Oxford: Basil Blackwell

Beretta, A. and Davies, A. 1985 'Evaluation of the Bangalore project'. *ELT Journal* 39/2: 121–7

Bever, T. 1970 'The cognitive basis for linguistic strctures'. In Hayes, J. R. (ed.) *Cognition and the Development of Language* New York: Wiley

Bever, T. and Townsend, D. 1979 'Perceptual mechanisms and formal properties of main and subordinate clauses'. In Cooper, W. E. and Walker, E. C. T. (eds) *Sentence Processing: Psycholinguistic Studies Presented to Merril Garrett* Hillsdale, N. J.: Lawrence Erlbaum

Bialystok, E. 1978 'A theoretical model of second language learning'. *Language Learning* 28: 69–83

Bialystok, E. 1982 'On the relationship between knowing and using linguistic forms'. *Applied Linguistics* 3/3: 181–206

Bialystok, E. 1984 'Strategies in interlanguage learning and performance'. In Davies, A., Criper, C. and Howatt, A. P. R. (eds) *Interlanguage* Edinburgh: Edinburgh University Press, pp. 37–48

Bialystok, E. 1988 'Psycholinguistic dimensions of second language proficiency'. In Rutherford, W. and Smith, M. S. (eds) *Grammar and Second Language Teaching* Rowley, Mass.: Newbury House

Bialystok, E. 1990 'The competence of processing'. Paper presented at the colloquium on the Scope and Theory of Second Language Learning, TESOL Convention, San Francisco, March

Bialystok, E. and Ryan, E. B. 1985 'Towards a definition of metalinguistic skill'. *Merrill–Palmer Quarterly* 31: 229–51

Bialystok, E. and Sharwood Smith, M. 1985 'Interlanguage is not a state of mind: an evaluation of the construct for second-language acquisition'. *Applied Linguistics* 6/2: 101–17

Bobrow, D. G. and Norman, D. A. 1975 'Some principles of memory schemata'. In Bobrow, D. G. and Collins, A. M. (eds) *Representation and Understanding: Studies in Cognitive Science* New York: Academic Press

Bolinger, D. 1968 *Aspects of Language* New York: Harcourt Brace Jovanovich

Book, W. F. 1925 *Learning to Typewrite* New York: Gregg

Breen, M. P. 1987 'Contemporary paradigms in syllabus design'. *Language Teaching* 20/2: 81–92; 20/3: 157–74

Broughton, G. 1968 *Success with English* Harmondsworth: Penguin

Brown, G., Anderson, A., Shillcock, R. and Yule, G. 1984 *Teaching Talk* Cambridge: Cambridge University Press

Brown, R. 1970 'The first sentences of child and chimpanzee'. In *Psycholinguistics: Selected Papers* New York: Wiley, p. 222

Brumfit, C. J. 1979 ' "Communicative" language teaching: an educational perspective'. In Brumfit, C. J. and Johnson, K. (eds) *The Communicative Approach to Language Teaching* Oxford: Oxford University Press, pp. 183–91

Brumfit, C. J. 1981 'Notional syllabuses revisited: a response'. *Applied Linguistics* 2/1: 90–2

Brumfit, C. J. 1984a *Communicative Methodology in Language Teaching* Cambridge: Cambridge University Press

Brumfit, C. J. 1984b 'The Bangalore procedural syllabus'. *ELT Journal* 38/4: 233–41

Burt, M. and Dulay, H. 1980 'On acquisition orders'. In Felix, S. (ed.) *Second Language Development* Tübingen: Gunther Narr, pp. 265–327

Bygate, M. 1994 'Adjusting the focus: teacher roles in task-based learning of grammar'. In Bygate, M., Tonkyn, A. and Williams, E. (eds) *Grammar and the Language Teacher* London: Prentice-Hall, pp. 237–59

Bygate, M., Tonkyn, A. and Williams, E. 1994 (eds) *Grammar and the Language Teacher* London: Prentice-Hall

Byrne, D. 1976 *Teaching Oral English* Harlow: Longman

Canale, M. and Swain, M. 1980 'Theoretical bases of communicative approaches to second language teaching and testing'. *Applied Linguistics* 1: 1–47

Candlin, C. N. 1987 'Towards task based language learning'. In Candlin, C. N. and Murphy, D. (eds) *Language Learning Tasks* Englewood Cliffs, New Jersey: Prentice-Hall

Carmichael, L., Hogan, H. P. and Walter, A. 1932 'An experimental study of the effect of language on the reproduction of visually perceived form'. *Journal of Experimental Psychology* 15: 73–86

Carr, H. A. 1930 'Teaching and learning'. *Journal of Genetic Psychology* 37: 189–218

Carrell, P. L. and Esterhold, J. C. 'Schema theory in ESL reading pedagogy'. In Carrell, P. L., Devine, J. and Eskey, D. (eds) *Interactive Approaches to Second Language Reading* Cambridge: Cambridge University Press, pp. 73–92

Carroll, J. B. 1966 'The contribution of psychological theory and educational research to the teaching of foreign languages'. In Valdman, A. (ed.) *Trends in Language Teaching* New York: McGraw Hill, pp. 93–106

Carroll, J. B. 1973 'Implications for aptitude testing research and psycholinguistic theory for foreign language teaching'. *Linguistics* 112: 5–14

Carroll, J. B. and Casagrande, J. B. 1958 'The functions of language classifications in behavior'. In Maccoby, E. E., Newcomb, T. M. and Hartley, E. L. (eds) *Readings in Social Psychology* New York: Holt, Rinehart and Winston

Cellerier, G. 1980 'Cognitive strategies in problem solving'. In Piatelli-Palmarini, M. (ed.) *Language and Learning* London: Routledge and Kegan Paul, pp. 67–72

Cherry, C. 1957 *On Human Communication* Boston, Mass.: MIT Press

Chomsky, C. 1969 *The Acquisition of Syntax in Children from 5 to 10* Cambridge, Mass.: MIT Press

Chomsky, N. 1964 'Formal discussion of Miller and Ervin's paper'. In Bellugi, U. and Brown, R. (eds) *The Acquisition of Language* Chicago: University of Chicago Press, pp. 35–9

Chomsky, N. 1965 *Aspects of the Theory of Syntax* Cambridge, Mass.: MIT Press

Chomsky, N. 1980 'On cognitive structures and their development: a reply to Piaget'. In Piatelli-Palmarini, M. (ed.) *Language and Learning* London: Routledge and Kegan Paul, pp. 35–52

Chomsky, N. 1981 *Lectures on Government and Binding* Dortrecht: Foris

Chomsky, N. 1986 *Knowledge of Language* New York: Praeger

Chomsky, N. 1987 'The nature, use and acquisition of language'. 'Open Forum' Lecture, Open University, Milton Keynes, April

Chomsky, N. 1988 *Language and Problems of Knowledge* Cambridge, Mass.: MIT Press

Chomsky, N. and Halle, M. 1968 *The Sound Pattern of English* New York: Harper and Row

Clahsen, H. 1984 'The acquisition of German word order. A test case for cognitive approaches to second language development'. In Anderson, R. W. (ed.) *Second Languages* Rowley, Mass.: Newbury House

Clahsen, H. 1988 'Paramaterized grammatical theory and language acquisition: a study of the acquisition of verb placement and inflection by children and adults'. In Flynn, S. and O'Neill, W. (eds) *Linguistic Theory in Second Language Acquisition* Dortrecht: Kluwer, 47–75

Clahsen, H. and Muysken, P. 1986 'The availability of universal grammar to adult and child learners'. *Second Language Research* **2**: 93–119

Clahsen, H., Meisel, J. and Pienemann, M. 1983 *Deutsch als Zweitsprache. Der Spracherwerb ausländischer Arbeiter* Tübingen: Gunter Narr

Clark, H. H. and Clark, E. V. 1977 *Psychology and Language* New York: Harcourt Brace Jovanovich

Cohen, A. D. 1983 'Reformulating compositions'. *TESOL Newsletter* **17/6**: 1–5

Colley, A. M. and Beech, J. R. 1989 'Acquiring and performing cognitive skills'. In Colley, A. M. and Beech, J. R. (eds) *Acquisition and Performance of Cognitive Skills* Chichester: John Wiley, pp. 1–16

Colville, F. M. 1957 'The learning of motor skills as influenced by knowledge of mechanical principles'. *Journal of Educational Psychology* **48**: 321–7

Comrie, B. and Keenan, E. 1978 'Noun phrase accessibility revisited'. *Language* **55**: 649–64

Cook, G. 1994 'Language play in advertisements: some implications for applied linguistics'. In Graddol, D. and Swann, J. (eds) *Evaluating Language* Clevedon: BAAL/Multilingual Matters, pp. 102–16

Cook, V. J. 1985 'Chomsky's universal grammar and second language learning'. *Applied Linguistics* **6/1**: 2–18

Cook, V. J. 1988 *Chomsky's Universal Grammar* Oxford: Blackwell

Cook, V. J. 1991a *Second Language Learning and Language Teaching* London: Edward Arnold

Cook, V. J. 1991b 'Review of Lydia White's *Universal Grammar and Second Language Acquisition*'. *System*

Cook, V. J. 1993 *Linguistics and Second Language Acquisition* Basingstoke: Macmillan

Cook, V. J. and Newson, M. 1995 *Chomsky's Universal Grammar* Revised edition, Oxford: Blackwell

Corder, S. P. 1981 *Error Analysis and Interlanguage* Oxford: Oxford University Press

Craik, K. J. W. 1943 *The Nature of Explanation* Cambridge: Cambridge University Press

Cromer, R. F. 1991 *Language and Thought in Normal and Handicapped Children* Oxford: Blackwell

Crookes, G. 1989 'Planning and interlanguage variation'. *Studies in Second Language Acquisition* 11: 367–83

Crookes, G. and Gass, S. M. 1993a *Tasks and Language Learning: Integrating Theory and Practice* Clevedon: Multilingual Matters

Crookes, G. and Gass, S. M. 1993b *Tasks in a Pedagogical Context: Integrating Theory and Practice* Clevedon: Multilingual Matters

Crossman, E. R. F. W. 1959 'A theory of the acquisition of speed-skill'. *Ergonomics* 2: 153–66

Crossman, E. R. F. W. 1960 'The information capacity of the human motor system in pursuit tracking'. In Legge, D. (ed.) *Skills* Harmondsworth: Penguin

Crystal, D. 1987 *The Cambridge Encyclopedia of Language* Cambridge: Cambridge University Press

Dechert, H. W. 1984 'Second Language productions: six hypotheses'. In Dechert, H. W., Möhle, D. and Raupach, M. (eds) *Second Language Productions* Tübingen: Gunter Narr, pp. 211–30

Dechert, H. W. 1987 'Understanding producing'. In Dechert, H. W. and Raupach, M. (eds) *Psycholinguistic Models of Production* Norwood, N. J.: Ablex Publishing Corporation, pp. 229–34

Dechert, H. W. 1989 'On the natural order of events'. In Dechert, H. W. and Raupach, M. (eds) *Transfer in Language Production* Norwood, N. J.: Ablex Publishing Corporation, pp. 237–70

Dechert, H. W. 1992 ' "The study of neurolinguistics made me notice what school grammar is" '. In Leirbukt, O. and Lindemann, B. (eds) *Psycholinguistische und didaktische Aspekte des Fremdsprachenlernens* Tübingen: Gunter Narr

Demyankov, V. Z. 1983 'Understanding as an interpreting activity'. *Voprosy yazykoznaniya* 32: 58–67

Dinnsen, D. A. and Eckman, F. 1975 'A functional explanation of some phonological typologies'. In Grossman, R. (ed.) *Functionalism* Chicago: University of Chicago Press

Dornic, S. 1979 'Information processing in bilinguals: some selected issues'. *Psychological Research* 40: 329–48

Dreyfus, H. L. and Dreyfus, S. E. 1986 *Mind over Machine: The Power of Human Intuition and Expertise in the Era of the Computer* New York: The Free Press

Dulay, H. and Burt, M. 1973 'Should we teach children syntax?' *Language Learning* 23/2: 245–58

Dulay, H. and Burt, M. 1974 'Natural sequences in child second language acquisition'. *Language Learning* 24/1: 37–53

Eckman, F. 1977 'Markedness and the contrastive analysis hypothesis'. *Language Learning* 27: 315–30

Ellis, R. 1985a *Understanding Second Language Acquisition* Oxford: Oxford University Press

Ellis, R. 1985b 'Sources of variability in interlanguage'. *Applied Linguistics* 6/2: 118–31

Ellis, R. 1987 'Interlanguage variability in narrative discourse: style shifting in the use of the past tense'. *Studies in Second Language Acquisition* 9: 12–20

Ellis, R. 1989 'Sources of intra-language variability in language use and their relationship to second language acquisition'. In Gass, S., Madden, C., Preston, D. and Selinker L. (eds) *Variation in Second Language Acquisition, Vol. 2* Clevedon: Multilingual Matters, pp. 22–45

Ellis, R. 1990 *Instructed Second Language Acquisition* Oxford: Blackwell

Ericsson, K. A. and Smith, J. 1991 'Prospects and limits of the empirical study of expertise: an introduction'. In Ericsson, K. A. and Smith, J. (eds) *Towards a General Theory of Expertise* Cambridge: Cambridge University Press, pp. 1–38

Faerch, C. and Kasper, G. 1983 'Plans and strategies in foreign language communication'. In Faerch, C. and Kasper, G. (eds) *Strategies in Interlanguage Communication* Harlow: Longman, pp. 20–60

Faerch, C. and Kasper, G. 1985 'Procedural knowledge as a component of foreign language learners' communicative competence'. In Bolte, H. and Herrlitz, W. (eds) *Kommunikation im Sprachunterricht* Utrecht: Rijksuniversiteit, pp. 167–99

Faerch, C. and Kasper, G. 1986 'Cognitive dimensions of language transfer'. In Kellerman, E. and Sharwood Smith, M. (eds) *Crosslinguistic Influence in Second Language Acquisition* New York: Pergamon, pp. 49–65

Felix, S. W. 1986 *Cognition and Language Growth* Dortrecht: Foris

Fitts, P. M. 1964 'Perceptual-motor skill learning'. In Melton, A. W. (ed.) *Categories of Human Learning* New York: Academic Press

Fitts, P. M. and Posner, M. I. 1967 *Human Performance* Belmont, Calif.: Brooks Cole

Fodor, J. A. 1980 'Fixation of belief and concept acquisition'. In Piatelli-Palmarini, M. (ed.) *Language and Learning* London: Routledge and Kegan Paul, pp. 143–9

Fodor, J. A. 1983 *The Modularity of Mind* Cambridge, Mass.: MIT Press

Gallwey, W. T. 1974 *The Inner Game of Tennis* New York: Random House

Gardner, R. A. and Gardner, B. T. 1969 'Teaching sign language to a chimpanzee'. *Science* 165: 664–72

Gass, S. 1979 'Language transfer and universal grammatical relations'. *Language Learning* 27: 327–44

Gass, S. 1984 'The empirical basis for the universal hypothesis in interlanguage studies'. In Davies, A. and Criper, C. (eds) *Interlanguage: Proceedings of the Seminar in Honour of Pit Corder* Edinburgh: Edinburgh University Press

Gass, S. and Ard, J. 1984 'Second language acquisition and the ontology of language universals'. In Rutherford, W. (ed.) *Second Language Acquisition and Language Universals* Amsterdam: John Benjamins

Gasser, M. 1990 'Connectionism and universals of second language acquisition'. *Studies in Second Language Acquisition* 12: 179–99

Gawain, S. 1978 *Creative Visualisation* London: Bantam Books

Gilhooly, K. J. and Green, A. J. K. 1989 'Learning problem-solving skills'. In Colley, A. M. and Beech, J. R. 1989 (eds) *Acquisition and Performance of Cognitive Skills* Chichester: John Wiley, pp. 85–112

Gleitman, L. R., Gleitman, H. and Shipley, E. F. 1972 'The emergence of the child as grammarian'. *Cognition* 1: 137–64

Gradman, H. 1971 'Limitations of contrastive analysis predictions'. *Working Papers in Linguistics* 3: 11–15

Green, B. and Gallwey, W. T. 1986 *The Inner Game of Music* London: Pan Books

Greenberg, J. H. (ed.) 1963 *Universals of Language* Cambridge, Mass.: MIT Press

Gregg, K. R. 1984 'Krashen's monitor and Occam's razor'. *Applied Linguistics* 5: 79–100

Grierson, H. J. C. 1945 *Rhetoric and English Composition* London: Oliver and Boyd

Griffiths, R. 1991 'Pausological research in an L2 context: a rationale, and review of selected studies'. *Applied Linguistics* 12/4: 345–62

Halliday, M. A. K. 1961 'Categories of the theory of grammar'. *Word* 17: 241–92

Halliday, M. A. K. 1970 'Language structure and language function'. In Lyons, J. (ed.) *New Horizons in Linguistics* Harmondsworth: Penguin, 140–65

Halliday, M. A. K. 1973 'Towards a sociological semantics'. In *Explorations in the Functions of Language* London: Edward Arnold, 72–102

Hatch, E. and Hawkins, B. 1985 'Second language acquisition: an experiential approach'. In Rosenberg, S. (ed.) *Advances in Applied Sociolinguistics, Vol. 2* New York: Cambridge University Press, pp. 241–83

Hatch, E., Polin, P. and Part, S. 1970 'Acoustic scanning or syntactic processing'. Paper presented to Western Psychological Association, San Francisco

Henning, G. H. 1979 'Remembering foreign language vocabulary: acoustic and semantic parameters'. *Language Learning* 23: 185–96

Herriot, P. 1970 *An Introduction to the Psychology of Language* London: Methuen

Hockett, C. F. 1960 'The origin of speech'. *Scientific American*, September: 203

Holding, D. H. 1965 *Principles of Training* Oxford: Pergamon Press

Holding, D. 1989 'Skills research'. In Holding, D. (ed.) *Human Skills* Chichester: John Wiley, pp. 1–16

Hornstein, N. and Weinberg, A. 1981 'Case theory and preposition stranding'. *Linguistic Enquiry* 12: 55–91

Huey, E. B. 1968 *The Psychology and Pedagogy of Reading* Cambridge, Mass.: MIT Press

Hulstijn, J. H. 1990 'A comparison between the information-processing and the analysis/control approaches to language learning'. *Applied Linguistics* 11/1: 30–45

Hulstijn, J. H. and Hulstijn, W. 1984 'Grammatical errors as a function of processing constraints and explicit knowledge'. *Language Learning* 34/1: 23–43

Hyltenstam, K. 1982 'Language, typology, language universals, markedness and second language acquisition'. Paper presented at the Second European-North American Workshop of Second Language Acquisition Research, Göhrde, Germany, 22–9 August

Hymes, D. 1970 'On communicative competence'. In Gumperz, J. J. and Hymes, D. (eds) *Directions in Sociolinguistics* New York: Holt, Rinehart and Winston, pp. 269–93

Inhelder, B. 1980 'Language and knowledge in a constructivist framework'. In Piatelli-Palmarini, M. (ed.) *Language and Learning* London: Routledge and Kegan Paul, pp. 132–7

Johnson, H. 1992 'Defossilizing'. *ELT Journal* **46/2**: 180–9

Johnson, H. W. 1961 'Skills = speed × accuracy × form × adaptability'. *Perceptual and Motor Skills* **13**: 163–70

Johnson, K. 1979 'Communicative approaches and communicative processes'. In Brumfit, C. J. and Johnson, K. (eds) *The Communicative Approach to Language Teaching* Oxford: Oxford University Press

Johnson, K. 1980a 'The "deep end" strategy in communicative language teaching'. *MEXTESOL* **4/2**: 34–42. Reprinted in Johnson, K. 1982 *Communicative Syllabus Design and Methodology* Oxford: Pergamon Institute of English, pp. 192–200

Johnson, K. 1980b 'Making drills communicative'. *Modern English Teacher* **7/4**: 23–5. Reprinted in Johnson, K. *Communicative Syllabus Design and Methodology* 1982 Oxford: Pergamon Institute of English, pp. 156–62

Johnson, K. 1982a *Now for English* Walton-on-Thames: Thomas Nelson

Johnson, K. 1982b *Communicative Syllabus Design and Methodology* Oxford: Pergamon Institute of English

Johnson, K. 1983a 'Communicative writing practice and Aristotelian rhetoric'. In Freedman, A., Pringle, I. and Yalden, J. (eds) *Learning to Write: First Language/Second Language* Harlow: Longman, pp. 247–57

Johnson, K. 1983b 'Syllabus design: possible future trends'. In Johnson, K. and Porter, D. (eds) *Perspectives in Communicative Language Teaching* London: Academic Press, pp. 47–58

Johnson, K. 1983c 'The application of functional syllabuses'. In Johnson, K. and Morrow, K. (eds) *Functional Materials and the Classroom Teacher* Oxford: Modern English Publications, pp. 16–20

Johnson, K. 1986 'Language teaching as skill training'. Paper delivered at the Second Colloquium on Language Teaching, Centre for Applied Language Studies, University of Reading, May, mimeo

Johnson, K. 1988 'Mistake correction'. *English Language Teaching Journal* **42/2**: 89–96

Johnson, K. and Morrow, K. 1981 *Communication in the Classroom* Harlow: Longman

Judd, C. H. 1908 'The relation of special training to general intelligence'. *Educational Review* **36**: 28–42

Kahneman, D. 1973 *Attention and Effort* Englewood Cliffs, N.J.: Prentice-Hall.

Karmiloff-Smith, A. 1986 'Stage/structure versus phase/process in modelling linguistic and cognitive development'. In Levin, I. (ed.) *Stage and Structure: Reopening the Debate* Norwood, N.J.: Ablex Publishing Corporation, pp. 164–90

Karmiloff-Smith, A. 1992 *Beyond Modularity* Cambridge, Mass.: MIT Press

Katz, N., Baker, E. and Macnamara, J. 1974 'What's in a name? A study of how children learn common and proper names'. *Child Development* 45: 469–73

Keele, S. W. 1973 *Attention and Human Performance* Pacific Palisades, Calif.: Goodyear

Kellerman, E. 1979 'Transfer and non-transfer: where are we now?' *Studies in Second Language Acquisition* 2: 37–57

Kiparsky, P. 1974 'Remarks on analogical change'. In Anderson, J. M. and Jones, C. (eds) *Historical Linguistics* Amsterdam: North Holland

Köpcke, K.-M. 1989 'Erwerb morphologischer Ausdrucksmittel'. *Zeitschrift für Sprachwissenschaft* 6

Koster, J. 1978 *Locality Principles in Syntax* Dortrecht: Floris

Krashen, S. D. 1977 'The monitor model for adult second language performance'. In Burt, M. K., Dulay, H. C. and Finocchiaro, M. (eds) *Viewpoints on English as a Second Language* New York: Regents, pp. 152–61

Krashen, S. D. 1982 *Principles and Practice in Second Language Acquisition* Oxford: Pergamon Institute of English

Krashen, S. D. 1983 BBC *Horizon,* 'A Child's Guide to Language'

Krashen, S. D. and Terrell, T. D. 1983 *The Natural Approach* New York: Pergamon and Alemany

Langacker, R. W. 1987 *Foundations of Cognitive Grammar* Stanford, Calif.: Stanford University Press

Langley, P. and Simon, H. A. 1981 'The central role of learning in cognition'. In Anderson, J. R. (ed.) *Cognitive Skills and Their Acquisition* Hillsdale, N.J.: Lawrence Erlbaum

Lawler, J. and Selinker, L. 1971 'On paradoxes, rules and research in second language learning'. *Language Learning* 21: 27–43

Legge, D. and Barber, P. J. 1976 *Information and Skill* London: Methuen

Lenneberg, E. H. 1966 'The natural history of language'. In Smith, F. and Miller, G. A. (eds) *The Genesis of Language* Cambridge, Mass.: MIT Press

Lennon, P. 1984 'Retelling a story in English as a second language'. In Dechert, H. W., Möhle, D. and Raupach, M. (eds) *Second Language Productions* Tübingen: Gunter Narr, pp. 50–68

Levenston, E. A. 1978 'Error analysis of free composition: the theory and the practice'. *Indian Journal of Applied Linguistics* 4/1: 1–11

Liceras, J. M. 1989 'On some properties of the "pro-drop" parameter: looking for missing subjects in non-native Spanish'. In Gass, S. M. and Schachter, J. (eds) 1989 *Linguistics Perspectives on Second Language Acquisition* Cambridge: Cambridge University Press, pp. 109–133

Levelt, W. J. M. 1978 'Skill theory and language teaching'. *Studies in Second Language Acquisition* 1: 53–70

Levelt, W. J. M. 1989 *Speaking* Cambridge, Mass.: MIT Press

Long, M. H. 1985 'A role for instruction in second language acquisition: task-based language training'. In Hyltenstam, K. and Pienemann, M. (eds) *Modelling and Assessing Second Language Acquisition* Clevedon: Multilingual Matters, pp. 77–100

Long, M. H. in press *Task-Based Language Teaching* Oxford: Basil Blackwell

Long, M. H. and Crookes, G. 1993 'Units of analysis in syllabus design: the case for task'. In Crookes, G. and Gass, S. M. (eds) *Tasks in a Pedagogical Context: Integrating Theory and Practice* Clevedon: Multilingual Matters, pp. 9–54

Lyons, J. 1968 *Introduction to Theoretical Linguistics* Cambridge: Cambridge University Press

MacKay, D. M. 1972 'Formal analysis of communicative processes'. In Hinde, R. A. (ed.) *Non-Verbal Communication* Cambridge: Cambridge University Press

Mackey, W. F. 1965 *Language Teaching Analysis* Harlow: Longman

Mandler, J. M. 1983 'Representation.' In Flavell, J. and Markman, E. (eds) *Handbook of Child Psychology Vol. 3* New York: Wiley

Mandler, J. M. 1988 'How to build a baby: on the development of an accessible representational system'. *Cognitive Development* 3: 247–64

Matthews, A., Spratt, M. and Dangerfield, L. 1985 *At the Chalkface* London: Edward Arnold

Mazurkewich, I. 1984 'The acquisition of the dative alternation by second language learners and linguistic theory'. *Language Learning* 34: 91–109

McDonough, S. H. 1981 *Psychology in Foreign Language Teaching* London: Allen and Unwin

McLaughlin, B. 1987 *Theories of Second-Language Learning* London: Edward Arnold

McLaughlin, B. 1990 'Restructuring'. *Applied Linguistics* 11/2: 113–28

McNeill, D. 1966 'The creation of language by children'. In Lyons, J. and Wales, R. J. (eds) *Psycholinguistic Papers* Edinburgh: Edinburgh University Press, pp. 99–115

Miller, G. A., Galanter, E. and Pribram, K. H. 1960 *Plans and the Structure of Behavior* New York: Holt, Rinehard, Winston

Möhle, D. 1984 'A comparison of the second language speech production of different native speakers'. In Dechert, H. W., Möhle, D. and Raupach, M. (eds) *Second Language Productions* Tübingen: Gunter Narr, pp. 26–49

Möhle, D. and Raupach, M. 1983 *Planen in der Fremdsprache* Bern: Lang Verlag

Möhle, D. and Raupach, M. 1987 'The representation problem in interlanguage theory'. In Lorscher, W. (ed.) *Perspectives on Language in Performance* Tübingen: Gunter Narr, pp. 1158–73

Möhle, D. and Raupach, M. 1989 'Language transfer of procedural knowledge'. In Dechert, H. W. and Raupach, M. (eds) *Transfer in Language Production* Norwood, N. J.: Ablex Publishing Corporation, pp. 195–215

Morrow, K. 1981 'Teaching the "general" student'. In Johnson, K. and Morrow, K. (eds) *Communication in the Classroom* Harlow: Longman, pp. 52–8

Moulton, W. 1962 *The Sounds of English and German* Chicago: University of Chicago Press

Munby, J. 1978 *Communicative Syllabus Design* Cambridge: Cambridge University Press

Muñoz-Liceras, J. 1983 *Markedness, Contrastive Analysis and the Acquisition of Spanish Syntax by English Speakers* PhD Thesis: University of Toronto

Naiman, N., Fröhlich, H., Stern, H. and Todesco, A. 1978 *The Good Language Learner* Ontario Institute for Studies in Education: Research in Education Series, 7

Neves, D. M. and Anderson, J. R. 1981 'Knowledge compilation: mechanisms for the automization of cognitive skills'. In Anderson, J. R. (ed.) *Cognitive Skills and Their Acquisition* Hillside, N.J.: Lawrence Erlbaum Associates, pp. 57–84

Newmark, L. 1979 'How not to interfere with language learning'. In Brumfit, C. J. and Johnson, K. (eds) *The Communicative Approach to Language Teaching* Oxford: Oxford University Press, pp. 160–6

Newmark, L. and Reibel, D. A. 1968 'Necessity and sufficiency in language learning'. *International Review of Applied Linguistics* **6/2**: 145–64

O'Connell, D. C. and Kowal, S. 1980 'Prospectus for a science of pausology'. In Dechert, H. W. and Raupach, M. (eds) *Temporal Variables in Speech: Studies in Honour of Frieda Goldman-Eisler* The Hague: Mouton, pp. 3–10

Oldfield, R. S. 1959 'The analysis of human skills'. In Halmos, P. and Iliffe, A. (eds) *Readings in General Psychology* London: Routledge and Kegan Paul

O'Mahoney, M. and Muhiudeen, H. 1977 'A preliminary study of alternative taste languages using qualitative description of sodium chloride solutions: Malay versus English'. *British Journal of Psychology* **68**: 275–8

O'Malley, J. M. and Chamot, A. U. 1990 *Learning Strategies in Second Language Acquisition* Cambridge: Cambridge University Press

O'Malley, J. M., Chamot, A. U. and Walker, C. 1987 'Some applications of cognitive theory to second language acquisition'. *Studies in Second Language Acquisition* **9**: 287–306

Paulston, C. B. 1981 'Notional syllabuses revisited: some comments'. *Applied Linguistics*, **2/1**: 93–5

Peterson, L. R. 1975 *Learning* Glenview, Ill.: Scott, Foresman

Petitto, L. A. 1987 'On the autonomy of language and gesture: evidence from the acquisition of personal pronouns in American Sign Language'. *Cognition* **27**: 1–52

Phinney, M. 1981 *Syntactic Constraints and the Acquisition of Embedded Sentential Complements* PhD thesis: University of Massachusetts, Amherst

Piaget, J. 1954 'Language and thought from the genetic point of view'. In Adams, P. (ed.) *Language in Thinking* Harmonsdworth: Penguin, 1972: pp. 170–9

Piaget, J. 1968 'The stages of the intellectual development of the child'. In Wason, P.C. and Johnson-Laird, P. N. (eds) *Thinking and Reasoning* Harmondsworth: Penguin, pp. 355–63

Piaget, J. 1980 'Open discussion of Fodor's paper: "Fixation of belief and concept acquisition"'. In Piatelli-Palmarini, M. (ed.) *Language and Learning* London: Routledge and Kegan Paul, pp. 143–9

Piatelli-Palmarini, M. (ed.) 1980 *Language and Learning* London: Routledge and Kegan Paul

Pienemann, M. 1985 'Learnability and syllabus construction'. In Hyltenstam, K.

and Pienemann, M. (eds) *Modelling and Assessing Second Language Acquisition* Clevedon, Avon: Multilingual Matters, 23–76

Pienemann, M. 1989 'Is language teachable?' *Applied Linguistics* **10**: 52–79

Politzer, R. L. 1961 *Teaching French: An Introduction to Applied Linguistics* Boston: Ginn & Co

Pollock, J.-Y. 1989 'Verb movement, universal grammar, and the structure of IP'. *Linguistic Enquiry* **20**: 365–424

Poulton, E. C. 1957 'On prediction in skilled movements'. *Psychological Bulletin* 54, 467–78

Prabhu, N. S. 1983 'Procedural syllabuses'. Paper delivered at the eighteenth SEAMO/RELC Seminar, Singapore, April

Prabhu, N. S. 1984 'Communicative teaching: "communicative" in what sense?' Paper delivered at the SEAMO/RELC Conference on Communicative Language Teaching, Singapore, April

Prabhu, N. S. 1985 'Guided and unguided grammar construction'. Paper delivered at the BAAL seminar on grammar teaching, Bath

Prabhu, N. S. 1986 'The Bangalore Project', interview by K. Johnson. Video, Centre for Applied Language Studies, University of Reading

Prabhu, N. S. 1987 *Second Language Pedagogy: A Perspective* Oxford: Oxford University Press

Premack, D. 1980 'Open discussion of Chomsky's paper: "the linguistic approach"'. In Piatelli-Palmarini, M. (ed.) *Language and Learning* London: Routledge and Kegan Paul, pp. 109–30

Premack, D. 1986 *Gavagai! Or the Future History of the Animal Language Controversy* Cambridge, Mass,: MIT Press

Premack, D. 1988 'Does the chimpanzee have a theory of mind?' In Byrne, R. and Whitten, A. (eds) *Machiavellian Intelligence* Oxford: Clarendon Press, p. 161

Premack, A. J. and Premack, D. 1972 'Teaching language to an ape'. *Scientific American* **227**: 92–9

Putnam, H. 1980 'What is innate and why'. In Piatelli-Palmarini, M. (ed.) *Language and Learning* London: Routledge and Kegan Paul, pp. 287–309

Raupach, M. 1987 'Procedural learning in advanced learners of a foreign language'. In Coleman, J. and Towell, R. (eds) *The Advanced Language Learner* London: CILTR, pp. 123–56

Reed, G. F. 1968 'Skill'. In Lunzer, E. A. and Morris, J. F. (eds) *Developments in Human Learning* New York: Staples, pp. 104–43

Richards, J., Platt, J., and Weber, H. 1985 *Longman Dictionary of Applied Linguistics* Harlow: Longman

RIE 1980 *Newsletter 4 (Special Series)* Regional Institute of English, South India, Bangalore, mimeo

van Riemsdijk, H. 1978 *A Case Study in Syntactic Markedness* Lisse: Peter de Ridder Press

Ritchie, W. (ed.) 1978 *Second Language Acquisition Research* New York: Academic Press

Rizzi, L. 1990 *Relativized Minimality* Cambridge, Mass.: MIT Press

Rogers, M. 1994 'German word order: a role for developmental and linguistic factors in L2 pedagogy'. In Bygate, M., Tonkyn, A. and Williams, E. (eds) *Grammar and the Language Teacher* London: Prentice-Hall, pp. 132–59

Rosch, E. 1977 'Human categorization'. In Warren, N. (ed.) *Advances in Cross-Cultural Psychology Vol. 1* London: Academic Press

Rossman, T. 1981 'The nature of linguistic processing in reading a second language'. PhD thesis: Concordia University

Rost, M, 1990 *Listening in Language Learning* Harlow: Longman

Rubin, J. 1975 'What the good language learner can teach us'. *TESOL Quarterly* **9**: 41–51

Rumelhart, D. E. and Norman, D. A. 1981 'Analogical processes in learning'. In Anderson, J. R. (ed.) *Cognitive Skills and Their Acquisition* Hillside, N.J.: Lawrence Erlbaum, pp. 335–59

Rutherford, W. E. 1982 'Markedness in second language acquisition'. *Language Learning* **32**: 85–107

Rutherford, W. E. 1987 *Second Language Grammar: Learning and Teaching* Harlow: Longman

Rutherford, W. E. and Sharwood Smith, M. 1985 'Consciousness-raising and universal grammar'. *Applied Linguistics* **6**: 274–82

Ryle, G. 1949 *The Concept of Mind* London: Hutchinson

Sanders, G. 1977 'A functional explanation of elliptical coordinations'. In Eckman, F. (ed.) *Current Themes in Linguistics* Washington, D.C.: Hemisphere Publishing Corporation, pp. 241–70

Schachter, J. 1988 'Second language acquisition and its relationship to universal grammar'. *Applied Linguistics* **9/3**: 219–35

Schank, R. and Abelson, R. 1977 *Scripts, Plans, Goals, and Understanding* Hillsdale, N.J.: Lawrence Erlbaum

Scherer, G. A. C. and Wertheimer, M. 1964 *A Psycholinguistic Experiment in Foreign Language Teaching* New York: McGraw Hill

Schmidt, M. 1980 'Coordinate structures and language universals in interlanguage'. *Language Learning* **26**: 67–76

Schmidt, R. W. 1983 'Interaction, acculturation, and the acquisition of communicative competence'. In Wolfson, N. and Judd, E. (eds) *Sociolinguistics and Second Language Acquisition* Rowley, Mass.: Newbury House

Schmidt, R. W. 1990 'Consciousness in second language learning'. *Applied Linguistics* **11/2**: 129–58

Schmidt, R. W. and Frota, S. 1986 'Developing basic conversational ability in a second language: a case study of an adult learner of Portugese'. In Day, R. (ed.) *Talking to Learn: Conversation in Second Language Acquisition* Rowley, Mass.: Newbury House

Schneider, W. and Shiffrin, R. 1977 'Controlled and automatic human information processing: 1. detection, search and attention'. *Psychological Review* **84/1**: 1–66

Schumann, J. 1978 *The Pidginization Process: A Model for Second Language Acquisition* Rowley, Mass.: Newbury House

Segalowitz, N. 1986 'Skilled reading in the second language'. In Vaid, J. (ed.) *Language Processing in Bilingual Psycholinguistic and Neuropsychological Perspectives* Hillsdale, N.J.: Lawrence Erlbaum

Seidenberg, M. S. 1985 'Evidence from great apes concerning the biological bases of language'. In Marras, A. and Demopoulous, W. (eds) *Language Learnability and Concept Acquisition* Norwood, N.J.: Ablex Publishing Corporation

Selinker, L. and Lamendella, J. 1978 'Two perspectives on fossilization in interlanguage learning'. *Interlanguage Studies Bulletin* **3**: 143–91

Shaffer, L. H. 1975 'Control processes in typing'. *Quarterly Journal of Experimental Psychology*, **27**: 419–32

Shiffrin, R. M. and Dumais, S. T. 1981 'The development of automatism'. In Anderson, J. R. (ed.) *Cognitive Skills and Their Acquisition* Hillside, N.J.: Lawrence Erlbaum, pp. 111–40

Shiffrin, R. M. and Schneider, W. 1977 'Controlled and automatic human information processing: 2. Perceptual learning, automatic learning and a general theory'. *Psychological Review* **84**: 127–90

Sinclair, H. 1972 'A possible theory of language acquisition within the general framework of Piaget's developmental theory'. In Adams, P. (ed.) *Language in Thinking* Harmonsdworth: Penguin, pp. 364–73

Sinclair, H. 1971 'Sensorimotor action patterns as a condition for the acquisition of syntax'. In Huxley, R. and Ingram, E. (eds) *Language Acquisition: Models and Methods* New York: Academic Press, pp. 121–36

Sinclair, H. 1987 'Language: a gift of nature or a homemade tool?' In Modgil, S. and Modgil, C. (eds) *Noam Chomsky: Consensus and Controversy* Falmer

Sinclair, J. and Coulthard, M. 1975 *Towards an Analysis of Discourse* Oxford: Oxford University Press

Skehan, P. 1994 'Interlanguage development and task-based learning'. In Bygate, M., Tonkyn, A. and Williams, E. (eds) *Grammar and the Language Teacher* London: Prentice-Hall, pp. 175–99

Slobin, D. I. 1973 'Cognitive prerequisites for the development of grammar'. In Ferguson, C. A. and Slobin, D. I. (eds) *Studies of Child Language Development* Now York: Holt, Rinehart and Winston, pp. 175–208

Smith, N. and Tsimpli, I. M. 1991 'Linguistic modularity? A case study of a "savant" linguist'. *Lingua* **84**: 315–51

Smith, N. and Tsimpli, I. M. 1995 *The Mind of a Savant* Oxford: Blackwell

Smith, S. M., Brown, H. O., Toman, J. E. P. and Goodman, L. S. 1947 'The lack of cerebral effects of d-Tubercurarine'. *Anesthiology* **8**: 1–14

Smolak, L. and Levine, M. P. 1984 'The effects of differential criteria on the assessment of cognitive–linguistic relationships'. *Child Development* **55**: 973–80

Snow, C. E. and Ferguson, C. A. (eds) 1977 *Talking to Children: Language Input and Acquisition* Cambridge: Cambridge University Press

Stern, H. H. 1983 *Fundamental Concepts of Language Teaching* Oxford: Oxford University Press

Stevick, E. 1976 *Memory, Meaning and Method* Rowley, Mass.: Newbury House

Summers, J. J. 1989 'Motor programs'. In Holding, D. (ed.) 1989 *Human Skills* Chichester: John Wiley, pp. 49–70

Swan, M. 1994 'Design criteria for pedagogic language rules'. In Bygate, M., Tonkyn, A. and Williams, E. (eds) *Grammar and the Language Teacher* London: Prentice-Hall, pp. 45–55

Tarallo, F. and Myhill, J. 1983 'Interference and natural language processing in second language acquisition'. *Language Learning* 33: 55–76

Tarone, E. 1983 'On the variability of interlanguage systems'. *Applied Linguistics* 4/2: 141–63

Thiersch, C. 1978 *Topics in German Syntax* PhD thesis, MIT

Towell, R. 1987 'Variability and progress in the language development of advanced learners of a foreign language'. In Ellis, R. (ed.) *Second Language Acquisition in Context* Englewood Cliffs, N.J.: Prentice-Hall, pp. 113–28

Towell, R. and Hawkins, R. 1994 *Approaches to Second Language Acquisition* Clevedon: Multilingual Matters

Trim, J. L. M., Richterich, R., van Ek, J. A. and Wilkins, D. A. 1980 *Systems Development in Adult Language Learning* Oxford: Pergamon Institute of English

Underwood, M. 1990 *Task Related Variability in Past Tense Morphology: A Longitudinal Study* MA dissertation, Institute of Education, University of London

Vigil, N. A. and Oller, J. W. 1976 'Rule fossilization: a tentative model'. *Language Learning* 26/2: 281–95

Watson, J. B. 1930 *Behaviourism* Chicago: University of Chicago Press

Welford, A. T. 1952 'The psychological refractory period and the timing of high speed performance: a review and a theory'. *British Journal of Psychology* 43: 2–19

Welford, A. T. 1970 'On the nature of skill'. In Legge, D. (ed.) *Skills* Harmondsworth: Penguin, pp. 21–32

Welford, A. T. 1968 *Fundamentals of Skill* London: Methuen.

White, L. 1982 *Grammatical Theory and Language Acquisition* Dortrecht, Holland: Foris Publications

White, L. 1983 'Markedness and parameter setting: some implications for a theory of adult second language acquisition'. In Eckman, F., Moravcsik, E. and Wirth, J. (eds) *Proceedings of the 12th Annual University of Wisconsin-Milwaukee Symposium on Markedness* New York: Plenum Press

White, L. 1986 'Implications of parametric variation for adult second language acquisition: an investigation of the pro-drop parameter'. In Cook, V. J. (ed.) *Experimental Approaches to Second Language Learning* Oxford: Pergamon Press, pp. 55–72

White, L. 1991 'Second language competence versus second language performance: UG or processing strategies?' In Eubank, L. (ed.) *Point Counterpoint: Universal Grammar in the Second Language* Amsterdam: John Benjamins

White, R. V. and Arndt, V. 1991 *Process Writing* Harlow: Longman

Whorf, B. L. 1956 *Language, Thought, and Reality* Cambridge, Mass.: MIT Press

Widdowson, H. G. 1978 'The acquisition and use of language system'. In Valdman, A. (ed.) *Studies in Second Language Acquisition Vol. 2*, Indiana University Linguistics Club

Wilkins, D. A. 1976 *Notional Syllabuses* Oxford: Oxford University Press

Wilkins, D. A. 1981 'Notional syllabuses revisited'. *Applied Linguistics* 2/1: 83–9

Winograd, T. 1975 'Frame representations and the declarative–procedural controversy'. In Bobrow, D. G. and Collins, A. M. (eds) *Representation and Understanding: Studies in Cognitive Science* New York: Academic Press, pp. 185–210

Wode, H. 1984 'Some theoretical implications of L2 acquisition research and the grammar of interlanguages'. In Davies, A. and Criper, C. (eds) *Interlanguage: Proceedings of the Seminar in Honour of Pit Corder* Edinburgh: Edinburgh University Press

Wolfe, S. 1981 *Bilingualism: One or Two Conceptual Systems?* PhD thesis: San Francisco State University

Wright, T. and Bolitho, R. 1993 'Language awareness: a missing link in language teacher education?' *ELT Journal* 47/4: 292–304

Yalden, J. 1983 *The Communicative Syllabus: Evolution, Design and Implementation* Oxford: Pergamon Institute of English

Zobl, H. 1984 'Cross generalisations and the contrastive dimension of the interlanguage hypothesis'. In Davies, A. and Criper, C. (eds) *Interlanguage: Proceedings of the Seminar in Honour of Pit Corder* Edinburgh: Edinburgh University Press, pp. 79–97

Index